Child sexual abuse and the Internet:

Tackling the new frontier

Edited by

Martin C. Calder

RHP

First published in 2004 by:

Russell House Publishing Ltd.

4 St. George's House

Uplyme Road

Lyme Regis

Dorset DT7 3LS

Tel: 01297-443948

Fax: 01297-442722

e-mail: help@russellhouse.co.uk

www.russellhouse.co.uk

British Library Cataloguing-in-publication Data:

A catalogue record for this book is available from the British Library.

ISBN: 1-903855-35-7

Typeset by Sheaf Graphics Ltd, Sheffield

Printed by Cromwell Press, Trowbridge

About Russell House Publishing

RHP is a group of social work, probation, education and youth and community work practitioners and academics working in collaboration with a professional publishing team.

Our aim is to work closely with the field to produce innovative and valuable materials to help managers, trainers, practitioners and students.

We are keen to receive feedback on publications and new ideas for future projects.

For details of our other publications please visit our web site or ask us for a catalogue. Contact details are on this page.

To my bright and beautiful daughters,
Stacey and Emma, who inform my writing
in so many ways

Martin C. Calder
December 2003

Child sexual abuse and the Internet: Tackling the new frontier

Contents

Contributor details

Anthony Beech is a reader in Criminological Psychology at the University of Birmingham and is a fellow of the British Psychological Society. Over the last 10 years he has been the lead researcher of the STEP (Sex Offender Treatment Evaluation Project) team. Here he has been involved in treatment evaluation and the development of systems to look at treatment need and treatment change in sex offenders. He has taken a keen interest in process issues in sex offender therapy. He has written widely on the topics of assessment and treatment of sexual offenders and other related subjects.

Martin C. Calder MA, CQSW is a team manger of the Child Protection Unit in the City of Salford Community and Social Services Directorate. He has written extensively in the area of sex offenders and is driven to provide accessible, evidence-based frameworks for operational use. He also acts as an independent social work trainer and consultant and is contactable at martinccalder@aol.com

Sean Hammond BA, MA, PhD is currently a lecturer in the Department of Applied Psychology, University College Cork where he is also a member of the COPINE team and director of the postgraduate programme in Forensic Psychology. Before joining UCC Dr Hammond was a senior clinical scientist at Broadmoor Hospital where he was head of the Clinical Decision Making Support Unit. His primary expertise is in psychometrics with particular application to forensic and clinical settings especially the assessment of personality disorder and sexual offenders.

Robert E. Longo MRC, LPC is Corporate Director of Special Programming and Clinical Training for New Hope Treatment Centers, Charleston, South Carolina. He also serves as a consultant, educator, trainer, and author dedicated to sexual abuse prevention and treatment. Robert was previously a director of the Safer Society Foundation, Inc. and the Safer Society Press from 1993 to 1998. He has published four books, five workbooks, more than 40 chapters and articles in the field of sexual abuse treatment, and pioneered the adult sexual offender workbook series formerly published by the Safer Society Press and now published by NEARI Press.

David Middleton is Head of Sex Offender Programmes for the National Probation Service. He was formally the Manager of the specialist Sex Offender Unit in the West Midlands Probation Service. In 2000 the unit was awarded the Wates Foundation Award for Reducing Re-offending and the treatment programme was the first community based sex offender treatment programme to be accredited by the Correctional Services Accreditation Panel. David is an honorary tutor in Forensic Psychology at the University of Birmingham and a member of the editorial board of *Child Abuse Review*.

Rachel O'Connell is the Director of Research at the Cyberspace Research Unit at the University of Central Lancashire.

Prior to working at the University of Central Lancashire Rachel managed an EU funded project entitled COPINE (Combating Paedophile Information Networks in Europe), based at University College Cork, Ireland. The particular focus of the Project was the sexual exploitation of children through the Internet. The Project staff worked closely with law enforcement and other agencies in this field in the development of practice related initiatives, as well as undertaking collaborative research into the nature of offending, and victim related issues.

In January 2000 Rachel, on behalf of the Cyberspace Research Unit, University of Central Lancashire, secured a grant of £500,000 from the European Commission to involve children in the development of web based educational tools designed to equip children and young people with the tools, knowledge and skills required to navigate safely on the Internet. The ONCE project had partners in Belgium, Greece and Ireland and developed a set of materials, FKBKO (For Kids by Kids Online), which are available and are being promoted widely: http://www.fkbko.net

The Cyberspace Unit is currently the UK co-ordinator within SafeBorders, another European Commission funded project working towards a multinational awareness campaign about a safer Internet. The Unit has also carried out research for the Home Office and the Department for Education and Skills in the UK.

Rachel is well known for her work researching on-line criminal activity, and investigating these activities using forensic computing and also psychological approaches such as criminal profiling. She has good working relationships with various members of law enforcement agencies.

Rachel sits on the Home Office Task Force and Department for Education and Skills Schools Internet Safety Strategy Group. She frequently speaks at on-line safety and child welfare conferences, and is regarded as an expert in her field by both the British and Irish media.

Ethel Quayle is a lecturer with the Department of Applied Psychology, University College Cork, Ireland, and a researcher with the COPINE Project. Her professional background is as a clinical psychologist and she is course director for two postgraduate courses in cognitive behaviour therapy. Her research with the COPINE project has as its focus an understanding of the function of Internet child abuse images in the offending process and she is currently managing two projects that seek to develop assessment and intervention materials for working with such offenders. She has published widely in this area.

Joe Sullivan MA (Crim), BA (Hons), CQSW, Dip Psych is Principal Therapist with the Lucy Faithfull Foundation. He is based at the Wolvercote Clinic, which is a specialist residential facility for the assessment and treatment of adult male sexual abusers. He is an honorary tutor in Forensic Psychology at the University of Birmingham and is currently researching a PhD in Forensic Psychology exploring sexual offenders who use their employment or profession as a means to target, manipulate and sexually abuse the children with whom they work. His work at the Wolvercote clinic includes the residential assessment and treatment of adult male perpetrators and non-residentially he provides assessment and treatment programmes for alleged male and female sexual offenders, families of offenders and adult survivors of sexual abuse. He has published and presented papers to national and international conferences on the techniques he uses for engaging, assessing and treating sexual offenders.

Bill Thompson PhD is a forensic criminologist, and a lecturer in Human Sexuality at Reading University. He specialises in case reviews and child interview methodologies; teaching both subjects on a post qualifying social work course for six years. He is currently working on the genesis of false allegations. Miscarriages of justice that have been overturned as a result of his work include the landmark *AJE -v- HMA* appeal in Scotland. He sat on the expert's panel in the recent Home Affairs Committee Inquiry into Care Homes Investigation Methodologies. He has written numerous articles on pornography and is the author of *Soft-core*.

Andy Williams PhD lectures in Criminology, and Youth Culture, at the Institute of Criminal Justice, Portsmouth. He has recently completed his PhD study of media myths concerning the Paulsgrove anti-paedophile 'vigilante riots' and the lessons to be drawn for Multi Agency Public Protection Panels. He is currently writing *Snuff, Sex, and Satan: the Social Psychology of Moral Panics and Crusades*.

Introduction

Martin C. Calder

Sexual abuse has reached epidemic proportions in many countries and procedurally we have been asked to embrace children involved with prostitution, organised abuse, children and young people who sexually abuse and female genital mutilation. More recently we have been asked to respond to the growing concern about the emergence of sexual abuse on the Internet. Indeed, the latest version of *Working Together* says the following:

> *The Internet has now become a significant tool in the distribution of child pornography. Adults are now using the Internet to try to establish contact with children with a view to grooming them for inappropriate or abusive relationships. As part of their role in preventing abuse and neglect, ACPCs may wish to consider activities to raise awareness about the safe use of the Internet by children, for example, by distributing information through education staff to parents, in relation to both school and home-based use of computers by children.*
>
> *When somebody is discovered to have placed child pornography on the Internet, or accessed child pornography, the police should normally consider whether that individual might also be involved in the active abuse of children. In particular, the individual's access to children should be established, within the family and employment contexts and in other settings (e.g. work with children as a volunteer). If there are particular concerns about one or more specific children, there may be a need to carry out s.47 enquiries in respect of those children.*
>
> (DoH, 1999: 73).

Once again, there is no substantial guidance being offered centrally so the responsibility for procedures and practice guidance appears to remain with local authorities and their Area Child Protection Committees. However, as with many new areas of concern, practice cannot wait until the necessary research has been undertaken and a body of theory and knowledge develops.

Many experienced workers have had to ask questions as to the transferability of material generated in other areas of child sexual abuse and in doing so have encountered some problems. For example the introduction of men convicted of Internet-related sexual crimes to the community-based sex offender treatment programmes (SOTP) and the difficulties of applying Finkelhor's model of child sexual abuse (Finkelhor, 1984) thus compounding denial problems across many offenders. Workers have also had to grapple with the issue of crossover from 'hands-off' sexual crime to 'hands-on' sexual abuse of children resident in their family.

This book is a preliminary attempt to organise some of the emerging practice wisdom, small-scale research findings and theory development into a useful and accessible text for frontline busy practitioners. It represents a small building block as we endeavour to construct a larger and safer platform for effective and informed developments.

In the opening chapter, I try to review the available UK-based literature which has a practice-orientated focus as opposed to the more research-based, academic material emanating from the United States. One of the biggest problems facing frontline workers is developing sufficient knowledge about the Internet and its associated terminology and capabilities to undertake investigative and assessment work confidently. The material is structured in such a way that it mirrors the intervention process and will enable workers to use it as a primary guidance tool in their work. I try and differentiate the potential the Internet holds, and should be applauded, from its more sinister use by people who want to sexually harm children and young people. For some time the great driving request from practitioners has been to offer some clear guidance on whether Internet sexual crimes correlate in any way with hands-on sexual offending. Whilst I address this issue as far as our knowledge base allows, we also need to look to other research findings about hands-off sexual offending and the modus operandi of such perpetrators as articulated by Rachel O'Connell in Chapter 3. Although considerable space could have been taken up referring to the impact on partners and children of Internet sexual offenders, this was not explored further as there is significant material of relevance in Calder, Peake and Rose, 2001.

In Chapter 2 one of the country's pioneers in this area of work, Ethel Quayle, reminds us that the child is at the centre of the misuse of the Internet: either when they are groomed by the offender or otherwise when the picture of their abuse is available and downloaded by millions of other people. She attempts to guide us through the nature of such offending, the characteristics of the offenders and the relationship between viewing such images and the commission of contact offences.

In Chapter 3, Rachel O'Connell explores the challenges encountered as a result of the widespread penetration and the associated communicative capabilities of the Internet which are set to become much more complex and potentially dangerous, as computing and mobile technologies converge and multi-media real-time communication via mobile applications will become the norm. Her chapter presents an exposé of a range of child-sex related risks associated with both existing and emerging communication technologies. She categorises, and then explores, six main areas of concern i.e. children, parents, educators, teachers, law enforcement, and the industry. She explores a number of key technical issues, which act to both constrain but also potentially liberate both the fixed and mobile Internet industry in terms of implementing security features designed not only to enhance children's safety but also to

deter criminal activity. Arguably, a baseline understanding of these technical issues is imperative if Internet safety experts are to adopt a more proactive role in, for example, working with the product developers of new technologies. A second theme involves an outline of issues associated with the development of programmes of education designed to empower children, parents and teachers with the tools, knowledge and skills they need to navigate the Internet safely. She concludes by calling for strategic action and outlines a vision of how we might harness the knowledge generated as a result of our experiences and furthermore proposes that we ought to co-ordinate activities so that a clearer, louder and infinitely more effective voice is heard by the key players with respect to the need to put systems in place to augment children's safety on-line. We are at a critical point at the cusp of the roll out of the next evolution in communication technologies, and now is the time to act in order to ensure a safer future for children on-line.

In Chapter 4, Rob Longo addresses issues associated with young people with sexual behaviour problems and the Internet. With the growth of Internet users and access to a growing number of web sites and a variety of materials, there exists a concern about access to adult-oriented materials by under-aged persons. This is especially concerning as it pertains to young people with sexual behaviour problems. A growing number of young people with sexual behaviour problems who are referred to treatment programmes and treatment providers have histories of going on-line to access sexually oriented materials, including pornography and chat rooms. His chapter also addresses recommendations for the future regarding ways to assess and guide these patients and clients about the potential hazards associated with the use of on-line adult-oriented web sites, ways to reduce the incidence of children and teens accessing these materials, and proposed treatment issues.

The book then moves into a second section geared at looking in some more detail at the assessment and treatment issues faced when working with Internet sexual offenders. Joe Sullivan and Anthony Beech explore the issues facing professionals conducting risk assessments of Internet sex offenders and look at how the research challenges the early stereotypes. They offer us an overview of the various assessment techniques employed and outline some additional tools which might assist workers to understand and intervene in the fantasy world of the Internet sex offender. The chapter links nicely into Chapter 6 from Sean Hammond who explores the psychometric assessment of Internet sex offenders.

David Middleton then takes us through the current treatment approaches to child sexual abuse and the Internet, attempting to look at successful treatment approaches, therapist characteristics and treatment style. The final chapter explores false allegations against

alleged Internet sex offenders and the authors take us through a personal account of the experience of one author at the hands of a police investigation.

I hope that this book provides some useful information to empower workers faced with the challenge of assessing and managing the people who misuse the Internet for sexual gain.

References

Calder, M.C., Peake, A. and Rose, K. (2001). *Mothers of Sexually Abused Children: A Framework for Assessment, Understanding and Support*. Lyme Regis: Russell House Publishing.

DoH (1999). *Working Together to Safeguard Children*. London: The Stationery Office.

Finkelhor, D. (1984). *Child Sexual Abuse: New Theory and Research*. New York: Free Press.

Chapter One

The Internet: Potential, Problems and Pathways to Hands-on Sexual Offending

Martin C. Calder

Introduction

The aim of this chapter is to:

- Explore the emergence of the Internet and with it the huge potential if utilised appropriately.

- Explore what the Internet is and how big an area it has become.

- Identify some of the pitfalls and problems associated with regulating such a global network.

- Review some of the emerging theory and research in relation to causation, assessment and intervention of sex offenders who utilise the Internet. Whilst space dictates that I focus primarily on adult male offenders, the issues for children and young people do receive some attention given that there has to be a preventive focus as well.

- Specifically explore some of the potential cross-over issues between 'hands-off' Internet sexual crime and 'hands-on' sexual offending.

The primary audience is frontline workers and their managers who are starting to get the throughput of cases from Operation Ore and other major international operations.

The Internet: what are we talking about?

The Internet is a worldwide network of smaller computer networks and individual computers all connected by cable, telephone lines or satellite links. It is thus a decentralised, global medium of communication that links people around the world. No single entity administers it and it is timeless and spaceless. There is no single point at which all the information is stored or from which it is disseminated and it is said that it would not be technically feasible for any one entity to control all of the information contained therein (Arnaldo, 2001: 55).

The Internet has a number of components that have the ability to deliver an enormous array of information. These include:

- WWW stands for 'World Wide Web'. When people talk about surfing the Internet, they are actually talking about surfing the Web. The Web is a network of millions of sites that is accessible through a 'graphical' interface, the web browser (i.e. Internet Explorer). To locate these sites the user needs to know the name of the location. The name is referred to as URL (Universal Resource Locator). The URL commands tell the computer of the Internet Service Provider (ISP) (such as AOL or Freeserve), which remote computer to connect to. The Web is a section of the Internet where information is cross-linked to other related information, allowing one to jump from one web 'site' to another. It is also rich in graphics and sound and with the introduction of new applications, the Web has become interactive and increasingly loaded with multi-media content. The Web is the most popular and fastest growing feature of the Internet and accounts for more than 90% of Internet usage (Arnaldo, 2001: 56). It allows linkages across many sites that are related to a particular topic and these can relate to sex, violence, drugs etc.

- E-mail for electronic communication: continues to develop with the capacity to send voice, video and other forms of attachments around the world in an almost instantaneous manner.

- A newsgroup is a discussion about a particular subject consisting of notes written to a central Internet site and redistributed through Usenet (a worldwide network of news discussion groups). Users can send post ('text'), picture and sound files to existing newsgroups and respond to previous posts, as well as create new newsgroups. There are some 30,000 such groups on the Internet covering a wide range of topics, the vast majority of which are innocent and appropriate.

- Bulletin board systems are for posting of information on almost any topic one could imagine. Bullet Board Systems (BBS) are similar to newsgroups but with more real time involvement. Durkin and Bryant (1995) talk of them as high tech party lines, by which users can send and receive text, engage in conversations, and both upload and download files.

- Internet Relay Chat (IRC) is the exchange of typed, graphic, video or audio messages. One site acts as the storeroom for the messages (chat site or rooms) which a group of users can read and respond to from anywhere on the Internet. Users can also participate in a private chat (direct client to client) which bypasses the need for a server and thereby raises the level of security of the communications. Chats can either be ongoing or scheduled for a particular time and duration. Unlike web sites, newsgroups and e-mails, chat channels exist only in real time. As such, when all the users have logged off, the channel no longer exists. There are numerous chat channels, all of which have a variety of 'rooms' you can enter. These rooms can be created by either the service providing access or by the members. When members enter a chat area they nominate a pseudonym which can be frequently changed. This makes it very difficult to trace a person (Blundell et al., 2002).

The potential of the Internet

Technology is changing the options available to media audiences and the Internet is frequently identified as the most striking example of this digital revolution. As Carlsson (2001) has noted, the Internet is now taking the transition into a new phase – from being considered merely as a technology to representing a medium of information and communication. The Internet is rapidly becoming as vital a part of life as the telephone, and a key to many powerful tools. It combines global communications with an incredible range of resources and is well on the way to becoming the world's library (Mars, 2001). Indeed, everything on the Internet is global. When one accesses an item on the Internet people everywhere in the world can also access it. Something published on the Internet can be read by everyone, immediately and worldwide. This global aspect of the Internet is one of its best qualities – it offers worldwide communication in real time and at little cost. People can talk to others without regard to geographical borders and without the constraints imposed by the traditional national and international telecommunications carriers (Arnaldo, 2001: 56).

The Internet provides unparalleled opportunities to learn about the world and to learn about almost any topic that we choose to explore, including human sexuality. Wide public access is provided in libraries, Internet cafes as well as on home-based terminals. The accessibility of the Internet continues to grow and it is very much a medium for the young. Denying children access will leave them increasingly disadvantaged with their peers. We need to facilitate their access to and knowledge about it: it is exceedingly educational and almost indispensable in today's society.

For young people who can filter out accurate from distorted information, the Internet can be an incredibly rich source of information particularly about topics generally not discussed with parents, or in sex education classes, such as falling in love, breaking up, orgasms, and how to sexually pleasure a partner. A recent content analysis of questions submitted to a sexuality information website for teenagers, sxetc.org, found just that. The kind of questions most frequently asked by teenagers pertained to issues related to sexual pleasure; exactly those areas that adults and schools omit talking about. However, for those teenagers less able to tell fact from fiction, the Internet, with its vast amount of distorted sexual stimuli (pornography and otherwise), may only serve to propagate more misinformation and reinforce exaggerated beliefs about sexuality.

There are many benefits that can be derived from the development of on-line relationships and on-line relationships that become sexual. The research (Cooper et al., 1999) suggests that the Internet can:

1. Facilitate the formation of romantic relationships.

2. Improve the chances of finding an optimal partner.

3. Highlight that relationships can develop on attachments, not simply physical appearance.

4. Improve one's skills in interpersonal communication.

Katz and Apsden (1997) have forecast that the Internet will promote better social relationships as people will be freed from the constraints of time and place. Among home Internet users, 96.6% of women and 93.6% of men have reported using the Internet to communicate with family and friends, thus maintaining social ties (Hughes and Hans, 2001). Hampton and Wellman (2000) also found that rather than replacing face-to-face ties, computer-mediated ties supported and strengthened neighbourhood ties. The Internet can foster relationships between family members and social networks via on-line support groups that deal with family-related issues such as divorce, death or having a child with special needs (Mickelson, 1997). The Internet continues to have a very positive impact in the promotion of networking and the strengthening of partnerships which will give

results on the ground and an effective voice at an international level.

The presence of home-based computers may well facilitate a better home-work balance, with the number of people working from home increasing.

It can be used for healthy sexual expression. For example, the Internet offers the opportunity for the formation of on-line or virtual communities where isolated or disenfranchised individuals e.g. gay males and lesbians can communicate with each other around sexual topics of shared interest; it offers educational potential; and it may allow for sexual experimentation in a safer forum, thus facilitating identity exploration and development (Cooper et al., 2000). It is assisting in the dissemination of sexual knowledge through informational sites (Sexuality Information and Education Council of the United States (SIECUS) (www.siecus.org), 'Go ask Alice!' (www.goaskalice.columbia.edu) and the Kinsey Institute Sexuality Information Service for Students (KISISS) (www.indiana.edu/~kinsey).

The Internet can be used to counter the potential influence of paedophiles through outreach information aimed at families, parents of young children and children themselves, on protections to be taken when surfing a highway full of unknowns and through reminders of the law and the risks incurred by transgressors (Auclaire, 2001).

It is a phenomenal educational tool. Although few studies have confirmed that the use of computers enhances educational achievement, there are many laudable initiatives to encourage Internet use in schools.

In summary, the potential includes:

• Breaking down national and international barriers.

• The potential for the development and maintenance of relationships (Cooper, 1998).

• The development of deeper, more personal interactions as users are better able to self-disclose and take greater interpersonal risks (Parks and Floyd, 1999).

- The use of the Internet for advocacy and networking, especially among gay and lesbian groups (Carey, 1996).
- The development of support groups, communities and on-line sex therapy (Cart, 1997).
- The use of the Internet in data collection for research into sexuality-related topics (Binik et al., 1999).
- The delivery of counselling, disease control and prevention services (Acevedo et al., 1998).
- Rheinhold (1993) views the Internet as a positive force that will foster greater communication and better access to education, promote global understanding and make the world a better place to live.

The size of the Internet and the size of the problem

It is virtually impossible to determine the size of the Internet at any given moment, although reasonable estimates suggest that as many as 350 million people around the world can, and do, access this enormously flexible interactive communication medium. It has grown massively since its origins in 1969. In 1981, fewer than 300 computers were connected to the Internet, but by 1996 over 9,400,000 host computers were estimated to be connected, with 60% of them in the United States. The use of the Internet has increased 50% a year since 1990. The rate of growth for new Internet service is estimated to be 25% every three months (Cooper, 2000).

Today around one in two children in the UK has domestic access to the Internet, and four in five have used it at home, school or elsewhere (Livingstone, 2002). Between 1999 and 2002 there was an expected 155% increase in use among 5–12 year-olds and 100% among teenagers. There is every indication that 50% of children, even as young as aged five, will be on-line within the next few years, confirming that

the Internet is a technology that differentiates the young from the old (Donnerstein, 2002). Indeed, recent figures suggest that nearly five million children in the UK regularly use the Internet (Internet Crime Forum, 2001).

Sex is the most frequently searched for topic on the Internet. If we use a search engine and type in the words 'sex pictures' we will access a list of almost 2 million sites that contain these words and often the pictures the child is seeking. There is no block to such material for children and young people unless certain blocking software has been applied.

Computers act as an aid for those who are sexually interested in children and allow for the production, viewing, storage and distribution of child pornography. Accompanying the growth of the Internet is the number of people who are drawn into using Internet access to obtain sexual satisfaction. In April 1998 some 9 million users (15% of the on-line population) accessed one of the top five 'adult' web sites and in August 1999 some 31% of the total on-line population visited an adult web site (Cooper, 2000).

The passive involvement in child pornography through browsing and downloading is very difficult to detect as many users simply 'lurk' in the background and download the pictures they require. This reflects a hidden layer of activity, as does the medium of private e-mail.

Internet sexual abuse represents a small part of international incidence but it is a rapid growth area. This may be fuelled further by technical advancements such as 3D graphics, improved video compression, increased band width and encryption. A significant amount of material can be stored on relatively small diskettes. For example, a floppy disc could hold 700 pages and a CD can hold up to 650 typed novels (Jones, 2002). Given that you could store a half a million pages on a gigabyte and the average home computer has a 20 gigabyte capacity, the task of law enforcement is an uphill struggle.

There are estimated to be one million pornographic images of children on the

Internet, many of them featuring children from third world countries being abused by affluent sex tourists from the west (Wellard, 2001). Since 1996, ISPs have removed 20,000 pornographic images of children from the Internet. But with an estimated 200 more being posted each day, many of them through news groups, it is clear that the providers are only touching the tip of the iceberg. In the US, there may be as many as 2,000 convictions a year for on-line offences against children (Wellard, 2001).

One in five children aged under 17 years has visited pornographic websites (Richardson, 2001). Finkelhor et al. (2000) found that 19% of young people reported being approached for sex through the Internet media at least once a year. One in seven of these reported that the offender also attempted to contact them by telephone or postal mail. These figures correspond with those from Australia where 27% of children believed that they had been contacted by a sexual predator whilst using a chat room (NAPCAN, 2001). It is now known that an offender may lurk in Internet chat rooms, gathering information until an opportunity arises to move the conversation with the child to a private chat room or to a mobile phone and then ultimately to arrange a real life meeting (Aftab, 2000). In 2002 one in five 9–16 year-olds used chat rooms and one in ten chat room users have met in person somebody they communicated with on-line. More disturbingly, three-quarters of those who went to face-to-face meetings were not accompanied by an adult. A third did not know where to report unpleasant experiences and would not have told parents (Millar, 2003).

Although there are difficulties gauging the extent of child pornography on the Internet, Costello (2001) has estimated that 14 million pornographic sites exist, some of which carry an estimated one million pornographic images of children (Wellard, 2001).

There have been a number of high profile cases that have brought media and public attention to the problems of sexual abuse associated with the Internet revolution. For example, Gary Glitter, the disgraced former

rock star, who was convicted in 1999 for downloading child pornography from the Internet, was deported from Cambodia to Thailand in 2002 for alleged further sexual indiscretions.

There has also been significant interest in the fallout of certain high-profile police cases largely through some of the people identified. What must be remembered is the size of the collections seized in such operations. For example, to become a member of the secret Wonderland Club, an international paedophile ring linked to the Internet, applicants had to present a minimum of 10,000 images of child pornography. When the police smashed the group in 2001, at least 180 people had succeeded in supplying this enormous collection. The police investigation, entitled Operation Cathedral, resulted in 50 convictions around the world, seven of which were in England. Those seven men alone distributed more than 750,000 images of child sexual abuse.

Operation Ore is the British end of the US Justice Department's Operation Avalanche, which was sparked when the US postal service closed down Landslide Promotions, thought to have been used by 75,000 people worldwide in the late 1990s. On the site subscribers could access child pornography via a button marked 'child porn', click here', linking to other sites with titles such as Cyber Lolita, I am 14 and Child Rape. These showed the abuse of captive children. In August 2002 a Texas computer consultant, Thomas Reedy, was sentenced to a total of 1355 years for running the Internet child porn empire, which had a turnover of more than $1.4 million a month and his wife is serving 14 years for her role in a business with 250,000 subscribers on three continents. Operation Ore identified 7,000 British users of an American pornographic website of which 1,300 people have already been arrested, including a judge, magistrates, dentists, hospital consultants, soldiers and a teacher, along with more than 50 police officers (including two officers involved in the investigation into the murder of Holly Wells and Jessica Chapman). Pete Townsend, lead guitarist of The Who, was arrested on suspicion of possessing and making indecent images of children and that he paid to enter an Internet site containing child pornography. 40 children in the UK were taken into protective custody following the investigations.

Sex and the Internet

There are a number of differing types of sex-related use of the Internet:

- The search for sexual educational materials (healthy sexual interactions).
- The buying or selling of sex-related goods (sex toys).
- Seeking out materials for entertainment or masturbatory purposes (pornographic pictures or images).
- Seeking out sexual partners for long-term or short-term relationships and encounters (dating agencies or prostitution).
- Illegal seeking out of individuals for sexually-related Internet crimes (sexual harassment, cyber-stalking, children) (Donnerstein, 2002). The harassment of children represents a form of emotional abuse. Finkelhor et al. (2000) found that 6% of the young people in their sample had experienced harassment through the Internet in the form of threats of harm or humiliation. One third of these children felt either very or extremely afraid by the behaviour and 18% were very or extremely embarrassed.
- Commercial exploitation of children: advertising on-line is emerging and tends to be more tailored to the child's profile, enhancing the likelihood of a sale.
- Promotion of child sexual tourism: The Internet advances such offences with Internet facilitators assisting with access to child prostitutes, the location of child sex tourism operators and the sale and trafficking of children. Aloysius (2001) reported that at least 600 Sri Lankan boys are presently directly advertising their services on the Internet.

- Trafficking: Mail order brides are openly accessible, where young women are offered alongside a rating scale of compliance and ability to carry out domestic duties. You can then easily order your bride over the Internet. A similar system applies to children, though child pornography is often coded and a decoder is needed for access (Mullins, 1997).

Child Pornography and the Internet: Old Problem, New Technology

What is child pornography?

This is an important question and much time could be spent addressing it. For the purposes of this chapter, let us agree that it is a complex area and that legal definitions of both child and pornography differ globally, and may even differ among legal jurisdictions within the same country (Healy, 1997). Edwards (2000) defined child pornography as a record of the systematic rape, abuse and torture of children on film and photograph and other electronic means.

Pornography on the Internet

Around 1% of all material on the Internet is pornographic material but a small percentage of an almost infinite amount is a large quantity of material.

(Jauch, 1997).

The advent of the Internet has meant that child pornography is far more accessible and available to those with even minimal computer skills. Should we wish, and most of us do not, we can now see it for ourselves. And so can our children. Virtual pornography, virtual flashing and virtual soliciting for pornographic ends or sex are but a keystroke away. And once caught in this mire, it is sometimes difficult to get out (Jones, 2001).

The Internet has removed the communication constraint in a similar way that air travel removed the proximity constraint for paedophiles seeking access to child prostitutes abroad. The Internet with its growing capacity to exchange in real time written messages, telephone calls, data, sound, still and moving pictures, has broken the traditional communication barriers and makes incalculable quantities of information of all kinds and all forms instantly available to anyone with a personal computer – at any time and place in the world. The dynamics of producing, collecting, trading and distribution of child pornography has thus been transformed. Also the scope for the selection of particular pictures that cater for specific desires has also increased. Child pornography has thus grown into a massive industry that systematically promotes the abuse of children. The Internet can facilitate abuse by allowing access to children in a way that was not previously possible. It is an anonymous tool and brings people from all over the world together in one place. Before it came into being it was a difficult task for an abuser to meet a child or meet someone who could obtain a child for them. This is the danger of the Internet – not that it creates sex offenders but, rather, that it provides an opportunity for those minded to abuse children to do so in a way that exposes them to less risk, thus reducing the likelihood of detection and potentially leading to an increase in actual child abuse (Gillespie, 2002).

The Internet is a very attractive place for producers and consumers of child pornography for a number of reasons:

- Technology makes constant updating very easy – some services claim to update their material biweekly.

- It reaches a global audience faster than any other media. Child pornography is available on the Internet in many different formats ranging from pictures, anime (cartoon) and video to sound files and stories. Most pornographic material is distributed via e-mail, newsgroups or World Wide Web pages. It can also be distributed during conversations in chat rooms and interactive home pages, and personally via diskettes or CD-ROMS (Blundell et al., 2002).

- Pictures and film clips can be downloaded into the computer and have an advantage over film in that their quality does not deteriorate with age or with transfer to another computer. The development of live video conferencing has raised child pornography to an even higher level, giving the impact of three-dimensional virtual reality and enabling the viewer to participate interactively and give orders on how a scene should be played.

- It provides digital-quality photographs at far less expense than the earlier paper catalogues. There are continual developments in this arena. The next generation of camera-equipped handsets (to take secret photographs of naked and half-dressed children) are now widely available. These latest phone cameras will also allow people to take pictures quickly and unobtrusively and often without the subjects knowing. They can then be transmitted straight onto the Internet offering high quality pictures. Multimedia messaging (MMR) phones allow the transmission of moving pictures in the same way. Phone usage will ensure greater anonymity.

- Those who distribute pornography seek security in the anonymity perceived to be offered by the Internet, enabling the user to invent virtually any identity and route a message through different countries in order to avoid detection (Calcetas-Santos, 2001). The advent of scanners and digital cameras has allowed for the development of home-based rather than commercially-based pornography. This is now considered safer by many.

- The Internet has also moved to a point of sophistication so that you can download whole movies and replay them, thus by-passing traditional controls such as the British Board of Film Classification. Video conferencing also has the potential to grow quickly and resulting in more real time child abuse.

- Computers also allow offenders to modify images. 'Morphing' (or pseudo-imaging) is common in child pornography and involves superimposing the face of a desired child on the body of another person. Images may not actually involve children at all. These pictures may then be posted on the World Wide Web without the victim's knowledge and may be used to trade with other offenders (Zwicke, 2000).

Exploring the problems of Internet technology

O'Connell (2001) noted that the Internet provides a uniquely safe, easily accessible, distribution medium that operates on at least three levels simultaneously:

- The technology facilitates the anonymous, rapid dissemination of an immediate and constant supply of illegal child pornography pictures in an environment supportive of any rationalisations for their behaviour.

- It enables the creation and maintenance of a sense of deviant behaviour. The presence of complex social structures in the computer underground indicates that on a social organisational level, adults with a sexual interest in children act as 'colleagues'. The pictures in themselves act as a form of currency, legitimising activity and creating social cohesion (Taylor et al., 2001).

- The children portrayed in child pornography images often present with smiles or neutral expressions designed to reinforce rationalisation and justification processes for adult sexual interest in children. This arises from a perception from the pictures of willing sexual behaviour.

The Internet allows paedophiles:

- Instant access to other predators worldwide.
- Open discussion about their sexual desires.
- Shared ideas about ways to lure victims.
- Mutual support of their adult-child sex philosophies.
- Instant access to potential child victims worldwide.
- Disguised identities for approaching

children, even to the point of presenting oneself as a member of teen groups.

- Ready access to 'teen chat rooms' to find out how and who to target as potential victims.
- Means to identify and track down home contact information.
- Ability to build a long-term Internet relationship with a potential victim, prior to attempting to engage the child in physical contact.

The evolution of professional concern about the dark side of the computer revolution

Calder (1999) has charted in detail the emergence of the professional response to child sexual abuse, noting that it has stuttered and then become resurrected when a new dimension unfolded. For example, in the 1990s there was an acknowledgement of ritual abuse, 'sex tourism', the child murders and abuse (Fred and Rosemary West), paedophile rings and sexual abuse within residential and foster care (Calder, 1999b). We are now facing the latest challenge in the form of the Internet and the video recorder:

> *The Internet, a medium of a new and different sort, has added a late-twentieth century twist, a new virtual variable to the problem of sexual abuse of children, specifically as regards pornography and paedophilia.*
>
> (Jones, 2001).

Theoretical Developments: Understanding the Internet Sex Offender

Internet sexual crime: some preliminary categorisations

Cooper et al. (1999) described three categories of people who use the Internet for sexual pursuits:

- **Recreational users:** who access on-line

sexual material more out of curiosity or for entertainment purposes and are not typically seen as having problems associated with their on-line sexual behaviour.

- **Sexual compulsive users:** who, due to propensity for pathological sexual expression, use the Internet as one forum for their sexual activities? Research indicates that this group spent an estimated 15 to 25 hours on-line per week pursuing sexual material (Cooper, Delmonico and Burg, 2000).

- **At-risk users:** who, if it were not for the availability of the Internet, may never have developed a problem with on-line sexuality? These people spend an estimated 10 hours per week on-line pursuing sexual material.

Whilst many of the people who use the Internet for sexual satisfaction will be recreational users, a significant proportion will have pre-existing sexual compulsions and addictions that are now finding a new outlet.

Lanning (1998) identified three categories of computer offender:

- **Situational offender (dabbler):** usually either a typical adolescent searching on-line for pornography and sex or an impulsive or curious adult with a newly found access to a wide range of pornography and sexual opportunities. Their behaviour is not as long-term, persistent, and predictable as that of preferential offenders.

- **Preferential offender:** usually either a sexually indiscriminate with a wide variety of deviant sexual interests or a paedophile with a definite preference for children. The main difference between them is that the pornography/erotica collection of the sexually indiscriminate preferential offender will be more varied, usually with a focus on their particular sexual preference or paraphilias. This group tends to be serial offenders who prey on children through the operation of sex rings or the collection, creation or distribution of child pornography.

- Other **miscellaneous offenders** include: media reporters who erroneously believe they can go on-line and traffic in child pornography as part of a news expose; pranksters who disseminate false or incriminating information to embarrass the targets of their dirty tricks; older boyfriends attempting to sexually interact with adolescent boys or girls; and concerned citizens who go overboard doing their own private investigations into the problem.

The Internet entices people to act in ways that they would not normally act. Orzack (1998, 1999) compiled a list of symptoms specific to computer addiction:

- Experiences pleasure, gratification or relief while engaged in computer activities.

- Preoccupation with computer activity, including thinking about the experience, making plans to return to the computer, surfing the web, having the newest and fastest hardware.

- Needing to spend more and more time or money on computer activities to change mood.

- Failure of repeated efforts to control these activities.

- Restlessness, irritability, or other dysphoric moods such as increase in tension when not engaged in computer activities.

- Need to return to these activities to escape problems or relieve dysphoric mood.

- Neglect of social, familial, educational or work obligations.

- Lying to family members, therapists, and others about the extent of time spent on the computer.

- Actual or threatened loss of significant relationships, job, financial stability, or educational opportunity because of computer usage.

- Show physical signs such as backaches, migraines, neglect of personal hygiene or eating irregularities.
- Changes in sleep patterns.

The presence of at least five of the list represents a persistent and recurrent misuse of the computer.

Identifying Internet pornography users: a generalised framework

Whilst little empirical data exists, the current research identifies men aged 25–50 years, who tend to be better educated, have a higher IQ, are more likely to be employed and to be in a relationship than are individuals who commit hands-on offences against children (Blundell et al., 2002). Few successfully stop accessing child pornography despite assertions to the contrary, and thus treatment needs to be mandatory. Restrictions on access via the removal of the home computer may be replaced by public facility access (libraries, Internet cafes, etc.)

Schwartz and Southern (2000) identified the following generalisation from the characteristics and interests of cyber-sex abuse patients in their sample:

Cybersex abusers are	• Heavy users of the Internet • Generally married • Frequently college-educated professionals • Survivors of sexual abuse • Depressed
Male cybersex abusers are	• Middle aged • Generally older than the female cyber-sex abusers • Similar to heavy users of the Internet • More likely to be chemically dependent than the female cyber-sex abusers • More likely to be involved in recovery than the female cyber-sex abusers • More likely to be involved in sexual compulsivity or be labelled a sex addict
Female cybersex abusers are	• Generally younger than male cyber-sex abusers and heavy users of the Internet • Similar to all (non-problematic) users of the Internet • More likely to present PTSD than male cyber-sex abusers • Generally involved in compulsive overeating or bulimia • Similar to male cyber-sex abusers in terms of interests in paraphilias, romance/dating and swinging.

Is there an identifiable modus operandi (MO)?

The Internet allows for highly dis-inhibited sexual behaviour (Dabet, 1998). People are more likely to allow themselves to behave in ways that are different from ordinary, everyday life, and to express previously unexplored aspects of their personalities, which can be likened to the wearing of a mask.

Taylor et al. (2001) identified a series of stages that people move through in their offending behaviour when downloading pornography from the Internet. This is directly linked to the offender's engagement with the Internet. Setting events for downloading including histories of early sexualised behaviour; inadequate adult socialisation; dissatisfaction with current persona; and an acquisition of a computer and Internet skills. Initial contact with the Internet was often accompanied by accessing adult pornographic sites before a search for child pornography. Accessing such material facilitates engagement with a virtual community, further normalising the collection of such material, as well as promoting further engagement with the Internet and its corresponding technology. This is then followed by a steady increase in on-line behaviour and a reduction in other outside engagement. Increasingly large quantities of material are rapidly collected and then different types of collecting behaviour emerges linked to time spent sorting and cataloguing images. For those people who download and go on to engage in social contacts on the Internet, the process of sustaining that engagement requires credibility. The latter is often achieved through the exchange or trade of material such as pictures, text or fantasy stories. Collecting also leads to an increase in fantasy and sexual activity, particularly masturbation in relation to images or through engaging in mutual fantasies with others while on-line. In this sense, the Internet lowers sexual inhibitions. The illegality of the materials being downloaded can magnify and heighten the sexual arousal. With the acquisition of technical skills comes a sense of mastery and

control and this provides them with greater prestige and status which in turn facilitates more contacts. The continued exchange of images acts as a form of social reinforcement which validates and legitimises their activity. As such, there is a very real potential change in the offender's beliefs, values and cognitive styles when using the Internet. Many perpetrators may have been abused and seek to repeat their abusive experience with them in control for a change.

Blundell et al. (2002) found that the longer the fantasy is maintained and elaborated on, the greater the chances that the behaviour will be acted out in real life. Escalation is recognisable if someone progressed from viewing child pornography to using chat rooms to contact children for sexual conversations; leading to telephone contact with the hope of engaging in mutual masturbation or sexualised conversations.

Grooming refers to the process by which a child is befriended by a would-be abuser in an attempt to gain a child's trust and confidence, enabling them to get the child to acquiesce to abusive activity (Wyre, 2000). It is frequently a prerequisite for an abuser to get access to a child. Whilst it is difficult to know how big a problem grooming over the Internet is, van Dam (2002) suggests that in the US, 5–20% of children have been subjected to unwarranted approaches while on the Internet and it is unlikely to be different in the UK. The Internet does certainly provide new and distinct opportunities for sex offenders to facilitate abusive behaviour. It enables the abuser to be anonymous at the beginning of the encounter, building up the child's trust, so that when the offender introduces himself in person, the child is less concerned (Gillespie, 2002). Day trips, offers of acting or modelling contracts, invitation to play computer games and other carrots are used to gradually introduce the children into photographic and abuse networks. Later they will be used to recruit and coerce other children when accepting rewards can put them in an even more invidious position. Offenders can send pornographic material to potential victims in the grooming phase. Typically children are instructed in the most efficient methods of destroying or hiding the evidence of the file transfer. They may be advised to: download the file to diskettes rather than the hard drive; rename the disk or file so that it will appear innocuous; or change the file extension after it has been downloaded so that the file will not open until it has been changed back to the correct extension. Alternatively, offenders may set up sub-identifications and assign passwords to allow other users to enter their account and download images from their e-mail and send and receive information. This allows pornography to be passed from the offender's main account to the sub-account that was set up for the victim, leaving no overt trace on the victim's personal computer as all communications have occurred within the Internet account of the offender (Zwicke, 2000).

Morahan-Martin and Schumacher (2000) noted that the Internet can be used to alter mood in the context of feeling down, anxious or isolated. Internet communication can lessen social risk and lower inhibitions without the demands of traditional friendship (Turkle, 1995).

The Internet also enables multiple self-representations (Quayle, 2002). Quayle and Taylor (2001) explored self-representation on the Internet in some detail. They found that the Internet plays a unique role in allowing individuals to self-represent aspects that might otherwise remain hidden or dormant. The expression of sexual interest is facilitated by the ability to represent oneself in whatever way one wants in apparent anonymity. People can present themselves as a child or an adult, as a male or a female, and with different preferences. Lamb (1998) in a study of how chat rooms may be used by paedophiles reported that most visitors were not as described and showed no restraint in what they wanted to say or do. Most people self-represent through verbal exchange and sometimes photographs. However, if the purpose is sexual, then the absence of non-verbal cues makes the process of first impression formation take on new forms. This

is largely expressed through the language chosen, speed of writing, timing of the response, and style of writing, use of punctuation and use of emotions (Mantovani, 2001). The Internet also allows for multiple representations of identity that need bear no relationship with other social cues that are normally so salient in the off-line world (Quayle, Holland et al., 2000).

Collections of child pornography: a framework for analysis

Quayle and Taylor (2002) reported that it can generate strong group dynamics expressed through issues of status, expertise and apprenticeship. Child pornography plays a role in that status in the community is achieved through amassing a large organised collection, through distributing parts of missing series of photographs and through providing new pictures via postings. Their research confirmed that the Internet plays an important role in collecting behaviour related to child pornography. Material was often collected even when it has no arousing properties for the individual but because is part of a series or is new. Collections can be very large and may be the result of most child pornography on the Internet being free.

Collections of child pornography can be categorised along a continuum ranging from everyday and perhaps accidental pictures involving either no overt erotic content, or minimal content (such as the depiction of a child in their underwear) to pictures showing actual rape. Such a continuum might be helpful in characterising the nature of a given collection as well as elucidating factors that may enable and sustain offender behaviour.

Taylor et al. (2001) identified the following ten levels of severity with descriptions:

Level	Name	Description of picture qualities
1	Indicative	Non-erotic and non-sexualised pictures showing children in their underwear, swimming costumes, etc., from either commercial sources or family albums; pictures of children playing in normal settings, in which the context or organisation of pictures by the collector indicates inappropriateness.
2	Nudist	Pictures of naked or semi-naked children in appropriate nudist settings, and from legitimate sources.
3	Erotica	Surreptitiously taken photographs of children in play areas or other safe environments showing either underwear or varying degrees of nakedness.
4	Posing	Deliberately posed pictures of children fully, partially clothed or naked (where the amount, context and organisation suggest sexual interest).
5	Erotic posing	Deliberately posed pictures of fully, partially clothed or naked children in sexualised or provocative poses.
6	Explicit erotic posing	Emphasising genital areas where the child is either naked, partially or fully clothed.
7	Explicit sexual activity	Involves touching, mutual and self-masturbation, oral sex and intercourse by child, not involving an adult.
8	Assault	Pictures of children being subject to a sexual assault, involving digital touching, involving an adult.
9	Gross assault	Grossly obscene pictures of sexual assault, involving penetrative sex, masturbation or oral sex involving an adult.
10	Sadistic/bestiality	a. Pictures showing a child being tied, bound, beaten, whipped or otherwise subject to something that implies pain. b. Pictures where an animal is involved in some form of sexual behaviour with a child. (Reproduced by permission of Ethel Quayle)

They pointed out that in relation to collections of pictures, even level one images can be sexualised and fantasised over, and may be used to both promote and sustain sexual fantasy. The lack of knowledge of victimisation at level three does not diminish its gravity in any way.

Collections of pictures are rarely a random aggregation of individual images. Most pictures occur as part of a series and it is usual for such series to have a narrative or thematic link. The narrative might be an aid to fantasy and filling gaps in the series may be highly reinforcing to the collector. Locating a picture, or a series of pictures, at some point on the continuum needs to be considered in the context of other issues related to a collection. These include the size of the collection and the obsessional qualities relating to its organisation, and storage, the principle themes illustrated, the presence of new or private material, and the age of the children depicted in the pictures. Taylor (1999) suggested that the age of children in new pornography is reducing (especially girls) with the implication that such victims may be less able to disclose the abuse than would older children.

Thomas and Wyatt (1999) have noted that users of the Internet can quickly move into becoming the producers.

Identifying vulnerable children

Gillespie (2002) identifies procurement as the second major child protection issue raised by the use of the Internet. This is where an offender approaches someone to persuade them to find a child for the offender to abuse. It may involve financial instruction. Procuring differs from grooming in that the adult who wants to abuse the child does not communicate directly with the child but, rather, communicates to a third party in the hope that the third party will obtain a child for him.

Sexual offenders often target children with particular characteristics. These may be children in the care of the state; children who have experienced prior abuse; emotionally immature children with learning or social difficulties and problems with peer friendships; children isolated in their families; children at a loose end on the streets, whose parents do not have interest or time for them; love or attention deprived children; children with strong respect for adult status; children from single parent families; children who will co-operate for a desired reward (such as money, computer games); children who have been previously sexually abused and are displaying learned behaviour which a paedophile will spot; and children with low self-esteem (adapted from Stanley, 2001).

Issues relevant to the risk from the Internet include the trusting nature of children and their naivety, tied in with curiosity, rebellion and independence, making children the perfect target. Troublesome and rebellious children – as well as nice children – do things 'behind their parents' backs'. They will engage in conversation that is titillating and exciting and naughty. Children will be fascinated by pornographic imagery. Unfortunately, even if it appears initially innocent, the offender gradually moves in to one where the child can feel guilty, responsible and unable to tell anyone. Approaching safeguards from an angle that children seek loopholes within these safeguards is one of the ways forward (Wyre, 2001). Mitchell et al. (2001) found that children over 14 years who were 'troubled' (defined as being exposed to negative life events, maltreated and/or depressed) were more likely to be solicited. This marries with most of the literature which highlights that adolescents, more than children, are at greater risk of seduction from offenders.

Lanning (1998) noted that children are often interested in and curious about sexuality and sexually explicit material and will sometimes seek out information on-line. They will often be moving away from the total control of their parents and trying to establish new relationships outside the family. Sex offenders targeting children will exploit and use these characteristics and needs. Adolescent boys confused about their sexual orientation are at high risk of being contacted.

It is rare that children report sexual solicitation, even when the offender attempts to contact them outside the Internet. Mitchell et al. (2001) found that only 25% reported a sexual approach to their parents whilst only 10% were reported to the police.

Mapp (1994) identified some characteristics of assistance to parents in identifying children who may be involved in Internet organised abuse: they may have disturbed sleep patterns, or a change in behaviour, perhaps anti-social or criminal, which is not just a phase or they may show sexuality inappropriate for their age. In practical terms, they may have inexplicable gifts or money.

The impact on the child

Using the Internet for crimes against children makes them twice victims, the first when they were actually abused, the second time when this abuse is seen by thousands or millions and forever on the screen. Regardless of the content of the picture, each time that an image of a child is accessed for a sexual purpose, it victimises the individual concerned. This makes the treatment and recovery much more difficult as they may continue to be available on the Internet and this inhibits any recovery. Some offenders may use pornographic images as a trophy of the abuse and they might even be used as an aid to blackmail in order to ensure the child's silence or co-operation in future assaults.

Finkelhor et al. (2000) found that 25% of those who had been solicited for sexual purposes reported being extremely afraid or upset, with children aged 10–13 years reporting the greatest adverse impact. The majority of these children reported at least one symptom of stress in the form of avoidance behaviours, intrusive thoughts or physical symptoms.

Clearly the impact of sexual material will impact differently according to the child's developmental level and their reason for viewing the content. There is also likely to be an effect of desensitisation through prolonged access.

Child pornography is a permanent record of the abuse and even if the perpetrator is arrested and some copies seized, the children are left with the fear that other copies could surface anywhere in the world at any time. Once photographed, the pictures are deliberately used to silence and hold them. If they tell, they are warned, the pictures will be shown to their parents or teachers etc. They may also be used to desensitise other children.

Symantec (2003) conducted a study of 1,000 US youngsters between the ages of seven and 18 about their experiences with spam e-mail. They found that 80% receive inappropriate spam e-mails touting on-line drugs and porn on a daily basis, with half saying it made them feel uncomfortable and offended. One in five children opened and read spam, and more than half of them checked their e-mail without parental knowledge. Nearly half had received links to pornographic web sites, two-thirds had received information on dating services and four-fifths received sweepstake messages.

The impact on the family of sexual activity on the Internet

Schneider (2000) found that:

- The effects of an average 11 hours per week on the computer can leave the partner and the children feeling lonely, ignored, unimportant, neglected or angry.

- The specific nature of the access (sexual matters) leads to lies being told and often a sense of betrayal and distrust develops in the partner.

- Their sexual relationship is affected because of the Internet use but also through a comparison by the spouse of the body and sexual performance with the on-line women.

- Children can potentially be exposed to pornography and may develop unhealthy attitudes toward sex and children.

The response by the partner to a realisation of the on-line access is:

- **Ignorance or denial:** the partner recognises that there is a problem in the relationship but is unaware of the contribution of their on-line activities to the problem. They accept the man's denials, explanations and promises. She tends to ignore and explain away her own concerns and may blame herself for the sexual problems. Self-esteem is likely to suffer. Later in this stage, suspicions may increase accompanied by snooping or detective behaviours.

- **Shock or discovery of the on-line activities:** When the partner learns of the on-line activities they often experience strong emotions of shock, betrayal, anger, pain, hopelessness, confusion and shame. These may be aggravated by continued on-line activity post-discovery. Their feelings of shame, self-blame and embarrassment emerge and often prevent the partner from talking with others, compounding their isolation. They often cover up for the on-line user.

- **Problem-solving attempts:** the partner may snoop, bargain, control access to the computer, give ultimatums, obtain information about their behaviour and ask for full disclosure after each repeat episode. This often provides some illusion of control. Where they are computer literate there is much more chance of regulation and successfully tracking the on-line activities.

The relationship between child pornography and contact sexual offences

In pre-Internet days the link between the possession of pornography and actual abuse was very strong. A Chicago police study in the mid 1980s found that in almost all cases of child pornography the cache of photographs seized included images of the person arrested abusing children, while US customs concluded that 80% of those who use child pornography are abusers (Taylor, 2001). A study carried out by the US Postal Inspections Service found that in 36% of cases of possession of pornographic material featuring children, the individuals concerned were also involved in actual abuse (Wellard, 2001).

Can we import these figures and use them in a UK context?

It has been argued that there are three groups of people who use the Internet: those who see it out of curiosity, are turned off by it and never do it again; those who use it for masturbation and fantasy; and those who see it and then act out their fantasies (Wellard, 2001).

Dobson (2003) noted that preliminary work in the UK points to the fact that between one in three and one in five of those arrested for possessing child pornography will be found to

be abusing children. Since many sex offenders do feature problems in self-regulation and this feature is being found around Internet usage, the potential for crossover cannot be discounted. Authors such as Goldstein (1999) suggest that pornography is a by-product of sexual offences, used by offenders to facilitate the seduction of new victims and an inevitable part of the process of organised abuse (Itzin, 1997). Many assume that pornographic images play an important part in sexual fantasy and are used for purposes of arousal. Seto et al. (2001) have argued that the use of pornography causes offending through mediating variables such as anti-social personality, physical aggressiveness, offence-supportive attitudes and beliefs, or conditioned sexual responding to cues of non-consent.

Quayle and Taylor (2002) established that child pornography downloaded on the Internet does act as a means of sexual arousal and is used as an aid to masturbation both off and on-line and for the majority it resulted in an increase in masturbatory behaviour. Respondents were highly selective in the material they chose, seeking out content that was arousing for them and which fit with individual fantasies. Given the scope of child pornography available on the Internet, none had any difficulty in finding material that met their own sexual proclivities.

Quayle (2002) identified how contact offences can be induced through material seen on the Internet:

- **Imitation:** where offenders replay with a victim what they have witnessed on the computer.

- **Permission giving:** The offender is given more courage and ideas from what they see on the computer, especially regarding the escalation of their offending behaviour.

- **Reinforcing existing feelings:** Makes the offender want to act on them. The transition from hands-off to hands-on offending can be very quick and direct, with rapid progression through asking for their age, previous experience of sex and whether she would like to meet him.

Conversely, pornography may be seen as fulfilling a positive function for some offenders in that it may prevent the commission of a contact offence. Here, since the Internet has the potential to provide people with options for communication other than directly with people (Kennedy-Souza, 1998), it is likely that we will continue to see the emergence of offenders for whom there has been no direct contact with children, and whose crimes are exclusively related to downloading pornographic pictures of children (Holmes et al., 1998).

Quayle (2002) concluded that whilst there is little support for a direct causal link, individuals who are already predisposed to sexually offend are most likely to show an effect of exposure to pornography and are the most likely to show the strongest effects. What may be relevant is the significance of the pornography for the offender. The exposure thus influences but does not cause the offending. What appears to be clear is that someone accessing child pornographic images will at the very least be desensitising themselves and this is a concern in its own right. Blundell et al. (2002) found that the longer the fantasy is maintained and elaborated on, the greater the chances that the behaviour will be acted out in real life. Escalation is recognisable if someone progressed from viewing child pornography to using chat rooms to contact children for sexual conversations; leading to telephone contact with the hope of engaging in mutual masturbation or sexualised conversations.

The effect of pornography on the propensity to offend continues to be widely debated: you can believe that it is a harmless substitute or that it promotes offending behaviour. The step from child pornography to sexual contact with children is a huge one, but the desire for such contact is arguably implicit in the use of the pornography. What does seem to be clear is that someone found to be in possession of child pornography who is a father should rightly start alarm bells ringing in child protection circles.

Assessment issues

All assessment has to capture and take account of the function that the Internet plays in facilitating sexual fantasy and its transfer to the off-line world (Quayle, 2002). We also have to be alert to early intervention as the potential for change is greater when we are dealing only with behaviour on the Internet rather than hands-on offences which show a pattern of entrenched behaviour.

Quayle and Taylor (2002b) provided us with some useful guidelines for conducting a semi-structured interview that offers workers a framework for assessment:

1. Action

- What are the number of total hours that the individual spends on-line in any one week, and the proportion of this time that was spent in contact with others sexually interested in children or in downloading images?

- What has been the level of general disruption in their lives that being on-line has played, particularly in relation to work or real-life social relationships?

- Has there been a reduction (where appropriate) in sexual interest with their partner?

- Has there been emotional withdrawal from family members and friends?

- Is there a preoccupation with accessing the Internet such that there are ongoing difficulties in concentrating?

- How many Internet media are being accessed (web sites, chat rooms, e-mail, newsgroups)?

- What do they do with each and what level of pleasure is associated with these activities?

- What nicknames are used and what do they mean to the person?

- How is material retrieved from the Internet, saved and organised (in particular, how is it stored, how are files labelled, what changes are made to existing file names)?

- How much time is spent off-line with collected material, either editing or sorting, or for use as an aid to masturbation?
- Have images been exchanged with others (how has this been done, what volume and what purpose did this serve)?
- Have images been created through scanning from existing pictures or by digital camera?
- Have any fantasies been acted out with real children (which may or may not be of an explicitly sexual nature)?
- What are the person's existing social networks and levels of emotional support?
- What level of social isolation is present?
- Has there been any contact in real life with people (adults or children) met on-line?

2. Reflection

- What level of preoccupation is there with regard to 'reliving' past experiences?
- How much time is spent thinking about their latest Internet experience (chat or image), or planning the next?
- Are details of other on-line people kept and reflected on?
- Does the person keep making promises to stop going on-line and then breaking them?
- Are there difficulties in concentrating on or keeping to off-line commitments?

3. Excitement

- Does the individual take risks in terms of accessing the material (either because of others in the house or same room) or storing it?
- Have images been downloaded while children were in the room or in close proximity?
- Have images been shared with others off-line (work colleagues, children)?
- Is there a sense of excitement in

anticipation of going on-line, or a sense of frustration or irritation when blocked from doing so?

- Does the person chat to others about real or imaged sexual encounters with children?
- Is there self-representation as other individuals (either same or other sex or age)?
- What attempts have been made to contact children through the Internet?

4. Arousal

- What level of masturbation is associated with on-line activities?
- Does masturbation take place on or off-line?
- What has been the increase or change in sexual activities since accessing the Internet?
- Does the individual engage in virtual sexual relationships with others (adults or children), for example through IRC?
- Has there been a change in the kinds of text or images accessed (age or other characteristics of the child, types of images and level of victimisation)?
- Does arousal happen to other non-child images?

The following interview schedule was also developed by the COPINE Project team and is available electronically if you contact them at copine@ucc.ie:

Downloading

1. How long have you had access to the Internet?
2. How soon after getting the Internet did you look for pornography?
3. What was the total number of hours spent on-line per week prior to arrest?
4. What proportion of this time was spent looking for or downloading child pornography?
5. What proportion of this time was spent

looking for or downloading other non-child pornography?

6. What Internet media were being accessed (web sites, chat rooms, bulletin boards, email, newsgroups, e-groups etc.). Give details of each.

7. What activities were associated with each medium?

8. What types of images were downloaded (for example posed photographs, action shots etc.)?

9. What was the preferred age ranges and sex of children in the images?

10. Were there any preferred series of pictures? If yes, please name.

11. Were video clips collected?

12. Was there any change in the types of images collected over the course of time on the Internet?

13. Were there any types of images that were not collected?

14. How was material retrieved from the Internet saved and organised (how was it sorted, how were files labelled, what changes were made (if any) to existing file names).

15. Were any security measures taken (for example, encrypting files).

16. How big was the collection overall? Give approximate numbers to each of the categories collected.

17. What software was used to enable downloading and cataloguing?

18. How would you describe the filing system used for the images?

19. How much time was spent off-line sorting images?

20. Has child pornography been purchased prior to accessing the Internet?

21. What level of sexual activity took place with partner (where appropriate) before accessing the Internet?

22. Has there been a change in level of sexual activity with partner (where appropriate) since going on-line?

23. What level of masturbation is associated with on-line activities?

24. Did sexual arousal happen in relation to non-child pornography?

25. Did masturbation take place on or off-line?

26. What fantasies were associated with looking at the photographs? Please give details.

27. Were there any fantasies of sexual contact with children off-line?

28. What was the level of disruption in home-life since accessing pornography on the Internet?

29. What was the level of disruption to social life?

30. Were other substances used (alcohol, drugs) while accessing pornography?

31. Was there a preoccupation with accessing the Internet, such that there were difficulties with concentration?

32. How much time was spent thinking about the last Internet experience?

33. Has work/appointments been missed in order to go on the Internet?

34. Has work/appointments been missed through being on the Internet?

35. Does any other member of the household know about you accessing pornography on the Internet?

36. Have you made any promises (to self or other) to stop going on-line?

37. Did you take risks when accessing pornography? For example, other people in the house or room. Finding places to store disks or CDs.

38. Have you downloaded pornography when children were in close proximity? Please give details.

39. Have images been shared with others off-line?

40. Was there a sense of excitement in anticipation of going on-line?

41. Was there a sense of frustration when blocked from going on-line?

42. Have you communicated with others on-line (through IRC or ICQ, for example).

43. Have any nicknames been used on-line, and if so what did they represent?

44. Have you ever pretended to be somebody else on-line?

45. Have you attempted to contact children through the Internet?

46. Have you exchanged information about children with other adults through the Internet?

47. Have you ever exchanged gifts with a child or adult that you met on-line?

48. Have you ever arranged to meet off-line anyone (child or adult) that you met on-line?

49. Have you accessed any paedophile support groups on-line?

50. Have you sold off-line any of the material you have downloaded?

Trading

1. How soon after going on-line did you start to trade images?

2. How did you trade images?

3. Who did you trade images with?

4. Did you ever request certain images and if so, how?

5. Did you trade through public channels?

6. Did you trade through private channels?

7. What images were you particularly interested in trading?

8. Did you ever commission any images?

9. What computer software did you use to make trading easier?

10. Did you belong to any trading groups or networks?

Producing

1. Have you ever taken any pornographic/erotic photographs of children prior to going on-line? If so, give examples.

2. Have you taken any pornographic/erotic photographs of children since going on-line? If so, give examples.

3. Do you have equipment such as a scanner or digital camera?

4. Have you posted on the Internet any images that you have taken of children?

5. Was the child part of your immediate family?

6. What age was the child?

7. What was the context for taking the photographs?

8. Did you copy the content of photographs/videos that you had seen on-line?

9. How many photographs/videos were taken?

10. Were all of them posted on-line?

11. Were any of them privately traded?

12. What influenced the decision to allow others access to your pictures?

13. How did you control the distribution of the images?

14. Were any of the pictures commissioned by others?

15. Did you produce photographs on your own or with somebody else? If so, who?

16. Where were the pictures taken?

17. Did the child see the images that were taken?

18. Did the child know that they were to be distributed on the Internet?

19. Were any of the images sold for money?

20. Was there any sexual contact with the child apart from taking the images?

21. Was there sexual contact with other children prior to taking photographs?

22. Was there sexual contact with children other than those in the photographs?

Reproduced by permission of Ethel Quayle

Mullins (1997) noted that workers intervening with such people will be seen as the enemy of free speech and anyone who upsets such people could potentially find their own image superimposed on a pornographic picture on the screen as a means of trying to attack and discredit. Like other victims, knowing that a person's picture is on the Internet plus even their name, address and other details can have a traumatic effect on the person as well as their family, friends and even their community.

David Delmonico (2000) has produced an Internet sex screening test (ISST) that is available from www.sexhelp.com that asks 34 questions about on-line and off-line sexual behaviour.

Summary

To the uninformed, the potential personal harms appear to outweigh any potential benefits from engaging in on-line sexual activities. However, we should not discourage our upcoming generations from using the Internet based upon the potential hazards. Instead, it is our responsibility as professionals and caregivers to assist and teach children ways to avoid inappropriate materials and web sites. We need to encourage appropriate and safe use of this medium, while assisting children and young people to feel comfortable navigating the information highway (Calder, 2002).

References

Acevedo, E., Delgado, G. and Segil, E. (1998) INPPARES Uses Internet to Provide Peruvians with Sexuality Information and Counselling. *Siecus Report*, 26: 14.

Aftab, P. (2000) *The Parent's Guide to Protecting Your Children in Cyberspace.* NY: Mcgraw-Hill.

Aloysius, C. (2001) The Media Response: A Journalist's View of The Problem in Asia. In Arnaldo, C.A. (Ed.) (2001) *Child Abuse on the Internet: Ending The Silence.* NY: Bergahn Books.

Auclaire, E. (2001) Paedophilia: The Work of Associations and The Role of The Media and Research. In Arnaldo, C.A. (Ed.) (2001) *Child Abuse on the Internet: Ending the Silence.* NY: Bergahn Books.

Australian Bureau of Statistics (2000) *Use of the Internet by Householders*, November 2000.

Binik, Y.M., Ma, H.K. and Kiesler, S. (1999) Ethical Issues in Conducting Sex Research on the Internet. *Journal of Sex Research*, 36: 82–90.

Blundell, B. et al. (2002) Child Pornography and the Internet: Accessibility and Policing. *Australian Police Journal*, March: 59–65.

Calcetas-Santos, O. (2001) Child Pornography on the Internet. In Arnaldo, C.A. (Ed.) (2001) *Child Abuse on the Internet: Ending the Silence.* NY: Bergahn Books.

Calder, M.C. (1999) *Assessing Risk in Adult Males Who Sexually Abuse: Frameworks for Assessment.* Lyme Regis: Russell House Publishing.

Calder, M.C. (1999b) Managing Allegations of Child Abuse Against Foster Carers. In Wheal, A. (Ed.) *The Companion to Foster Care.* Lyme Regis: Russell House Publishing.

Calder, M.C. (2002) Child Sexual Abuse and the Internet: Current Challenges to Child Care Professionals. Presentation to *Sexual Abuse and the Internet: From Research Findings to Effective Assessment and Management*, TUC Congress Centre, London, 30th October, 2002.

Carey, R. (1996) Betwixt and Between: an Organization's Relationship With Online Communications. *Siecus Report*, 25: 8–9.

Carlsson, U. (2001) Research, Information and Sensitizing The Public. In Arnaldo, C.A. (Ed.) *Child Abuse on the Internet: Ending the Silence.* NY: Bergahn Books.

Cart, C.U. (1997) Online Computer Networks. In Minkler, M. (Ed.) *Community Organizing and Community Building for Health.* New Brunswick: Rutgers University Press.

Cooper, A. (1998) Sexuality and the Internet: Surfing into the New Millennium. *Cyberpsychology Behaviour*, 1: 181–7.

Cooper, A. et al. (1999) Online Sexual Compulsivity: Getting Tangled in the Net. *Sexual Addiction and Compulsivity*, 6: 2, 79–104.

Cooper, A., Delmonico, D.I. and Burg, R. (2000) Cybersex Users, Abusers and Compulsives: Results of A Survey. In Cooper, A. (Ed.) *Cybersex: The Dark Side of the Force.* NY: Brunner/Mazel.

Costello, T. (2001) Gambling's Great Web of Lies. *The Age*, 3: April, 15.

Dabet, B. (1998) Text as Mask: Gender, Play and Performance on the Internet. In Jones, S.G. (Ed.) *Cybersociety 2.0: Revisiting Computer-Mediated Community.* Thousand Oaks, CA: Sage Publications.

Dobson, A. (2003) Caught in the Net. *Care and Health*, 11: February, 6–9.

Donnerstein, E. (2002) The Internet. In Strasburger, V.C. and Wilson, B.J. (Eds.) *Children, Adolescents and the Media.* Thousand Oaks, CA: Sage Publications.

Durkin, K.F. and Bryant, C.D. (1995) Log on to Sex: Some Notes on the Carnal Computer and Erotic Cyberspace as an Emerging Research Frontier. *Deviant Behaviour*, 16: 179–200.

Edwards, S.S. (2000) Prosecuting Child Pornography. *Journal of Social Welfare and Family Law*, 22: 1, 1–21.

Faulkner, N. and Finkelhor, D. (2000) *Internet Paedophile Overview*. www.soc-um.org/online.html

Finkelhor, D., Mitchell, K.J. and Wolak, J. (2000) *Online Victimisation: A Report on the Nation's Youth. Crimes Against Youth Research Centre*. Available Online at www.missingkids.com

Gillespie, A.A. (2002) Child Protection on the Internet: Challenges for Criminal Law. *Child and Family Law Quarterly*, 14: 4, 411–25.

Goldstein, S.I. (1999) *The Sexual Exploitation of Children: A Practical Guide to Assessment, Investigation and Intervention*. Boca Raton, FL: CRC Press.

Hampton, K.N. and Wellman, B. (2000) Examining Community in the Digital Neighbourhood. In Ishida, T. and Isbister, K. (Eds.) *Digital Cities: Technologies, Experiences and Future Perspectives*. NY: Springer-Verlag.

Healy, M. (1997) *Child Pornography: an International Perspective*. Available Online at www.usis.usemb.se/children/csec/215e.htm

Hughes, R. and Hans, J.D. (2001) Computers, the Internet and Families: A Review of the Role New Technology Plays in Family Life. *Journal of Family Issues*, 22: 6, 776–90.

Internet Crime Forum (2001) *Chatwise, Streetwise*. Available at www.internetcrimeforum.org.uk

Itzin, C. (1997) Pornography and The Organization of Intra-Familial and Extra-Familial Child Sexual Abuse: Developing A Conceptual Model. *Child Abuse Review*, 6: 94–106.

Jauch, M. (1997) *Pornography and the Internet: Child Protection Issues*. Presentation to a Michael Sieff Foundation Conference Child Sexual Exploitation, Pornography and Paedophilia, Cumberland Lodge, April 1997.

Jones, M. (2001) Introduction. In Arnaldo, C.A. (Ed.) *Child Abuse on the Internet: Ending the Silence*. NY: Bergahn Books.

Jones, T. (2002) *Policing the Internet*. Presentation to a Workshop 'The Internet and Sexual Offences Against Children', Greater Manchester Police Training School, 28th June, 2002.

Katz, J.E. and Aspden, P. (1997) A Nation of Strangers. *Communications of the ACM*, 40: 12, 81–6.

Kennedy-Souza, B.L. (1998) Internet Addiction Order. *Interpersonal Computing and Technology*, 6: 1–2.

Kraut, R. et al. (1998) Internet Paradox: A Social Technology that Reduces Social Involvement and Psychological Wellbeing. *American Psychologist*, 53: 1017–31.

Lamb, M. (1998) Cybersex: Some Research Notes on the Characteristics of Visitors to Online Chat Rooms. *Deviant Behaviour*, 19: 121–35.

Lanning, K.V, (1998) Cyberpaedophiles: A Behavioural Perspective. *The APSAC Advisor*, 11: 4, 12–7.

Livingstone, S. (2002) New Technology, New Policy, New Research Agenda. *Children Now*, Winter: 7–8.

Livingstone, S. (2002b) *Children's Use of the Internet: A Review of the Research Literature*. London: National Children's Bureau.

Mantovani, F. (2001) Networked Seduction: A Test-bed for the Study of Strategic Communication on the Internet. *Cyberpsychology and Behaviour*, 4: 147–54.

Mapp, S. (1994) Living in Fear. *Community Care*, 9–15th June: 16–17.

Mars, A. (2001) Children and Internet Access. *Care and Health*, 6th Sept: 14.

Mickelson, K.D. (1997) Seeking Social Support: Parents in Electronic Support Groups. In Kiesler S (Ed.) *Culture of the Internet*. Hillsdale, NJ: Lawrence Erlbaum.

Millar, S. (2003) Chat Room Danger Prompts New Safety Code. *The Guardian*, 6th Jan.

Mitchell, K.J., Finkelhor, D. and Wolak, J. (2000) Risk Factors for and Impact of Online Sexual Solicitation of Youth. *JAMA*, 285: 23, 3011–4.

Morahan-Martin, J. and Schumacher, P. (2000) Incidence and Correlates of Pathological Internet Use Among College Students. *Computers in Human Behaviour*, 16: 13–29.

Mullins, A. (1997) *Pornography and the Internet*. Presentation to a Michael Sieff Foundation Conference Child Sexual Exploitation, Pornography and Paedophilia, Cumberland Lodge, April 1997.

Mullins, A. (1997b) Children and Cyberspace. *Childright*, 136: 4–6.

NAPCAN (2001) Newsletter Number 2, November.

O'Connell, R. (2001) Paedophiles Networking on the Internet. In Arnaldo CA (Ed.) *Child Abuse on the Internet: Ending the Silence*. NY: Bergahn Books.

Orzack, M.H, (1998) Computer Addiction: What is It? *Psychiatric Times*, 15: 8.

Orzack. M.H. (1999) How to Recognise and Treat Computer.Com Addictions. *Directions in Clinical and Counselling Psychology*, 9: 13–26.

Parks, M.R. and Floyd, K. (1999) Making Friends in Cyberspace. *Journal of Comput. Medicated Comm*, 1: 1–12.

Quayle, E. (2002) *The Impact of Viewing on Offending Behaviour*. Presentation to a Workshop 'The Internet and Sexual Offences Against Children', Greater Manchester Police Training School, 28th June.

Quayle, E. et al. (2000) The Internet and Offending Behaviour: A Case Study. *The Journal of Sexual Aggression*, 6: 78–96.

Quayle. E., and Taylor. M. (2001) Child Seduction and Self-Representation on the Internet: A Case Study. *Cyber Psychology and Behaviour*, 4: 5, 597–609.

Quayle, E. and Taylor, M. (2002) Child Pornography and the Internet: Perpetuating a Cycle of Abuse. *Deviant Behaviour*, 23: 331–61.

Quayle, E. and Taylor, M. (2002b) Paedophiles, Pornography and the Internet: Assessment Issues. *British Journal of Social Work*, 32: 863–75.

Rheingold, H. (1993) *The Virtual Community: Homesteading on the Electronic Frontier*. Reading, MA: Addison-Wesley.

Richardson, T. (2001) UK Kids Take to Gambling and Porn. Available at www.theregister.co.uk/content/archive/18841.htm

Schneider, J.P. (2000) Effects of Cybersex Addiction on the Family: Results of a Survey. In Cooper, A. (Ed.) *Cybersex: The Dark Side of the Force*. NY: Brunner/Mazel.

Schwartz, M.F. and Southern, S. (2000) Compulsive Cybersex. In Cooper, A. (Ed.) *Cybersex: The Dark Side of the Force*. NY: Brunner/Mazel.

Sellier, H. (2001) The World Citizens' Movement to Protect Innocence in Danger. In Arnaldo, C.A. (Ed.) *Child Abuse on the Internet: Ending the Silence*. NY: Bergahn Books.

Seto, M.C., Maric, A. and Barbaree, H.E. (2001) The Role of Pornography in the Etiology of Sexual Aggression. *Aggression and Violent Behaviour*, 6: 35–53.

Stanley, J. (2001) *Child Abuse and the Internet*. Melbourne: Australian Institute of Family Studies.

Summit, R.C. (1990) The Specific Vulnerability of Children. In Oates, R.K. (Ed.) *Understanding and Managing Child Sexual Abuse*. Marrickville: Harcourt Brace Jovanovich.

Symantec (2003) *Children Upset by Spam E-Mail*. (14th June 2003) http://newsvote.bbc.uk/mpapps/pagetools/print/news.bbc.co.uk/2/hi/technology/29781

Taylor, M. (1999) *The Nature and Dimensions of Child Pornography on the Internet*. Paper Presented to Combating Child Pornography on the Internet, Vienna, 29.9.99–2.10.1999.

Taylor, M. (2001) Net is Not the Main Villain. *Community Care*, 15th–21st March: 14.

Taylor, M., Holland, G. and Quayle, E. (2001) Typology of Paedophile Picture Collections. *The Police Journal*, 74: 2, 97–107.

Taylor, M., Quayle, E. and Holland, G. (2001) Child Pornography, the Internet and Offending. *ISUMA*, 2: 2, 94–100.

Thomas, G. and Wyatt, S. (1999) Shaping Cyberspace: Interpreting and Transforming the Internet. *Research Policy*, 28: 681–98.

Turkle, S. (1995) *Life on the Screen: Identity in the Age of the Internet*. NY: Simon and Schuster.

Van Dam, C. (2002) *Identifying Child Molesters*. NY: Haworth Press.

Wellard, S. (2001) Cause and Effect. *Community Care*, 15th–21st March: 26–27.

Wyre, R. (2000) *Cycles of Behaviour in Sex Offending*. Milton Keynes: Ray Wyre Associates.

Wyre, R. (2001) Questions to Ray Wyre. *Care and Health*, 6: September 2001, 2–3.

Zwicke, L. (2000) *Crime on the Superhighway*. Available from www.geocities.com

Chapter Two

The Impact of Viewing on Offending Behaviour

Dr Ethel Quayle

Introduction

Cloaked in the anonymity of cyberspace, sex offenders can capitalize on the natural curiosity of children, seeking victims with little risk of interdiction. These offenders no longer need to lurk in parks and malls. Instead, they roam from chatroom to chatroom looking for vulnerable, susceptible children.

(Medaris and Girouard, 2002).

On the first of February, 2001, the FBI initiated an investigation after an undercover agent identified three e-groups involved in posting, exchanging and transmitting 'child pornography'. One web site depicted the group as the following, 'This group is for People who love kids. You can post any type of messages you like or any type of pics and vids you like too. PS if we all work together we will have the best group on the net' (Innocent Images, 2002). The global nature of such offending was illustrated by the fact that this operation, named Candyman in the US, identified 7,000 unique e-mail addresses, with 2,400 from outside of the United States. In August, 2001, the office of the US Attorney General announced the successful completion of Operation Avalanche (US Department of Justice, 2001). This operation began in 1999, when US Postal Inspectors discovered that a Texas company, Landslide Productions Inc., operated and owned by Thomas and Janice Reedy, was selling access to child pornography web sites. Customers from around the world paid monthly subscription fees via a post office box address or the Internet to access hundreds of web sites, which contained extremely graphic child pornography material (US Postal Inspection Service, 2003). Landslide Productions originally dealt with the sale of adult web sites, but as the business grew, most of the profits came from child pornography web sites, and in just one month the business grossed as much as $1.4 million.

The publicity related to such operations, and the names and professions of people identified, inevitably has drawn our attention to the fact that many people are accessing such images through the Internet and that these people may on occasion be those who might have been seen as 'pillars of the community'. It has also prompted us to ask questions about the nature of such offending, the characteristics of the offenders, and the relationship between viewing such images and the commission of contact offences. These are valid questions, and have influenced decisions about risk assessment and also about sentencing of offenders (Gillespie, 2003). However, in struggling to understand the problem it would often appear that we have lost sight of the child within the images. Child protection becomes an issue of protecting the child within the immediate social context of the offender, rather than protecting the child whose image depicts, often in a very graphic way, the commission of an offence. A further potential danger is that not only do we forget the child, but we also generate potential categories of 'good' and 'bad' offenders (those who are not known to have committed a contact offence as opposed to those who have). However, we might argue that the viewing of such material in and of itself increases the likelihood that children will be continue to be abused *in the service of providing pictures* for people to download (Taylor and Quayle, 2003).

It is apparent that many people access images that may be indicative of sexual interest in children, but which are still legal (Taylor et al., 2001), and it may be more useful to think of such images as lying along a continuum of victimisation. This is an important issue, and has been reflected in sentencing guidelines in the UK (Court of Appeal Criminal Division, 2002). It is important because offenders' collections of images reflect both their level of engagement with the material, and also provide visible evidence of sexual fantasy. Until recently, the term 'child pornography' has been used to describe these images, allowing comparison with the depictions of consensual sexual activity between adults that are so widely available from newsagents and video retailers. Many professionals working in this area have expressed the belief that such terminology is problematic and allows us to distance ourselves from the true nature of the material. A preferred term is abuse images (Jones, 2003), and its use will be reflected in this chapter.

We have no idea of the number of people accessing abuse images, as many operate within private Internet networks. We do know, from convicted offenders, however, that they are a very heterogeneous group and include people of all ages and from all social backgrounds. This may include people who have an existing offending history and others for whom there has been no previously acknowledged sexual interest in children. This clearly raises serious questions about the relationship between viewing abuse images and the commission of further offences. Both the function of abuse images and their relationship with contact offences remains unclear, and what little we know is based on research that largely predates the Internet. Many authors, such as Goldstein (1999), have suggested that 'child pornography' is a by-product of contact offences, or used by offenders to facilitate the seduction of new victims (Tyler and Stone, 1985). Itzin (1997) described pornography as central to child abuse and stated that, 'Pornography, in the form of adult and/or child pornography used to season/groom/initiate/coerce children into agreeing to be abused, or the production of child pornography (the records of children being sexually abused), is implicated in every form of child abuse, however it is organised' (p192). In this context Itzin appeared to be

focusing on the function of abuse images in relation to the further abuse of children. However, much of the literature related to abuse images has as its focus their role in sexual fantasy and the ways that they are used in relation to sexual arousal and masturbatory behaviour. For example, Lanning (1992) suggested that abuse images are used in a similar way to adult pornography in that they feed sexual fantasies, and act as a prelude to actual sexual contact with children. However, it is difficult to know whether this is an inevitable aspect of viewing abuse images, or whether it reflects the fact that those with an interest in deviant sexual behaviour are more likely to seek out material congruent to their sexual fantasies. It is also the case that much of what we do know about sexual interest in children relates to people who have been caught. Evidence from the Internet would seem to suggest that there are many more people who fantasise about children and who use images (pornographic or erotic) to aid those sexual fantasies, but who never come to the attention of law enforcement.

Goldstein (1999) differentiated between 'pornography' and 'erotica', in that the objects that form erotica may, or may not be, sexually oriented or related to a given child or children involved in a sexual offence. Any material that stimulates sexual arousal may be described as erotic, regardless of its content, and in the context of the Internet may include images that are in themselves legal. Both Lanning (1992) and Goldstein (1999) have emphasised that abuse images not only function as an aid to fantasy and masturbation but also serve to:

- Symbolically keep the child close.
- Remind the offender of what the child looked like at a particular age.
- Make the child feel important, or special.
- Lower the child's inhibitions about being photographed.
- Act as a memento that might give the offender status from other people that he associates with.

- Demonstrate propriety by convincing children that what the offender wants them to do is acceptable because he has engaged in a similar way with other children.
- Provide a vehicle for blackmail.
- Act as an aid to seduce children, by misrepresenting moral standards and by depicting activities that the offender wishes to engage the child in.

These functions clearly relate to the planned commission of a contact offence, and such collections of abuse images may be qualitatively different from those secured from the Internet, which are less likely to relate to a child known to the offender. In relation to the new technologies, there are people involved in both accessing and distributing child pornography who have no apparent history of child molestation (Quayle et al., 2000), and for whom the images serve as a kind of currency in the e-commerce of the Internet (Taylor and Quayle, 2003). However, it is unclear whether adults with a sexual interest in children use Internet abuse images and pornography more than the general population. A recent study by Demetriou and Silke (2003) established a website to examine whether people, who visited for the purposes of gaining access to legal material, would also attempt to access illegal or pornographic material. Over an 88-day period, 803 visitors entered the site and it was found that those sections purporting to offer illegal and/or deviant material were accessed by the majority of visitors. These authors suggested that 'On the Internet, the opportunity to commit crime is never more than three or four clicks away'. The combination of opportunity, ease, perceived anonymity and the immediacy of personal rewards created a situation where such behaviour 'is not simply common, it actually becomes the norm'. This is similar to the findings of Cooper et al. (2000) who talked about the triple A engine (access, affordability, anonymity) in the context of problematic on-line sexual behaviour. Tate (1990) suggested that the particular advantage of the Internet to the paedophile is its security, as a lifetime's collection can be hidden on a small amount of electric gadgetry, stacking the odds heavily against discovery.

One recent study that addressed the role of abuse images in the offending process is that of Proulx et al. (1999). Their study took as its focus pathways to offending in relation to extra-familial abuse. Their results suggested that within a population of child molesters, there were two distinct pathways to offending; coercive and non-coercive. People using a coercive pathway had generally used psychoactive substances (for example alcohol or drugs) before the commission of their offences. Of the thirty people in this group, all had molested female victims, whom were not perceived to be vulnerable and who were already well known to them. These offences were apparently unplanned and of relatively short duration. The number of offenders in the non-coercive pathway was smaller (fourteen), and had generally used 'pornography' and deviant sexual fantasies prior to committing their offence. All within this group had molested male victims, perceived by the offender as being vulnerable in some way, and whom did they not know. These offences differed from those of the other group in that they were planned, were of longer duration and involved non-coital activities without coercion. These results are clearly interesting and suggest differences between heterosexual and homosexual offenders that may relate to the duration of their deviant behaviour, which has allowed them to acquire a greater level of sophistication. It may also be that opportunistic offenders may have not been so engaged in the paedophile community, which would give them access to child pornography.

Proulx et al.'s (1999) study related to the use of abuse images as part of the commission of an offence, and are similar to the findings of Marshall (1988). In this study, 53% of their sample of child molesters deliberately used 'pornographic stimuli' as part of their planned preparation for offending. Carter et al. (1987) also examined the use of 'pornography' in the criminal and developmental histories of sex offenders. They found that all offenders had a similar prior exposure to pornography in childhood, but child molesters were more likely to use such child pornographic material prior to and during their offences and 'employ pornography to relieve an impulse to commit offences'. It is of interest that Carter et al. (1987) suggested that pornography might be used as a substitute for offending. Relevant to this, it is not unusual for offenders to suggest that abuse images were used as a way of controlling the urge to have sexual contact with a child (Quayle and Taylor, 2002). However, much of the research to date about the relationship between pornographies and contact offences has suggested that there is an association between induced sexual arousal and the depiction of sexual activities. Marshall (2000), in his review of the literature relating to the use of pornography by sexual offenders, concluded that pornography exposure may influence, but not be the sole cause of, the development of sexual offending, but for most 'its use is simply one of the many manifestations of an already developed appetite for deviant sexuality'. What is of significance for this discussion is that people with a sexual interest in children do not passively look at the material they are interested in, but engage with it sexually to the point of ejaculation.

It is, however, difficult to examine any purported causal relationship between viewing pornography and the commission of sexual aggression. We either have to rely on the use of historical accounts, or laboratory studies where the experimenter controls the amount of time the offender is exposed to material. It is also the case that many people with a sexual interest in children are highly selective in their choice of material, a factor largely ignored by experimenters, (Howitt, 1995). What this also highlights is that what is sexually stimulating does not necessarily relate to overt content but more to the way the offender perceives it, and identifies in some way with it. Seto et al. (2001) suggested that men who are sexually deviant, such as paedophiles, may preferentially seek out material that depicts content that is highly arousing to them. It may be, therefore, that subjective responses to pornography depend on how well the depicted content matches the individual's existing, preferred sexual scripts (Mosher, 1988).

However, the Internet has now emerged as one of the most versatile and accessible outlets for pornography, where those interested can access material with a minimum of cost, both financially and in terms of risk. Barron and Kimmel (2000) suggested, in the context of adult pornography, that there has been 'democratisation' with costs dropping and control of production becoming more diffuse. These authors found that there was evidence of an increase in the amount of non-consensual violent material available on the Internet, suggesting that men were more likely to be depicted in dominant positions as victimiser and not victim in far greater proportions than in magazines and videos. An important aspect of this study was that they suggested evidence of satiation with regard to the images downloaded. This meant that the consumer would seek out newer, more explicit and more violent forms of sexual material in order to achieve sexual arousal. While there is limited evidence to support this in relation to child abuse images, offender accounts do suggest that some offenders seek out more intensely stimulating pictures either by changing category (for example, to animal or torture), or to younger children (Quayle and Taylor, 2002).

However, the Internet cannot simply be viewed as just another way of offending. Holmes et al. (1998) suggested that the computer acts as a mechanism of metamorphosis in that fantasies are provided with the opportunities and resources to become more concrete. Fantasies may also take on a new realism that can be shared on-line with others who have similar interests. The Internet also provides anonymity, giving both pleasure from 'hiding' oneself and ones behaviour, along with the potential pleasure of playing another role (Chou and Hsiao, 2000).

What is also important in relation to the Internet is that for many people, engagement with this medium is not a passive response. For example, it can be used by individuals to alter mood in the context of feeling down, anxious or isolated (Morahan-Martin and Schumacher, 2000) and for those who have difficulty in relating to others, Internet communication can lessen social risk and lower inhibitions, without the demands of traditional friendship (Turkle, 1995). The Internet can also allow for multiple self-representations and may provide a context where both sexual experimentation and deviance can flourish (DiMarco, 2003; Lamb, 1998). For paedophiles, on-line communities show strong evidence of group dynamics (Lamb, 1998; Evans, 2001), expressed through issues of status, expertise and apprenticeship (Linehan et al., 2002). These authors noted that within one Internet community, abuse images played a role in that status within the community was achieved through amassing a large organised collection, through distributing parts of missing series of photographs and through providing new pictures via postings. As other authors have indicated, used in this way, abuse images both validated and justified paedophile behaviour and acted as a medium of exchange within a community (Healy, 1997; Durkin, 1997).

It is also the case that the Internet is an environment that challenges old concepts of regulation, which are reliant upon tangibility in time and space. It has been argued that conventional hierarchies are disrupted by a distributed, decentralised network in which power is spread among various people and groups. This may be a very positive aspect of the Internet for many marginalised groups, and increasingly we read accounts of people silenced through their political beliefs who are given a voice through the Internet. However, other groups that have been traditionally marginalised within our society, such as people with a sexual interest in children, may also be empowered by the Internet. Such empowerment is likely to be reinforced by anonymity but also by the fact that everybody's agenda can find a niche on the Internet. Feelings of empowerment may contribute to the development of personal beliefs about self-efficacy and control that serve to heighten dis-inhibition in the off-line world because fantasy and reality become blurred.

For most people, accessing the world of child abuse images is both illegal and difficult.

For the general public, it is a topic that generates a high level of emotion, but is not usually based on any actual contact with either the material or the offender. At its most simplistic, it is easy simply to take an undifferentiated approach to offending and see all offenders who use the Internet as being largely similar. From our own research in the COPINE Project, we have attempted to identify both the function of images for the offender and to generate a description of offending behaviours that can be understood within a process model of offending (Quayle and Taylor, 2003).

From an analysis of the accounts of offenders about their use of abuse images, we can identify six principal themes (Quayle and Taylor, 2002). Within the COPINE sample, all of these appear common across offenders, with the exception of where abuse images facilitate social relationships, as this is largely confined to offenders who have gone on to 'chat' on-line with others through IRC (Internet Relay Chat). The strongest theme to emerge in the analysis is the way that abuse images are used as a way of achieving sexual arousal. Many of the images that are accessed (but not all) are used for masturbatory purposes, and offenders are selective in the pictures that they use. Such selectivity might relate to specific age groups, physical types, gender of the child, or to a particular sexual activity and are often selected to fit with pre-existing fantasies, some of which may relate to earlier contact offences, or to new offending fantasies. This invariably, but not exclusively, involves masturbation to the fantasies, and levels of masturbation seem to be greater after the offender has gone on-line to access images.

It is interesting that following masturbation offenders often report that they stop looking at the pictures and either close the computer down or move on to some other non-sexual topic. More than this, for some, the images at this point themselves becomes almost aversive in the absence of sexual arousal. As referred to earlier, claims are made by offenders that such masturbation to child pornography is in fact a substitute for abuse, although invariably such accounts fail to acknowledge that the pictures being accessed are ones of child abuse.

Offending fantasies in relation to images are not always confined to looking at the pictures on screen, and at times do act as a blue print both for abuse and for the production of photographs. For some people, accessing such abuse images appears to reinforce existing fantasies and is used to give permission to act on them. It allows offenders to ignore what the child might be experiencing, and to not question cues such as crying or a child constantly covering her face with her nightdress. Sexual fantasies are also fuelled by the excitement that comes from a sense of doing something illegal.

The selection of abuse images for sexual purposes may also be made according to some sort of 'moral' or 'ethical' code, which varies according to the offender and also according to the circumstances. For example, many offenders prefer children who are smiling and who appear to be 'enjoying' the abuse. 'Smiling children' in images is often used by offenders to legitimise their abuse and make it appear as if it was consensual. This is similar to the findings of other studies that have examined the role that such images may play in the abuse of children (e.g. Silbert, 1989). Offenders may argue that they only retain images where the child looks happy, but such moral boundaries may be very flexible, in that if images of distressed children are accessed adventitiously, rather than searched for purposefully, then they may be kept by some offenders. The fact that non-preferred images are kept is often related to the way in which such images are used as currency for exchange.

A theme that relates to the collecting of abuse images overlaps with, but is not subsumed by, themes of arousal. Offenders often call themselves collectors, and use this to differentiate themselves from 'paedophiles', (Taylor and Quayle, 2003). Collecting abuse images in some ways is no different from any other items that people choose to collect, with one exception; the content of abuse images is illegal. Belk (1995) has suggested that collecting is a process, whose development

depends on what has gone before and the availability of items to be collected in the future. The process is an active and selective one, and all collections are held in sets of related but different items. There would be little value to the collection if all items were the same, or were a random hotchpotch. In any collection, the objects collected share common qualities but are non-identical. Most importantly there is a driven quality to collecting that Belk refers to as passionate. In the context of abuse images of children, it is relatively easy to access sufficient images to build up a collection. Along with this is the reduced risk and secrecy that comes from being able to store and catalogue such digital material without fear of discovery. Offenders can rapidly build up large collections, and it is not unusual for offenders to talk about collecting in excess of 40,000 images. Such rapid acquisition is also accompanied by the ability to trade or exchange images, while maintaining relative anonymity, and for some offenders this facilitates the building of community networks.

For many offenders, it seems that there is pleasure to be obtained from collecting pictures as part of a series, even when the images do not reflect their own sexual preferences. Such pictures may be talked about in a very dispassionate way with no reference made to the fact that these are pictures of children. For example, offenders may make comparisons between baseball cards, stamps and abuse images, which often serve to normalise the activity, and make it appear innocent in its intent.

In the context of collecting, not only is pleasure obtained from completing missing pictures in a series, but also in engaging with the material both on and off-line through sorting and cataloguing the images. Such cataloguing can be either simple or complex, depending whether access to the photographs is for individual use or for purposes of exchange. Where the material is kept only for personal use and there is no trading involved, sorting may still take place but in a much more rudimentary way. However, referring back to 'old' photographs in the collection takes second place to seeking out new material, which is an important aspect of collecting per se. To supply the demand by collectors of abuse images for new material, more photographs have to be taken that depict the on-going abuse of children. It is in the context of trading that accessing new or private collections requires the exchange of images that is of interest to other collectors. In many cases this may directly lead to the production of new material through the abuse of children in the offender's immediate social network.

For many Internet offenders, the photographs become an archive that they can refer back to when necessary, use for trading for new material, and have as a collection of artefacts that appear in series. For some people, completing the series is as much an end in itself as using the photographs for sexual pleasure although it can be associated with sexual pleasure when it enables fantasy. This is particularly important where there is a narrative theme to a series, such as pictures showing a child gradually removing their clothes.

However, collecting behaviour is not solely confined to child abuse images and for many offenders, (even those who identify their primary sexual orientation as paedophilia), it is part of a progression through collecting other forms of pornography. In the sample of those interviewed for the COPINE project, many offenders moved through a variety of pornographies, each time accessing more extreme material. This might refer to the age of the children in the photographs or to the actual activities being portrayed. It is worth noting that the use of hyperlinks means that websites containing pornographic but legal material may act as a portal to sites containing illegal images, such as child abuse.

It is important to note that by using the Internet, not only can such materials be accessed, but access can be rapid and movement can take place across categories. The density of the material that can be downloaded in any one session is high, and there is evidence that with this form of

collecting behaviour, where the collection is a stimulus for sexual behaviour, satiation may occur quite rapidly. This may also function to depersonalise the images even further, allowing the offender to see them simply as objects rather than images of children existing in an off-line world.

Offenders often talk about accessing the Internet, downloading images and organising their collections as high frequency, ritualised behaviour, which for many leads to huge collections of photographs. While earlier research in this area suggested that one feature of such collections is that they are permanent, in the context of the Internet, offenders will occasionally delete images, in part because they know that should they wish to do so they can access them again. What is different about the Internet in relation to collecting child pornography may relate to the volume of material that can be accessed and the fact that once the picture is on the Internet it will remain there, accessible as a part of somebody else's collection. Unlike where hard copy images are destroyed, it is always possible to access more of the same on the Internet.

Child abuse images and social relationships are almost exclusively seen in the context of offenders who trade images and who use IRC (Internet Relay Chat) or other synchronous forms of communication to link up with others. When on-line, those who trade images inevitably come into social contact with others similarly engaged, and clearly this is very important to some offenders. The exchange of images and the chat (which may or may not be sexually related) enables social cohesion and allows for the rapid acquisition of images through trading networks. Such networks have their own social hierarchies, associated with both the number of images, the ability to complete picture series and access to new or unusual material. Having abuse images is often a requisite for community membership, and is reinforced by having material to trade, by behaving correctly and by following the rules for trading. Once status has been achieved through membership of the group, trading may be reduced and instead the social function of the on-line exchanges and the ability to be on the inside and obtain special photographs is more important. However, not all offenders wish to trade and are members of a community. For some, limits here are bound up with ideas of doing wrong by being involved, while for others it relates to fears about security.

Using child abuse images to build social networks and relationships on-line serves a variety of complex functions. It may be used as a way of confirming sexual interests to others on-line, and it generates etiquette with regard to trading relationships, which results in gaining the trust of others. The importance of such relationships is often prioritised over the images, and may result in the indiscriminate saving of material in order to increase the likelihood of future exchange with others.

It is interesting that for many offenders, linking up with others on the Internet provides important social support that often replaces unsatisfactory relationships in the 'real world'. This is similar to the research by Morahan-Martin and Schumacher (2000) who described the Internet as providing an attractive alternative to a mundane or unhappy life. Accessing abuse images on the Internet may become part of a bid to create a secret and separate world, which has qualities unobtainable in the 'real' world and allows escape from many unpleasant realities. Through the Internet the unsatisfactory elements of life that are difficult to address or change can, for periods, be avoided and substituted for a world that is more controllable. Importantly, sexual satisfaction can be sought and gained and over which the respondent had perfect control, a quality often lacking in off-line sexual encounters.

When offenders talk of meeting their needs through the Internet, this often overlaps with talk of satiation and addiction, while some claim to be actively seeking abuse images as a way of controlling their interests, and as a way of dealing with emotions such as anger. While offenders often talk of addiction, it is unclear as to whether they feel they are addicted to the Internet or to the images, the two having

become inextricably intertwined. This problem has been reflected by debate in the psychological literature as to whether such behaviour is addictive (e.g. Griffiths, 2000), compulsive (Putman and Maheu, 2000) or simply problematic (Quayle and Taylor, 2003). Such terms are used to make sense of a loss of control, of high rate behaviour and are also used by offenders as a way of distancing oneself from ideas of personal agency. Such distancing is also seen in talk about the nature of sexual offences against children, with at least some offenders seeing themselves as someone who has done something illegal but who has not committed an offence against a child.

In understanding the function of abuse images for the offender and how this relates to the Internet, we can start to build on a conceptual model that allows us to examine offending activities that relate to abuse images as *a process*. This is important, as adult sexual interest in children on the Internet embraces both legal and illegal activates. For example, collecting abuse images is illegal, but talking about sexual fantasies or engaging in sexual role plays with other adults, generally speaking, is not. Similarly, sharing information about encryption software is not illegal, but giving information that allows access to children is likely to be. Many offenders move through a variety of offending behaviours, and we have to accept that some will move away from illegal activities back to those that we may consider undesirable but which are still legal. This may, for example, reflect a move to collecting images of murder victims or other pornographies. While most readers would see this as inappropriate, it is still a legal activity.

What are the offending behaviours that are associated with Internet abuse images? We can think of four broad classes of offending; downloading (which may include the commission of a contact offence); trading; production and Internet seduction. These are clearly not mutually exclusive categories, but all revolve around engagement with the Internet and the possession of abuse images. Downloading child abuse images is invariably a purposeful activity. While it is relatively easy to accidentally access adult pornography, this is rarely the case in relation to abuse images. We can conceptualise downloading as a largely passive way of collecting images, usually from web sites or from Newsgroups. However, although it may involve searching for material, such passive collecting is unlikely to include substantial social engagement with others, but may still result in the justification of such activity because of the evidence that there are large numbers of other people similarly engaged. Downloading may also be accompanied by the commission of contact offences and these may be in response to what is seen on-line, either through imitation or through permission giving.

Not all collectors of abuse images move from passive collecting to contact or communication with others. However social contact, and the 'reality' of such relationships, can be important in legitimising and normalising sexual interests. Contact with others is often sustained through credibility gained through trading activities related to abuse images. Such credibility is often related to the quality of the collector's image collection (the size of the collection or the ability to trade new or rare material). Taylor and Quayle (2003) have suggested that 'For those respondents who traded, or distributed, images, the notion of images as currency appeared to be important. They are currency in terms of trading for new material but they are also currency in maintaining existing on-line relationships and giving credibility. An important aspect of this is the notion of a community of collectors serving to normalise the process of collecting but also legitimising the downloading and saving of images that in other contexts may have been aversive to the respondent' (p185).

The drive for new material to trade may also provide the stimulus for the production of new material. Internet images of child abuse are still largely, but not exclusively, produced in a domestic context. The photographer is often an adult well known to the child and usually acting in a parental, or care giving, role. When offending takes place in these

circumstances, such offences relate to the need to sustain and increase credibility amongst others, and as a way of gaining more desired images of child abuse as well as an expression of sexual behaviour. Of significance here, newness of material is central in ensuring status within a trading community and is a source of power to the producer. He can decide what material is released and when, and to whom. Images may be created according to the producer's fantasies or his perception of the market, but can also be commissioned by others.

Clearly not all abuse images produced are used in the same way. For people who do not engage socially within the offending community, images may be a private commodity, to be viewed in privacy and which act as mementoes or trophies of the abuse. In the context of the Internet, seeing the images on-line may have acted to fuel fantasies about taking photographs, or may have given permission to the offender, enabling him to overcome both his internal and external inhibitors.

As already suggested pornography per se heightens sexual arousal and dis-inhibition and in the context of the Internet, may aid Internet seduction through fantasy manipulation and masturbation. This is largely accomplished through chat rooms. A study by Finkelhor et al. (2000) suggested that one in five children between the ages of 10 and 17 received sexual solicitation over the Internet, and that of those one in 33 received an aggressive solicitation. This involved being asked by an adult to meet, or being contacted on the telephone, or sent regular mail, money or gifts. Durkin (1997) suggested that there are four ways in which people with a sexual interest in children may misuse the Internet in this context: to traffic child pornography, to locate children to molest, to engage in inappropriate sexual communication with children, and to communicate with other paedophiles. Chat rooms may provide a perfect vehicle for all of these. For those with a sexual interest in children, life on-line operates in the context of the abuse of children both on-line and off-line, either in the production and exchange of abuse images or in attempted sexual engagement (Quayle and Taylor, 2001). There is a blurring of on-line and off-line activity, such that 'activities in cyberspace produce outputs for real life and vice versa' (Talamo and Ligorio, 2001). Cyberspace is an interactive arena and tools such as chat rooms offer new interactive resources. Within chat rooms, people can represent themselves in whatever way they want. They can change their age, gender, race, physical appearance and social background (DiMarco, 2003). If the purpose of self-representation is specifically sexual, as in the on-line seduction of children, then the absence of non-verbal cues (so important in the off-line world in terms of the impressions we make) increases the possibility of deception. Some children, already vulnerable, may be easy targets for such deception and provide the perfect victims, both on-line and off-line for those who wish to exploit them (Wolak et al., 2003). One published account of such an offender who used the Internet to attempt to seduce children, talked about other men engaged in the same activities as predators, masturbators and befrienders, all who would have used abuse images as part of their social exchange (Quayle and Taylor, 2001).

In this chapter, an attempt has been made to explore the functions that abuse images have for those who access them, within the context of a process model of related offending behaviours (Quayle and Taylor, 2003). What seems apparent from our own research in relation to Internet abuse images is the importance of process, which may reflect the interaction between the person and their social context. Such a model moves away from static conceptualisations of the offender and recognises that both internal and external factors play a part in the choices that individuals make with regard both to their offending and non-offending behaviour. It also moves us away from notions of simple causality with regard to the relationship between viewing abuse images and the commission of other offences. Itzin (2002) has presented a compelling argument that

pornography is 'instrumentally causal in the aetiology of sex offending'. As yet there is virtually no published data that allows us to make sense of the relationship between viewing Internet abuse images and the commission of contact offences. What little data there is would suggest that in incarcerated populations, levels of contact offences are high (e.g. Hernandez, 2000), as they might also be in private producing and trading networks. However, data from current operations indicate that it is highly unlikely that this will be the case across all Internet offender populations. Rather than seek causality between viewing and the commission of contact offences, it may be more useful to see the use of Internet abuse images as being instrumental and central to the sexual victimisation of children in its many forms.

References

Barron, M. and Kimmel, M. (2000) Sexual Violence in Three Pornographic Media: Toward a Sociological Explanation. *The Journal of Sex Research*, 37: 2, 161–8

Belk, R.W. (1995) *Collecting in a Consumer Society*. London: Routledge.

Carter, D. et al. (1987) Use of Pornography in Criminal and Developmental Histories of Sexual Offenders. *Journal of Interpersonal Violence*, 2: 2, 196–211.

Chou, C. and Hsiao, M.C. (2000) Internet Addiction, Usage, Gratification, and Pleasure Experience: The Taiwan College Students' Case. *Computers and Education*, 35: 65–80.

Cooper, A., McLoughlin, I. P. and Campbell, K.M. (2000b) Sexuality in Cyberspace: Update for the 21st Century. *CyberPsychology and Behaviour*, 3: 4, 521–36.

Court of Appeal Criminal Division (2002) *Regina -v- Mark David Oliver, Michael Patrick Hartney, Leslie Baldwin*. Neutral Citation Number: [2002] EWCA Crim 2766.

Demetriou, C. and Silke, A. (2003) A Criminological Internet 'Sting'. *British Journal of Criminology*, 43: 213–22.

DiMarco, H. (2003) The Electronic Cloak: Secret Sexual Deviance in Cybersociety. In Jewkes, Y. (Ed.) *Dot.Cons. Crime, Deviance and Identity on the Internet*. Portland, Oregon: Willan Publishing.

Durkin, K. (1997) Misuse of the Internet by Paedophiles: Implications for Law Enforcement and Probation Practice. *Federal Probation*, 61: 2, 14–8.

Evans, R.D. (2001) Examining the Informal Sanctioning of Deviance in a Chat Room Culture. *Deviant Behaviour: An Interdisciplinary Journal*, 22: 192–210.

Finkelhor, D., Mitchell, K.J. and Wolak, J. (2000). *Online Victimization. A Report on the Nation's Youth (6-00-020)*. Alexandria, VA: National Center for Missing and Exploited Children.

Gillespie, A.A. (2003) Sentences for Offences Involving Child Pornography. *Criminal Law Review*, Feb, 81–93.

Goldstein, S.L. (1999). *The Sexual Exploitation of Children. A Practical Guide to Assessment, Investigation, and Intervention*. Boca Raton: CRC Press.

Griffiths, M. (2000). Sex on the Internet. In Von Feilitzen, C. and Carlsson, U. (Eds.) *Issues, Concerns and Implications. Children in the New Media Landscape*. Goteborg: UNESCO.

Healy, M. (1997) *Child Pornography: An International Perspective*. Prepared as a working document for the World Congress Against Commercial Sexual Exploitation of Children. Retrieved from the World Wide Web: http://www.usis.usemb.se/children/csec/215e.htm

Hernandez, A.E. (2000) *Self-Reported Contact Sexual Offences by Participants in The Federal Bureau of Prisons' Sex Offender Treatment Program: Implications For Internet Sex Offenders*. Presented at the 19th Research and Treatment Conference of the Association for the Treatment of Sexual Abusers, San Diego, CA, November 2000.

Holmes, R., Tewksbury, R. and Holmes, S. (1998) Hidden JPGs: A Functional Alternative to Voyeurism. *Journal of Popular Culture*, 17–29.

Howitt, D. (1995) Pornography and the Paedophile: Is it Criminogenic? *British Journal of Medical Psychiatry*, 68: 15–25.

Innocent Images, Operation Candyman Phase 1 (2002). Available online at http://www.fbi.gov/pressrel/canyman/candymanhome.htm.

Jones, T. (2003) Personal Communication. Greater Manchester Abusive Images Unit.

Itzin, C. (2002) Pornography and the Construction of Misogyny. *The Journal of Sexual Aggression*, 8: 3, 4–42.

Itzin, C. (1997) Pornography and the Organization of Intrafamilial and Extrafamilial Child Sexual Abuse: Developing a Conceptual Model. *Child Abuse Review*, 6: 94–106.

Lamb, M. (1998) Cybersex: Research Notes on the Characteristics of the Visitors to Online Chat Rooms. *Deviant Behaviour*, 19: 121–35.

Lanning, K. (1992) *Child Molesters: A Behavioural Analysis*. Washington DC: National Center for Missing and Exploited Children.

Linehan, C. et al. (2002). Virtual Paedophile Communities. *Journal of Sexual Aggression*, in press.

Marshall, W.L. (2000). Revisiting the Use of Pornography by Sexual Offenders: Implications for Theory and Practice. *The Journal of Sexual Aggression*, 6: 1/2, 67–77.

Marshall, W.L. (1988) The Use of Sexually Explicit Stimuli by Rapists, Child Molesters and Nonoffenders. *Journal of Sex Research*, 25: 2, 267–88.

Medaris, M. and Girouard, C. (2002) Protecting Children in Cyberspace: The ICAC Task Force Program. *Juvenile Justice Bulletin*. U.S. Department of Justice. Available online at http://www.ncjrs.org/pdfiles1/ojjdp/191213.pdf.

Morahan-Martin, J. and Schumacher, P. (2000) Incidence and Correlates of Pathological Internet Use Among College Students. *Computers in Human Behaviour*, 16: 13–29.

Mosher, D.L. (1988) Pornography Defined: Sexual Involvement Theory, Narrative Context, and Goodness-of-fit. *Journal of Psychology and Human Sexuality*, 1: 67–85.

Proulx, J., Perreult, C. and Ouimet, M. (1999) Pathways in the Offending Process of Extrafamilial Sexual Child Molesters. *Journal of Research and Treatment*, 11: 2, 117–29.

Putman, D.E. and Maheu, M.M. (2000) Online Sexual Addiction and Compulsivity: Integrating Web Resources and Behavioural Telehealth in Treatment. *Sexual Addiction and Compulsivity*, 7: 91–112.

Quayle, E. and Taylor, M. (2001) Child Seduction and Self-representation on the Internet. *CyberPsychology and Behavior*, 4: 5, 597–608.

Quayle, E. and Taylor, M. (2002) Child Pornography and the Internet: Perpetuating a Cycle of Abuse. *Deviant Behaviour*, 23: 4, 331–62.

Quayle, E. and Taylor, M. (2003) Model of Problematic Internet Use in People With a Sexual Interest in Children. *CyberPsychology and Behavior*, 6: 1, 93–106.

Quayle, E. et al. (2000) The Internet and Offending Behaviour: A Case Study. *Journal of Sexual Aggression*, 6: 1/2, 78–96.

Seto, M.C., Maric, A. and Barbaree, H.E. (2001) The Role of Pornography in the Etiology of Sexual Aggression. *Aggression and Violent Behaviour*, 6: 35–53.

Silbert, M.H. (1989) The Effects on Juveniles of Being Used for Pornography and Prositution. In Zillman, D. and Bryant, C. (Eds.) *Pornography: Research Advances and Policy Considerations*. Hillside, NJ: Lawrence Erlbaum.

Talamo, A. and Ligorio, B. (2001) Strategic Identities in Cyberspace. *CyberPsychology and Behavior*, 4: 1, 109–20.

Tate, T. (1990) *Child Pornography*. St. Ives: Methuen.

Taylor, M. and Quayle, E. (2003) *Child Pornography: An Internet Crime*. Hove: Brunner-Routledge.

Taylor, M., Holland, G. and Quayle, E. (2001) Typology of Paedophile Picture Collections. *The Police Journal*, 74: 2, 97–107.

Turkle, S. (1995) *Life on the Screen: Identity in the Age of the Internet.* New York: Simon and Schuster.

Tyler, R.P. and Stone, L.E. (1985) Child Pornography: Perpetuating the Sexual Victimization of Children. *Child Abuse and Neglect*, 9: 313–8.

US Department of Justice (2001) Attorney General Ashcroft Announces the Successful Conclusion of Operation Avalanche. Available online at http://www.usdoj.gov/opa/pr/2001/August/385ag.htm.

US Postal Inspection Service and Operation Avalanche (2003) Available online at http://www.usps.com/postalinspectors/avalanch.htm.

Wolak, J., Mitchell, K.J. and Finkelhor, D. (2003) Escaping or Connecting. Characteristics of Youth Who Form Close Online Relationships. *Journal of Adolescence*, 26: 105–19.

Chapter Three

From Fixed to Mobile Internet: The Morphing of Criminal Activity On-line

Rachel O'Connell

Introduction

The evolution of the capabilities of communication technologies continues to astound and beguile – the potential is absolutely incredible and it is an exciting age to live in. We are now progressing towards an e-learning culture based on virtual learning environments – we can see the possibilities of children coming into schools with mobile devices with that fit in the palm of the hand, yet have the capabilities to allow access to vast amounts of information. These developments in technology require children and young people to evolve their learning styles and utilise greater depths of critical thinking, and so pushes their cognitive development beyond that which they may have utilised twenty years ago. They now need to have heightened skills of information retrieval in order to access and interpret data in a range of media, to critically analyse what they find, discriminate against information that may be biased or untrue, and to have the skills to create materials in this format to allow them to become active participants in the information society.

From a thematic perspective this chapter identifies a number of priorities:

● How children use the Internet.

● How both adults and adolescents with a sexual interest in children actually operate and exploit the capabilities of technologies to use them as a vehicle for abuse.

● How we might best address these issues whilst facilitating children having the optimal on-line experiences.

● How do we increase children's resiliency and reduce the risk of children being potential victims?

In many ways this chapter will be like a journey through the various communication technologies that have evolved in the last decade and seeks to explore the implications of the overlap of the on-line activities of both children as end-users and the end user with ill-intent. Most importantly this chapter seeks to signpost the most significant learning curves with respect to enhancing child safety in that time period and explores how we can utilise what we have learnt from our experiences to tackle the myriad of similar but also potentially much more challenging times ahead as 3G takes us into whole new realms of possibility which harbinger both positive and negative potentialities. Finally, this chapter calls for strategic action and outlines a vision of how we might harness the knowledge generated as a result of our experiences and furthermore proposes that we ought to co-ordinate activities so that a clearer, louder and infinitely more effective voice is heard by the key players with respect to the need to put systems in place to augment children's safety on-line. We are at a critical point at the cusp of the roll out of the next evolution in communication technologies and now is the time to act in order to ensure a safer future for children on-line.

An outline of children's reported experiences and expectations of chat rooms

In an attempt to define the nature of paedophile activity in children's chat rooms and more specifically, cyber child-sexual abuse, it is necessary to outline the kinds of social interactions that children report occurring in chat rooms. This process will help the reader to contextualise the latter sections of this chapter which outline why it is so easy for an adult with a sexual interest in children to harness and exploit the capabilities and features of children's chat rooms. To that end, the following paragraphs will focus on some of the most significant aspects of real-time interactions as explored in a study entitled 'Young People's Use of Chat Rooms: Implications for Policy Strategies and Programmes of Education' conducted by the Cyberspace Research Unit (CRU) on behalf of the Home Office.

Methodology and analysis

The sample consisted of 1,369 children between the ages of 9 and 16. 731 (53%) were males and 638 (47%) were females. The study, hereafter referred to as the CRU study, was conducted between March and May 2002 and largely involved 10 schools in the Lancashire region. 20% (n=259) of children reported that they used chat rooms on a regular basis. The findings of this study will be referred to heavily during this section of the chapter to explicate children's experiences of chat room's interactions.

Identity deception

The Internet affords users the facility to represent themselves in a variety of ways that can differ in varying degrees from actuality in terms of, for example, age, sex, personal interests and motivations for engaging in on-line conversation. In an adult context, it could be argued that identity deception as regarded by chat users is an almost expected aspect of social interactions. It is less clear if 'identity deception' is a concept with which children using children's chat rooms are familiar. Indeed, some Internet safety programmes advocate that children engage in low levels of identity deception when using chat rooms. For a more extensive discussion of the inherent flaws in such an approach please refer to O'Connell, (2001). The CRU study (2002) suggest that the vast majority of children who reported using chat rooms either reveal their real age or an age within plus or minus two years of their actual age whilst chatting, although a minority of children reported that

they sometimes pose as five-plus years older than their actual age. As will be outlined below adults with a sexual interest in children who like to groom children on-line can pose within two years of target child or choose a larger age difference of five years plus. When asked about whether or not they had encountered identity deception the following findings indicated that:

- More than one in every three chat users reported talking to someone who later revealed they were five years older than they had originally alleged, (35%, n=91).

- Less than one in every five chat users reported talking to someone who later revealed they were five years younger than originally said (19%, n=49).

- Only one in eight children reported feeling uncomfortable or worried when they found out the person they were chatting to was five years older (12%, n=31).

- Only one in every fifteen children reported feeling uncomfortable or worried when they found out the person they were chatting to was five years younger than they originally said (7%, n=18).

- Up to the age of 14, children seem to feel uncomfortable if the person reveals they are more than five years older but between 15–16 years old, children feel more uncomfortable if the person reveals they are more than five years younger than originally said.

These findings suggest that younger children feel uncomfortable by revelations of age deception when the person claims to be five years older than they had originally stated. Conversely, 14–16 year olds report that they feel uncomfortable when a person reveals that they are five years younger than they had originally stated.

Cyber flirting and cybersex

It is useful to remember that a large amount of teen chat revolves around cyber flirting and it is a useful medium in which children and teens become familiar with the language of friendship forming and relationships, and of these children:

- Two in every five of the total chat users reported that they had engaged in chat room conversations of a sexual nature with people they have only met on-line (40%, n=103).

- More than three in every five chat users would use a private chat room (64%, n=167).

- More than one in every two chat users reported that other chat users engaged them in conversations of a sexual nature (53%, (n=137) of total chat room users).

Scheduling and extending contact beyond initial point of contact

Conversations and contact via chat rooms can move rapidly from the chat room as users or participants in a conversation request or divulge details of e-mail addresses, IM programs and nicknames and mobile phone numbers. Recent Internet safety awareness campaigns in the UK have been explicit in trying to raise children's awareness of the need to guard their personal contact details in on-line contexts. The overall message of the campaign is to highlight children's awareness of identity deception in chat rooms and how it occurs. The main message is transmitted to viewers by depicting an adult, who is sitting near a computer, yet the details he communicates about himself are highly suggestive of a child.

Extension of activities from virtual into real world

In addition to conversations of a sexual nature, nearly one in every four of the total chat users reported that they have 'sometimes' been asked for a face-to-face meeting in the real world with a person they first met in a chat room (24%, n=61). Indeed, the findings of the study indicate that 10% of children who use

chat rooms reported attending a face-to-face meeting.

The next question to explore was the frequency of a match or indeed a mismatch between alleged on-line age and the actual age of the people whom children and young people met during face-to-face meetings. Interestingly, we found that:

- 55% (n=15) of the children who went to face-to-face meetings met up with people who were the same age as they said they were on-line.

- Six children reported meeting up with other people who were not the age they said they were on-line and the mismatches could be accounted for in terms of a difference of plus or minus two years to the age stated in the chat room, which was also within two years of respondent's age.

- Three 13 year-old girls reported that they had posed as chat users five years older than their actual age and arranged to meet with males five years older than the girls actual age. It is also reported by an 11 year-old boy who met up with a 16 year-old girl that she had been verbally abusive toward him during the meeting.

The expectations that children acquire of encountering conversations of a sexual nature between people who may be engaged in the processes of identity deception, and indeed, the seemingly high levels of reported experiences of alleged interactions with people engaged in identity deception coupled with the frequency with which chat users request face-to-face meetings, provides a perfect environment for adults with a sexual interest in children to camouflage their activities.

Exploitation through the Internet

The increasing number of child sexual abuse cases where the original point of contact is located in teen chat rooms suggests that for computer literate and indeed aspiring computer users with a sexual interest in children the easy accessibility of children in on-line virtual environments provides a host of previously unavailable opportunities and locations to groom, lure and seduce children. The wake up call for the UK in terms of grooming occurred in mid 2000, with Georgie, a girl from Milton Keynes, who'd been on-line chatting to a guy for six months, and thought she was in love with him. He began by telling her he was 15, and then he said he was 18, whereas he was actually 41. They arranged a meeting, which her mum drove her to. Her mum had spoken to this guy on the telephone previously, and she was relatively happy about a meeting. Georgie got out of the car. Her mother watched her for a moment in the rear view mirror and thought 'who is that guy walking towards my daughter?' They were both talking to each other on their mobiles to find each other. She realised that her daughter was in fact meeting a grown adult, acted quickly and got out of the car to warn him off. It raised the issue here in the UK that had happened in 1995, in America to Katie Tarbox. It took us in the UK that long to catch up.

Non-contact child-sexual abuse in chat rooms

Firstly, it would be wise to examine existing definitions of real world non-contact child sexual abuse and to recognise that there has been a lot of debate in this area. A comprehensive definition should reflect that non-contact sexual abuse encompasses the following types of activities:

- Photographing the child for sexual purposes.
- Showing the child pornographic materials.
- Sexualised talk with the child.
- Making fun of or ridiculing the child's sexual development, preferences, or organs.
- Verbal and emotional abuse of a sexual nature.

- Exposing genital area to child for sexual gratification.
- 'Peeping' in on child while dressing, showering, using the restroom.
- Masturbating in front of the child.
- Making the child witness others being sexually abused.

Furthermore, non-contact abuse encompasses a range of acts and can be defined in terms of 'inappropriate sexual solicitation'. One of the main advantages of chat rooms from a paedophile's perspective is that they afford access to children from the comfort of the paedophile's own home. As will be demonstrated later in this chapter, engaging in non-contact sexual abuse is a fairly common feature of paedophile's on-line activities. These activities are largely under reported and to date there has not been any substantive research into this area. Indeed, as far as the author is aware the concept of non-contact sexual abuse involving children in an on-line context has not previously been mentioned in child abuse literature. Furthermore, there appear to be a range of possible motives underpinning these activities. For example, for some paedophiles, cybersex with children seems to be an end point in itself, whereas for others this non-contact sexual abuse is merely a precursor to trying to set up a face-to-face meeting with a child for the purposes of sexual assault.

The findings of research regarding adult and adolescent child sex related activities in chat rooms outlined later indicate that in the context of interactions in chat rooms, non-contact child sexual abuse is certainly a dominant feature. Crucially, the importance of putting legislative means in place to tackle non-contact sexual abuse in chat rooms has recently been recognised by the UK government and this has been reflected in the recent White Paper, 'Protecting the Public',[1] the aim of which is to outline measures to reform the law in order to strengthen protection against sex offenders:

1. http://www.protectingthepublic.homeoffice.gov.uk/

The offence of adult sexual activity with a child will cover any sexual activity that takes place between an adult aged 18 or over and a child under 16 with the ostensible consent of the child. It will plug gaps in the existing law and will criminalise any activity with a child that a reasonable person would deem to be sexual or indecent in all the given circumstances. This will cover a range of behaviour including, for example, inducing a child to take off their clothes in circumstances, which would reasonably be considered as sexual and outside the bounds of normal family life. The offence will criminalise both direct physical sexual activity and non-contact activity. Where no contact takes place, the maximum penalty will be 10 years. The most serious behaviour involving direct physical contact will carry a maximum penalty of 14 years imprisonment.

Cyber-rape

An extension of the ideas around non-contact child sexual abuse, and perhaps a definitive feature of on-line chat room contexts, is the engagement of children by an adult – or an adolescent with a sexual interest in children – in the virtual enactment of their fantasies. Adults and adolescents who engage in cyber-rape fantasies will typically interact and engage with the child using an overt pattern of coercion, which may or may not be counterbalanced by intimacy and friendship. The express intention is to engage the child in a rape fantasy, and the enactment of this can involve explicit details of a range of sexual acts, which are often described with the inclusion of violence. In addition, in some instances a child's expressions of discomfort and fear often appear to drive the fantasy to a climactic end for the adult or adolescent with a sexual interest in children. Looking at both psychological theories of rape and inductive criminal profiles of rapists may be a useful mechanism to increase understanding of the motivations of people who engage in cyber rape scenarios.

The question is whether or not these people are motivated by a strong interest in child sex, or are they people simply exploiting the easy accessibility of potential victims that are more likely to acquiesce to these fantasies than perhaps adults might be? In other words, could the fact that the other 'participant' in the enactment of the rape fantasy is a child be less important to the cyber rapist than the actual rape fantasy? The answers to these kinds of questions are as yet unclear, but exploring rapist typologies does provide some clues about the motivations of cyber-rapists – the question is whether or not these motivations map well onto the realm of fantasy and non-contact sexual abuse. Some might argue that at one extreme, for example, that self masturbation to rape fantasies may be a cathartic process, or even that there is such a distance between fantasy and reality that a sizeable proportion of those who fantasise about raping a child or an adult would never act on this.

The Internet provides a forum, which is seemingly fantasy based and affords interaction with potential victims, and therefore shifts the rape fantasy into an interactive arena and leads to non-contact sexual abuse, which arguably can be psychologically extremely damaging.

Definition of grooming

Definitions of grooming, and indeed some definitions of non-contact sexual abuse, intimate the idea of solicitation for the purposes of the commission of a contact sexual abuse offence. For the purposes of clarity it would be wise to outline some of the definitions of grooming that are currently in existence and to explore how they might relate to an on-line environment. Under UK law, Section 1 of the Criminal Attempts Act 1981, grooming can be understood in terms of the steps leading up to the commissioning of a substantive sex offence as follows:

If with intent to commit an offence to which the section applies, the person does an act which is more than merely preparatory to the com-mission of the offence he is guilty of an attempt to commit the offence.

The proposed 'anti-grooming order' defines grooming in the following terms:

> *A course of conduct enacted by a suspected paedophile, which would give a reasonable person cause for concern that any meeting with a child arising from the conduct would be for unlawful purposes.*

The anti-grooming order is based on the Protection from Harassment Act 1997 model; the order would be backed by criminal law, and could result in prosecution and a maximum five-year jail sentence if breached. In effect, the proposed legislation would criminalise preparatory acts that are clearly leading to a criminal offence. The question that this new definition gives rise to is whether or not non-contact sexual abuse conducted via a chat room without the explicit or even implicit mention of a face-to-face meeting would actually sit under the proposed anti-grooming legislation? If there is no evidence of an individual engaging in a 'course of conduct' that suggests that they were attempting to arrange a face-to-face meeting that would result in a sexual assault, how would they sit in respect to the anti-grooming legislation?

Notwithstanding the apparent inclusion of non-contact sexual abuse under the grooming legislation, it would appear from the outline given in the Protecting the Public White Paper, that non-contact sexual abuse would actually become an offence in its own right carrying a maximum sentence of 10 years. The question is which piece of legislation would be applied if dealing with the 'hit and run' type approach that characterises on-line non-contact sexual abuse? If it were to fall under the proposed anti-grooming legislation and was deemed to be evidence of a 'course of conduct', it would carry a maximum tariff of five years. However, conceivably, a prosecution lawyer could argue that in the event of a paedophile never actually having made any explicit arrangements to meet with the child, that there was therefore no evidence of a 'course of conduct' and that the crime would not fall under the anti-grooming legislation. It might then fall under the Sexual Offences Act where it could carry a maximum

tariff of 10 years. As yet, no precedents in this regard have been set as the process of deliberating on the proposed legislation is ongoing at the time of writing this paper.

Definition of procurement

A crime that is closely related to grooming is committed where an offender approaches someone to persuade them to find a child for the offender to abuse; it may or may not involve a financial element. Procurement differs from grooming in that the adult who wants to abuse the child does not communicate directly with the child but rather communicates through a third party in the hope that the third party can obtain a child for him. The shortfall in legislative measures designed to tackle this kind of scenario became blatantly obvious in the Kenneth Lockley case (2000) and some of these shortcomings have been addressed in 'Protecting the Public' (available from www.protectingthepublic.homeoffice.gov.uk).

Cases relating to procurement

Kenneth Lockley approached what he thought was a procurement agency but was in fact an undercover FBI operation. When it was realised that Lockley wanted a child in the UK, the details were passed to the Paedophile Unit of the Metropolitan Police who continued the deception. Eventually a fake meeting was arranged and Lockley was arrested. He was subsequently charged with and convicted of the offence of attempting to incite an undercover police officer to procure a girl under the age of 21 for sexual purposes. The substantive element of this crime – procuring a girl under 21 – is an offence contrary to Section 234 of the Sexual Offences Act 1956, and is punishable by a maximum sentence of up to two years imprisonment. Reviews of the Sex Offences Act in 2000 have recommended that the offence is repealed and replaced with an offence of commercial exploitation of children. Interestingly, according to the BBC, Kenneth Lockley also posted child pornography on the

Internet.[2] The potential links between grooming children in an on-line context for the purposes of producing child pornography is also worth thinking about in terms of determining the possible motivations of people who groom children on-line.

Typology of grooming practices

Victim selection methods

In teen chat rooms the activities that precede the processes of initiating direct contact with a child may simply involve the adult providing a description of himself to all of the users of the public chat room so that he is masquerading as a particular kind of child, of a particular age in the hope of attracting an equivalent age and same or opposite sex child. Once these vital details are stated the adult simply waits for a child to respond and once a child has responded they will either choose to pursue the conversation with the child on the basis of the child's answers to a few initial vetting questions or not.

A different behaviour pattern can also be adopted whereby some adults will simply lurk in a chat room for some time assessing the conversation and each of the children participating in the conversation and only then will they choose to introduce themselves, often to one individual child whom they have been observing.

In paedophile chat rooms users exchange information with one another about how best to target a child that most closely matches an individual's predilections. The advice regarding selection and targeting involves paedophiles viewing children's public profiles on-line. Public profiles consist of on-line forms that chat service providers request children to complete, with typical information fields such as real name, age, location, and children are also invited to upload their photograph, and to give details about their hobbies and interests. In addition, if a child has created their own

web site they are requested to provide the URL. In effect, these forms provide paedophiles with enough information to satisfy their curiosity about the physical appearance of the child and proximity or otherwise to the paedophile to the child's physical location.

Throughout each of the phases there are clear and easily identifiable differences in the patterns of behaviour of the individuals, and these appear to relate closely to their motivations, which will be discussed later in the chapter. But, it is important to note that whilst the phases outlined here summarise the stages of the conversations, some adults will remain in one phase for longer periods than other adults and whereas some phases, for example the risk assessment phase, have specific and identifiable goals, the goals of other phases are psychological and relate closely to both the aims of the adult and his perceptions of how malleable a child is in terms of meeting his requirements. Very early in the initial friendship-forming phase the adult will suggest moving from the public sphere of the chat room into a private chat room in which rather than the one to many facility of a public arena, an exclusive one-to-one conversation can be conducted.

Methodology and analysis

A participant observation methodology was employed in this study, which involved over 50 hours of research in chat rooms conducted intermittently over five years. Methodological considerations were numerous and rigorous ethical procedures were formulated and implemented according to American Psychological Association (APA) guidelines both before and during research. The procedure involved the researcher entering chat rooms or channels intended for child or teen users and posing as either an 8, 10 or 12 year-old child, typically female. The researcher utilised the usernames: 'angel', or 'honez~~'

---

2. http://news.bbc.co.uk/1/hi/uk/760521.stm

and frequented both web based, and IRC based chat rooms and channels respectively. Details of the fictitious child's life were that she had moved to a new location, her parents were constantly fighting, and that she had not yet made friends with peers in her new school. Essentially, the hallmarks of a socially isolated child were the messages that were to be divulged to any other user with whom the researcher, posing as a child, engaged. Socio-linguistic analytical techniques were employed in order to explore how adults and adolescents with a sexual interest in children cybersex exploit and groom children on-line.

The following paragraphs provide a summary of the findings of an ongoing programme of research, which aims to explore the possibility of developing socio-linguistic profiling techniques designed to analyse the speech employed by people who engage in on-line grooming.

Friendship-forming phase

The friendship-forming phase involves the paedophile getting to know the child. The length of time spent at this phase varies from one paedophile to another and the number of times this stage of the relationship is re-enacted depends upon the level of contact the paedophile maintains with a child.

Relationship-forming phase

The relationship-forming phase is an extension of the friendship-forming phase, and during this phase the adult may engage with the child in discussing, for example, school and/or home life. Not all adults engage in this phase but generally those who are going to maintain contact with a child will endeavour to create an illusion of being the child's best friend. More typically an initial relationship-forming phase will be embarked upon and then interspersed in the conversations will be questions that relate to the following risk assessment phase.

Risk assessment phase

The risk assessment phase refers to the part of the conversation when a paedophile will ask the child about, for example, the location of the computer the child is using and the number of other people who use the computer. By gathering this kind of information it seems reasonable to suppose that the paedophile is trying to assess the likelihood of his activities being detected by for example the child's parents, guardians or older siblings.

Exclusivity phase

The exclusivity phase typically follows the risk assessment phase where the tempo of the conversation changes so that the idea of 'best friends' or 'I understand what you're going through and so you can speak to me about anything' ideas are introduced into the conversation by the adult. The interactions take on the characteristics of a strong sense of mutuality, i.e. a mutual respect club comprised of two people that must ultimately remain a secret from all others. The idea of trust is often introduced at this point with the adult questioning how much the child trusts him and psychologically people, especially children, respond to the tactic by professing that they trust the adult implicitly. This often provides a useful means to introduce the next phase of the conversation, which focuses on issues of a more intimate and sexual nature.

Sexual phase

The sexual phase can be introduced with questions like 'have you ever been kissed?' or 'do you ever touch yourself?' The introduction of this phase can appear innocuous enough because typically the adult has positioned the conversation so that a deep sense of shared trust seems to have been established and often the nature of these conversations is extremely intense. Therefore, from the child's perspective the conversations are not likely to be typical and perhaps the intensity of the conversation makes it more difficult for the child to navigate because they have entered a previously unfamiliar landscape of conversations of this nature. Alternatively, for children who have previously been sexually abused, and it seems reasonable to assume that there is a high likelihood that at least a percentage of the children using chat rooms will have previously encountered child sexual abuse, adults will modify their approach in a manner that affords them the greatest amount of leverage with a child. The 'you can talk to me about anything' is a relatively staple part of the conversations of those adults who intend to maintain a longer term relationship and for whom the child's apparent trust and love is a vital part of their fantasy life.

It is during this phase that the most distinctive differences in conversational patterns occur. For those adults who intend to maintain a relationship with a child and for whom it seems to be important to maintain the child's perception of a sense of trust and 'love' having been created between child and adult, the sexual phase will be entered gently and the relational framing orchestrated by the adult is for the child to perceive the adult as a mentor or possible future lover.

Certainly a child's boundaries may be pressed but often gentle pressure is applied and the sense of mutuality is maintained intact, or if the child signifies that they are uncomfortable in some way which implicitly suggests a risk of some sort of breach in the relationship precipitated by the adult pushing too hard for information, typically there is a profound expression of regret by the adult which prompts expressions of forgiveness by the child which tends to re-establish an even deeper sense of mutuality. During the relationship forming phase the adult may outline the rationale of the relationship to the child whilst also intimating his intentions. The rationale for intended activities may include, for example, 'forming a loving lasting relationship or friendship'. This rationale may or may not include an outline of future activities, for example 'maybe we could meet some day and I could show you how much I love you' or 'maybe you could take

photographs of you touching yourself'.

The nature of sexual conversation will vary from mild suggestions to explicit descriptions of, for example, oral sex. The focus may be on the child, i.e. adult asking child to touch itself and to explain what it feels like. The usual rationale for this approach is that the adult is somehow perceived as a mentor who will guide the child to a greater understanding of their own sexuality. This can sometimes be taken a little further with the promise that by engaging in these activities the child will grow to become a wonderful lover. The interaction may be about how to self-masturbate and if the adult is a different sex to the child he will explain the techniques a child could use if they were together so that the child could bring the adult to orgasm.

Cyber-sex

Fantasy enactment based on perception of mutuality

In terms of fantasy enactment based activities a range of differing approaches may be employed whereby the adult will fluctuate between inviting and emotionally black-mailing a child into engaging in cyber-sex which may involve descriptions of anything from mutual masturbation, oral sex or virtual penetrative sex. Typically, this persuasive approach seems to focus a great deal on the child feeling loved and the desire on behalf of the adult that the child will fall in love with the adult is often openly stated. Fantasy seems to be an important element of the adult's interactions with the child and for the fantasy to work there seems to be a need for the child to appear willing to engage in on-line sexual activities.

Fantasy enactment: overt coercion counterbalanced with intimacy

However, there my research findings indicate that at least some of the individuals who engage a child in the virtual enactment of their fantasies may adopt a far more overt pattern of coercion, which is sometimes counterbalanced by intimacy and friendship.

For example:

Adult: 'tell me how you would touch my c***k'

Child: 'I feel uncomfortable'

Adult: 'just do it, come on just do it, what are you waiting for?'

Child: 'I don't want to'

Adult: 'Don't let me down, come on now, I am touching you making you feel really good, I love you, come on you will like this, don't you want to make me happy'

Cyber-rape fantasy enactment: overt coercion, control and aggression

Furthermore, some individuals will resort to the use of aggressive phrases to coerce a child and this method will be replaced with much more directive and aggressive commands, e.g. *adult:* 'do as I f**king say right now bitch or you will be in big f**king trouble'

Post-fantasy enactment: damage limitation

These kinds of cyber-rape scenarios are sometimes characterised by a set of what could be termed as 'damage limitation' exercises by the adult or adolescent with a sexual interest in children. These involve very positive encouragement and high praise for a child and it seems reasonable to conclude that the intention is to reduce the risk of a frightened child divulging details of the on-line activities to anybody else. This damage limitation phase typically involves repetition of phrases by the protagonist of 'this is our secret' and 'I love you'.

Post-fantasy enactment: hit and run

More typically, especially in the case of very aggressive cyber-rapists, there is evidence of what could be termed a 'hit and run' mentality and rarely during the course of research was

the aggressive cyber-rapist interested in either damage limitation, extending contact or indeed in rescheduling. This raises issues about our understanding of the motivations of these offenders, the need for education for children and the possibility of low risks of detection due to perhaps guilt, embarrassment, shame and fear of an angry response from parents. Currently, there are low levels of provision of help lines for children where they could bring these activities to the attention of relevant authorities and receive adequate counselling and support. At present it is only possible to hypothesise about the possible psychological impact of these kinds of experiences on vulnerable children, but it seems reasonable to suggest that there is a likelihood that for some children at least, these experiences may have both short-term and long-term ill effects.

Adjusting for age

The level of duplicity engaged in by the adult means it is very difficult for a child to detect that firstly, they are not in fact talking to a child, and secondly to discover the true intentions of the adult. The patterns of conversation will vary slightly with the age of the child, but it would be contrary to evidence to assume that because a child is, for example, eight years old rather than 12 years old, that there is a very significant difference in the degree or extent of sexual suggestion or coercion employed. The variations relate to providing more explanations of what, for example, 'fingering' or 'touching oneself' actually means, but once those baseline levels of understanding have been achieved then the pattern of the conversation continues in a manner that closely approximates what is outlined above.

Broader implications

It seems reasonable to propose that the differing behaviour patterns suggest that adults and adolescents with a sexual interest in children may be gratifying differing sets of needs, desires and fantasies when interacting with children and teenagers in chat rooms.

The question is whether or not individuals have a stable style of interacting that remains consistent throughout their on-line interactions, or if there is some sense of progression as, for example, their skills in grooming become more refined, or the desire to enact in the real world a rape fantasy becomes greater than cyber based enactment?

What kind of harm does this cause to children in both the short and the longer term? Does exposure to non-contact child sexual abuse make them more susceptible to further abuse?

Verbal coercion, aggression, bullying and emotional blackmail are the stock trade of adult and adolescent child sex related activities. What impact does this have on children and what level of imitation and experimentation does it generate?

Exposures to rationalisations and justifications for child sex compounded, for example, by exposure to images of child pornography or indeed involving children in the production of both text and images based child pornography may have a long-term emotional blackmail quality which means that children may remain entrapped in a cycle of abuse and as in the real world may be used to recruit new children for either an individual or group of adults or adolescents with a sexual interest in children.

FKBKO programme of education

When the work of The ONCE project began, we conducted an audit of Internet safety web sites and discovered that there is a plethora of Internet safety websites, which tend to comprise of the typical safety messages as outlined at the beginning of this paper: 'don't give out personal details', 'tell your mum and dad if something negative happens', 'don't go to pornographic sites' and so on. A consideration of the scope of the Internet and other communication technologies, programmes and applications highlights the enormity of the technology, so the assumption that all potential risks and dangers associated with these technologies can be addressed in a handful of points about safety, is in fact, very naïve. The Cyberspace Unit strives

to counteract this with the production of FKBKO (www.fkbko.net), which has progressed considerably since the audit of sites.

Development of a measurement tool

We were very pleased to be involved in the evaluation of BECTa's pilot Internet Proficiency Scheme, which was intended to teach children at Key Stage 2 'discriminating behaviours' they could employ whilst using the Internet. This enabled us to develop an insight into how Internet safety programmes of education could be implemented in schools.

In order to assess the scheme, we measured the children's knowledge of Internet safety prior to exposure to the scheme, and then again afterwards so we could plot their learning curves. Interestingly we found some learning curves that were difficult to explain. Some children didn't benefit as well as others. Therefore we developed a measurement instrument that could be implemented and incorporated into a programme of education, which assesses a child's levels of experience in using the Internet, their exposure to Internet safety advice, and the levels of risk they engage in whilst using the Internet. This enables teachers to tailor their teaching specifically to the needs of each child, as academic ability is not the key indicator in terms of determining how knowledgeable children are about the Internet. For example, if you were teaching a child how to use Spam guards in an e-mail account but they've never used e-mail before, then it is going to be beyond their frames of reference and they will be unable to relate it to a familiar experience or analogy, and so they would require teaching about email from the very basics.

However, at the opposite end of the spectrum you may have a very knowledgeable 'high risk' child who has been using computers from an early age and regularly engages in high risk activities such as divulging personal contact details in a chat room, or sending photographs of themselves, and therefore you need to encourage them to employ critical thinking strategies about their Internet activities, and instead of challenging them and prohibiting certain activities without due explanation, rationalising why it might be risky to do certain things is more effective, and you adapt your teaching strategies to deal with that.

Educational materials

We now have the latest version of the FKBKO site that originated from the ONCE project. Part of the learning curve that occurred whilst evaluating the Internet proficiency scheme related to the efficacy of differentiating information into levels according to knowledge and experience, as your audience has different knowledge bases and you cannot feasibly 'cast the same net' over all children in any one teaching group. You need to bring them through a learning curve. Instead of fostering a kind of idea, a fear, that you're going to be a victim or you're vulnerable, it is far more constructive to increase resiliency through giving them the knowledge, the tools and skills to navigate the Internet safely.

A very practical example of this is that, on the FKBKO web site there is a section on mobile phones and mobile phone theft where children and young people are taught about the IMEI number that is uniquely allocated to each phone – this 15 digit number (which you can retrieve on all phones if you press *#06#) can be used in the event of your mobile phone being stolen, so it is important to keep a record of this number which can then be used to disable both your SIM card and your handset. This kind of approach counteracts the idea that you may be a victim of crime, and demonstrates that if this did happen, then there is positive action that you can take against the perpetrator.

Evolution of the mobile Internet

The increasing availability of 3G mobile phones means that we will shortly have video calling,

high-speed Internet access and MMS, even some handsets with camcorders in them. It is now a reality and the potential is enormous. But, we need to have education programmes in place to counteract the associated risks that these technological developments bring. We need to educate children about boundaries. A simple example of this is that like e-mail, a picture message that is taken and sent to one person for their viewing only, can in actual fact be forwarded onto many people which could have serious negative implications, as this picture is a record of an incident or moment in time that can be kept forever and even used as a visual weapon in, for example, cases of bullying or harassment. Therefore, existing programmes of education about Internet safety need to evolve in order to incorporate considerations such as these, and to ensure that we do not have a repeat situation of educational programmes at present, which have only just begun to realise the importance of educating children about elements of the Internet such as Instant Messaging, or peer-to-peer applications. The mobile Internet has evolved incredibly rapidly, with network speeds of 9.6 kilobytes in 1999 to 2 megabytes in 2002. This technology is going to be available to us sooner than we believe, and before it becomes within the reach of children we must ensure that we have effective programmes of education, amongst other strategies in place.

The Japanese experience

In Japan, mobile phones with 3G capabilities have been available for the last 18 months. 83% of high school students in Japan own mobile phones, and approximately one in five females and males report using dating sites,[3] where children post up 'advertisements' for a date on message board style web sites. This can leave them exposed to abuse. Crucially, children and young people are accessing these sites most commonly through their mobile phones.

---

3. Figures taken from a presentation by Yasumasa Kioka , Japanese National Police Agency, given at 'Children, Mobile phones and the Internet' experts meeting, Japan, March 2003. See http://www.iajapan.org/hotline/2003mobilepro-en.html

Approximately one in two females and one in four males reported attending face-to-face meetings. At a recent conference, the Japanese National Police Agency reported an unprecedented increase in child prostitution as a result of this, and an overall increase in crimes where there is a direct link between the use of a mobile phone and these cases. It seems logical to point out that one of our primary objectives ought to be to ensure that we do not have a repetition of the complacency that we currently encounter in the fixed Internet industry, who seem to have adopted the policy of adopting reactive strategies whereby change is brought about very slowly only in response to negative events for end users. It is only at this point that the industry appears willing to enter the public forum for debate and their agenda seems to pivot on two overarching concerns to ensure that any proposed best practice guidelines will not cost the industry money and that at no point must any notion of making such guidelines mandatory be allowed to progress in any dialogue.

In the UK, research conducted by the Cyberspace Research Unit with younger children[4] aged 7–11 (n=1,331) found that 1 in 3 children of this age group reported owning a mobile phone, and 5 in 7 say they use text messaging, which indicates how adept children are at picking up and utilising new technologies. One of the most interesting statistics from this research was that 1 in 5 children reported sending messages to mobile phones from the Internet, which demonstrates how children see this seamless integration between the two (the Internet and mobile phones), and so the boundaries between these two methods of communication are lessening.

Capabilities and associated risk factors

The increased risks we associate with 3G mobile phones are multi-faceted:

- **Mobility:** Internet safety guidelines tend to advise that you should keep a computer in a family room. However, if you have Internet access on your mobile phone this is no longer applicable – the mobility is always there, which leads to increased privacy.

- **Privacy:** Commonly, a PC belongs to the family and a parent or carer may well impose restrictions on content by installing filtering software, and also restrictions on time. However, most children and young people would regard their mobile phone as their own personal property, which is private and should not be interfered with by adults.

- **Scheduling:** Parents or carers can schedule the amount of time their children spend on-line when the computer belongs to the household, through rules and rotas amongst siblings. However, a private terminal precludes this level of control.

- **Unmonitored:** In addition to imposing time constraints, parents often install filtering software of some sort on the family PC so they can control the content – mobile Internet access may well remain unmonitored.

- **Preparedness:** Children possessing these phones will have increased opportunities for using them, such as increased use of MMS picture messaging. This in turn means that they become more visible.

- **Exposure:** This increased visibility introduces increased exposure, as pictures sent via MMS, email, or chat, can be easily forwarded via mobile phone, a facility that will widen the scope of paedophile networks and communities.

- **Exploitation:** We would be naïve to think that paedophiles will not try and exploit these new forms of communication technologies, and certainly there is evidence that paedophiles are aware of the advantages of contacting a child on a mobile phone and this is evidenced by the

---

4. 'Evaluation of BECTa's Internet Proficiency Scheme', September 2002, Cyberspace research Unit. Confidential report

fact that in a number of recent cases in the UK the paedophile has bought a mobile phone for his intended victim.

- **Vulnerability:** Children having access to these phones and the 'always on' capability they provide increases their vulnerability as people can easily see their on-line presence, and there's an increased vulnerability associated with this, as the increased amount of time spent on-line increases the child's visibility.

The next generation of mobile phones will facilitate children being able to create, send and receive photographs and video clips via their handsets in both a-synchronistic time frames and in real-time. These capabilities have enormous advantages but also potential down sides. For example, an adult with a sexual interest in children who is engaged in grooming a potential victim may be much more demanding in their requests for that victim to send a photograph of him or herself. It seems reasonable to predict that increases in children's responses to pressure to send images will not only enable paedophiles to be more selective about their targets according to their particular preferences, but also enable abuse to take place on a child's own personal handset – i.e. a paedophile may instruct a child to engage in sexual activities and to stream images to him in real time. Therefore, it seems reasonable to suggest that these increased capabilities and attendant greater levels of privacy will be associated with increasing the potential risks to child safety.

Pre-emptive strategies

Anticipating potential risks associated with children using 3G technology prompts us to look at devising strategies that ought to be employed whereby we can augment children's resiliency and in effect serve to off-set the impending risks. Some Internet safety experts anticipate that the guidelines developed in the context of the fixed Internet will extrapolate well into the mobile Internet environment.

Programmes of education

Arguably, one of the key strategies ought to be the development and delivery of programmes of education to address these issues for delivery in both school and a range of other environments. Clearly it would be completely naïve to assume that messages from existing programmes of education regarding the fixed Internet would suffice. As outlined earlier many of the Internet safety programmes that currently exist consist of little more than a handful of inoperable guidelines. Emerging technologies will affect people's lives at an existential level and it will no longer suffice to regard communication technologies as some kind of add-on to children's lives, or some additional element of their education or indeed as some kind of hindrance to efficient operation of the classroom as many teachers currently regard mobile phones.

Communication technologies are becoming integral parts of children's' lives and arguably this needs to be reflected in programmes of education which teach children how to recognise, establish and maintain the kinds of boundaries they ought to have with respect to, for example, recording and disseminating images using their handsets. Teaching strategies will have to include modules designed to enhance children's critical reasoning with a view to facilitating children making informed decisions about appropriate and safe use of communication technologies. In effect educators will be enhancing one of life's newest life skills, i.e. safe use of communication technologies. In addition, to be effective these programmes of education will need to grapple with these issues on a context by context analogy based methodology engaging children in the processes of making decisions about when and where and in what contexts it is certain actions are, and indeed are not appropriate.

This will involve bringing these technologies into the classroom. Whilst conducting research in schools during the previous two years many schools balked at the idea of talking to children about chat rooms –

they were seen as taboo and many schools did not want to accept responsibility for teaching children about them. However, acknowledging the issue and teaching children actively about the capabilities of technologies is an effective way of grounding their knowledge and enhancing their understanding of what might be dangerous or risky and empowering them with the tools, knowledge and skills to enhance their resiliency. We need to recognise that we are at the cusp of a huge evolution in terms of communication technology. There is a potential gap, a deficit in children and parent's knowledge, and we need to begin to counteract this gap.

Advice line

A practical strategy as regards sources of help for children who have had negative experiences would be the establishment of a 'one-stop shop' whereby children have a contact point, a source of help, similar to the Childline service in the UK. Indeed, Childline are receiving an increasing number of calls from children as a result of Internet or mobile phone related experiences. Such a service needs to be staffed by people who have the technical expertise and knowledge to be able to handle the issues and advise children about positive action they can take themselves in order to protect themselves and decrease their likelihood to be victims of such an incident.

Product development

Further preventative action that can be taken at this stage is to penetrate the product development level within mobile phone companies to ensure that the issue at the top of their agenda is child safety, and how to reduce risk. Past experience of working with the Internet industry has revealed to me, that oftentimes, there may be different teams of software engineers, sometimes in the same office, working toward developing new products, but firstly child safety is not on their agenda and secondly neither party

communicates with each other so there is no consistency in terms of the applications that they are developing or the safety features that are built in. Child safety is currently not an issue on their agenda and it needs to be. Whatever the fixed Internet industry might say in their defence, there certainly is not room for the product developers in the emerging mobile industry to exclude the issue. There can be no defence for the mobile industry such as that they did not realise that children were going to be using services such as chat, video calling and MMS, and that therefore they were going to be at risk. This is a given, and the only question now is what measures these companies take to enhance the number of safety features and the levels of product differentiation they engage into offsetting these risks.

Technical measures

In terms of investigative strategies, it is a problem when chat service companies don't store IP addresses, when their back end infrastructure is not conducive to investigating criminal activity. It is crucial that service providers are able to provide technical information to investigators, as in many cases this provides concrete evidence. If they do not have the back end infrastructure set up so that it records information in an accurate way to enable investigators to follow cyber trails, then investigations are severely hindered or sometimes even reach a dead end. Therefore, it is at this time in the developmental stage that we need to communicate with mobile companies to encourage them to talk to their software engineers and explore the options that are available to them. Forensic issues are very important. Law enforcement professionals with oceans of experience of dealing with technological investigations also have a great deal to contribute at initial product development stages and their expertise should be harnessed at this early stage, rather than trying to deal with problems as and when they occur at some point in the future. There is a need to establish best practice policies and to have 'keeping children safe' as an actual agenda item for these development teams.

Knowledge base

All these strategies need to be underpinned by a sound programme of research to investigate *how* children will be using these technologies. Few people could have anticipated the popularity of SMS messaging. It is vital to always monitor how the end user (i.e. the child) is going to use these things otherwise a plethora of policies will be of little use if they do not relate to how children and young people use these technologies in their everyday lives. There needs to be a reciprocal relationship between how the end users use the services and devices in order to inform the process of product development. There needs to be a shift in priorities to focus on overcoming the obstacles that are preventing us from getting information into schools and handling the issue so that mobile phone companies put to one side the fear they have of children as a huge customer base for them, and instead are seen to be acknowledging this fact and taking responsibility for the services they provide to the vulnerable by proactively working to protect them.

Conclusions

Clearly communication technologies have morphed the parameters of criminal activity in general and more specifically child sex related activities. In particular, with respect to victimology, communication technologies can be deemed to have the potentiality to alter the parameters on three levels, i.e. accessibility, vulnerability, and opportunity.

Typically, whilst parents are vigilant of the people children come in contact with in the real world they are not as readily vigilant of the adults children come into contact with in virtual worlds and this clearly has an impact on the accessibility of children. Furthermore, there is ample evidence that the Internet affords greater opportunity for adults or adolescents with a sexual interest in children to gain access to children, oftentimes whilst the child is at home with their parents. Communication via victim and predator can take place whilst both are in their respective real world homes but sharing a private virtual space. This fact ought to have a significant impact on our understanding of the scope and nature of child sexual abuse. Notwithstanding the evidence, some experts in the field of child abuse posit that current statistics suggest that child abuse is predominantly interfamilial and therefore the threat on-line adults or adolescents with a sexual interest in children pose is limited by virtue of the fact that they are ascribed to the category of 'stranger abuse'. But upon further examination, if the elements which contribute toward facilitating sexual abuse in the home are explored it would seem reasonable to suggest that key elements would include, easy accessibility of child, ease of hiding covert activities through use of emotional blackmail or threats of violence. It is increasingly important to recognise that the Internet affords users the ability to replicate these exact elements of an abusive relationship, crucially affording an adult or adolescent with a sexual interest in children using the Internet to gain access to a child's home environment.

In addition, not only do communication technologies afford ease of accessibility to children, they also provide the conduit by which adult or adolescents with a sexual interest in children can schedule contact with children and this gives greater opportunity to abuse children. Furthermore, in an off-line environment it seems reasonable to suggest that an adult with a sexual interest in children may need to invest a great deal in the processes of gaining access to a child, grooming a child and scheduling contact etc., but on-line typically they do not interact with adults of other children in the child's social circle and so it is possible to form an exclusive relationship rather quickly.

It seems reasonable to suggest that the Internet affords users with the potential to exploit a greater number of victims because it is easier and faster for an adult or adolescent with a sexual interest in children to establish whether or not he has identified a likely victim through a relatively short conversation on-line. In addition, he may in fact be conversing with more than one child at the same time. This raises questions about the number of children an individual may be grooming at any one time.

The potential for children to be vulnerable to greater levels of abuse also seems to be associated with on-line activity. For example, the easy accessibility of child pornography affords an adult or adolescent with a sexual interest in children the opportunity to expose a victim to child pornography as a means to lower inhibitions. Furthermore, an adult with a sexual interest in children may use that exposure as a means to coerce the child into keeping the activities secret by threatening to tell the child's parents that he/she has viewed pornography. Alternatively, an adult or adolescent with a sexual interest in children may encourage a child to create pornographic material using either a web cam or digital camera. This may begin as requests for images of, for example, the child's face, or of the child on holidays, i.e. images that would fall under the category of erotica before moving onto sexually explicit material – sexually explicit images include images of the child naked and in a sexually explicit position or engaged in sexual acts. Therefore, strictly speaking a child can become both the producer of child pornography and can be incited to initiate the processes of distribution of illegal material.

Members of on-line paedophile communities network with one another to share this kind of information about grooming practices, how best to avoid detection, and which chat programmes to exploit, i.e. ones with the minimum number of safety features to limit risk of detection, so there is in effect a co-operative element. In addition, from an adult with a sexual interest in children's perspective, there is the concept that chat rooms create the ideal environments for an adult with a sexual interest in children to practice and refine grooming skills, which may subsequently be transferred to real world environments.

Anecdotal evidence from paedophiles who operated in both on-line and off-line environments illustrate some of the co-operative strategies these adults have developed to maximise the opportunities in terms of gaining access to children via on-line grooming. For example, it emerged during treatment sessions with paedophiles at the Wolvercote clinic in the UK that as soon as one paedophile who was engaged in grooming a child on-line thought that the victim became suspicious the paedophile would let an associate know and the associate would then approach the child and try a different approach to grooming.

Clearly programmes of education regarding the Internet need to extend far beyond the usual target audiences of children, parents and teachers and we need to provide education for the criminal justice system, social workers, probation officers and all people who may be a point of contact for children who have been, or indeed who are being, abused on-line so that we are best placed to tackle these issues.

In addition, there is a whole cohort of key individuals who have not been mobilised to play a role in combating these activities and these include network engineers and the architects of the Internet. Typically the dominant narrative that pervades these peoples understanding of the Internet is that it is a vehicle for freedom of speech and that any attempts to introduce networking protocols to enhance child safety and to tackle criminal activity on-line inveigles upon that concept of free movement of information and ideas. Arguably, it is time for these architects of the networking protocols and capabilities of products that criminals exploit to broaden their perspective to perhaps extend their ideological viewpoints to incorporating children's freedom, to benefit maximally from this ethos and work toward limiting the potential harm by collaborating more effectively with experts in the field of combating paedophile activity on-line.

The issue of child abuse on-line has far reaching implications for society in general which significantly impacts on how we think about children, criminals, risk and vulnerability. We must not be discouraged by the idea of children being at risk or vulnerable, and instead we ought to focus on working toward enhancing resiliency of children, by empowering children and their carers with the tools, knowledge, and skills to navigate the Internet safely.

Furthermore, we need to equip the law enforcement sector with adequate skills, legislative measures and resources to tackle this problem effectively. Computer crime units are manned by people who often have a great deal of expertise in the field of forensic computing, profiling and the issues related to securing evidence from computer networks and arguably that experience needs to be exploited so that avenues of communication are created between those tackling illegal activities on-line and those involved in creating the very products and networks that criminals exploit. It is important to ensure that people who operate the criminal justice system have high levels of understanding of the complexities of on-line and related off-line child sexual abuse so that they are best placed to deliberate on cases involving the Internet.

The potentialities in terms of positive opportunities that both the fixed and mobile Internet afford are enormous and what is imperative is that we work toward maximising the positive elements whilst ensuring we create a safe environment in which children can benefit optimally.

References

Abel, G.G., Blanchard, E.B. and Barlow, D.H. (1981) Measurement of Sexual Arousal in Several Paraphilias: The Effects of Stimulus Modality, Instructional Set and Stimulus Content on the Objective. *Behavioral Research and Therapy*, 19: 25–33.

Abel, G.G. et al. (1988) Predicting Child Molesters' Response to Treatment. *Annals of the New York Academy of Sciences*, 528: 223–34.

Alexander, P.C. and Lupfer, S.L. (1987) Family Characteristics and Long-Term Consequences Associated With Sexual Abuse. *Archives of Sexual Behavior*, 16: 3, 235–45.

Best, J, and Luckenbill, D.F. (1994) *Organising Deviance* (2nd edn.). New Jersey: Prentice Hall.

Beech, A. et al. (1996) Treating Sex Offenders in the Community. *Home Office Research and Statistics Directorate, Research Bulletin*, 38: 21–5.

Collings, S.J. (1995) The Long-Term Effects of Contact and Non-Contact Forms of Child Sexual Abuse in a Sample of University Men. *Child Abuse and Neglect*, 19: 1–6.

Erickson, W.D., Walbek, N.H. and Seely, R.K. (1988) Behavior Patterns of Child Molesters. *Archives of Sexual Behaviour*, 17: 77–86.

Finkelhor, D. (1984) *Child Sex Abuse*. Free Press: New York.

Ford, C.S. and Beach, F.A. (1952) *Patterns of Sexual Behavior*. London: Eyre and Spotiswoode.

Freund, K. (1981) Assessment of Paedophilia. In Cook, M. and Howells, K. (Eds.) *Adult Sexual Interest in Children*. London: Academic Press.

Gibbens, T.C., Soothill, K.L., and Way, C.K. (1981) Sex Offenses Against Young Girls: A Long-Term Record Study. *Psychological Medicine*, 11: 351–7.

Grey, K.M. and Leslie, D.R. (1997) The Prevalence of Child Sexual Abuse: Integrative Review Adjustment for Potential Response and Measurement Biases. *Child Abuse Neglect*, 21: 391–8.

Groth, A.N. (1979) Sexual Trauma in the Life of Rapists and Child Molesters. *Victimology*, 4: 10–6.

Groth, A.N. and Birnbaum, H.J. (1978) Adult Sexual Orientation and Attraction to Underage Persons. *Arch. Sex. Behav.*, 7: 175–81.

Grubin, D. and Thornton, D. (1994) A National Programme for Assessment and Treatment of Sex Offenders in the English Prison System. *Criminal Justice and Behaviour*, 21: 55–71.

Grubin, D. and Wingate, S. (1996) Sexual Offence Recidivism: Prediction Versus Understanding. *Criminal Behaviour and Mental Health*, 6: 349–59.

Holmstrom, L.L. and Burgess, A.W. (1978) *The Victim of Rape: Institutional Reactions*. Chichester: Wiley.

Howitt, D. (1995) *Paedophiles and Sexual Offenses Against Children*. Chichester: Wiley.

Marshall, W.L. and Pithers, W.D. (1994) A Reconsideration of Treatment Outcome With Sex Offenders. *Criminal Justice and Behaviour*, 21: 10–27.

Marshall, P. (1994) Reconviction of imprisoned sex offenders. *Research Bulletin*, 36: pp23–29, Home Office, London.

Marshall, P. (1997) *The Prevalence of Convictions for Sexual Offending. Research Findings 55*. London: Home Office Research and Statistics Directorate.

MacCulloch, M.J. et al. (1983) Sadistic Fantasy, Sadistic Behaviours and Offending. *British Journal of Psychiatry*, 143: 20–9.

O'Connell, R. (2000a) Child Sex Iconography. Iconic Narratives of Child Sex Myths. In von Feilitzen, C. and Carlsson, U. (Eds.) *Children in the New Media Landscape; Games, Pornography, Perceptions.* UNESCO.

O'Connell, R. (2000b) Paedophile Information Networks in Cyberspace. In von Feilitzen, C. and Carlsson, U. (Eds.) *Children in the New Media Landscape; Games, Pornography, Perceptions.* UNESCO.

O'Connell, R. (2001a) Paedophilia and the Internet. In Arnaldo, C. (Ed.) *Child Abuse on the Internet: Ending the Silence.* Paris: UNESCO.

O'Connell, R. (2001b) Be Somebody Else But be Yourself at All Times: Degrees of Identity Deception in Chat Rooms http://www.once.uclan.ac.uk/idic.htm

O'Connell, R. (in preparation a) *The Use of Socio-Linguistic Profiling Techniques When Analysing Speech Patterns of Adults With a Sexual Interest in Children.*

O'Connell, R. (in preparation b) *Utilising Loglinear Regression Techniques to Explore the Selectivity Patterns Displayed by Adults and Adolescents With a Sexual Interest in Children With Respect to the Contents of Their Pornography Collections.*

Peters, S. D., Wyatt, G. E., and Finkelor, D. (1986) Prevalence. In Finkelhor, D. (Ed.) *A Sourcebook on Child Sexual Abuse.* Beverly Hills: Sage.

Quinsey, V.L. and Lalumiere, M.L. (1996) *Assessment of Sexual Offenders Against Children: (The APSAC Study Guides 1).* California: Sage Publications.

Sutton, M. and Mann, D. (1998) Netcrime: More Change in the Organisation of Thieving. *British Journal of Criminology* (in press).

Watkins, B. and Bentovim, A. (1992) Male Children and Adolescents as Victims. In Mezey, G.C. and King, M.B. (Eds.) *Male Victims of Sexual Assault.* Oxford: Oxford University Press.

Wisdom, C.S. and Ames, M.A. (1994) Criminal Consequences of Childhood Sexual Victimization. *Child Abuse and Neglect*, 18: 303–18.

Wyre, R. and Tate, T. (1995) *Murder of Childhood.* Harmondsworth: Penguin.

Zillmann, D. and Jennings, B. (1989) *Pornography: Research Advances and Policy Considerations.* New Jersey: Lawrence Erlbaum.

Chapter Four

Young People with Sexual Behaviour Problems and the Internet

Robert E. Longo

Introduction

Sexual abuse is a complex and multifaceted problem that expands well beyond criminal justice systems and thus, criminal sexual behaviour. If one were to consider a continuum; on one end there might be relatively harmless acts such as the verbal sexual abuse by one person of another (sexual harassing or sexualised comments), and on the other end the sexual torture or rape and murder of a human being (Carich and Calder, 2003).

Sexual abuse is a significant problem in societies throughout the world, and the occurrence of young people engaging in sexually abusive behaviour is growing. Sexual abuse however, crosses many boundaries and does not always constitute (a) an illegal behaviour or (b) a harmful act against another. Many young people with sexual behaviour problems are in fact abusive to others (rape, child sexual abuse), while others take advantage of people through their positions of trust or authority (sexual harassment of peers and other forms of youth violence, a babysitter forcing sex on a younger child, or a teenager pressuring a date to have sex).

Young people with sexual behaviour problems often engage in sexually abusive behaviours that may compromise themselves and others, e.g. youth who engage in prostitution. In many cases, however, young people with sexual behaviour problems are individuals whom frequently engage in sexual behaviour that results in harming themselves. On-line sexual behaviour is one such area.

One of the major tasks of those who assess and treat young people with sexual behaviour problems, is to acquire a detailed sexual history of the young person including whether or not the young person engages in deviant sexual fantasies, masturbation practices including the types of fantasies they masturbate to, and whether or not they use pornographic materials for fantasy and or masturbation.

Today's youth have access to the Internet, and with that access, if unrestricted, they have unlimited access to millions of pornography web sites. Therefore, as a general rule, when doing an assessment of a young person with sexual behaviour problems, the clinician or assessor should routinely ask the young person about use of the Internet and frequency of using the Internet to go to adult oriented or pornography web sites.

Use of the Internet for sexual purposes, which in most cases is legal for adults but remains illegal (in most cases) for minors, is becoming increasingly more available to those who would use it. Access to the Internet and specifically access to pornography and adult-oriented web sites is on the rise in America (Cooper et al., 1999).[1] Access to these web sites by young people also appears to be on the rise, and is illegal. Sparse literature is available that addresses youth and access to adult-oriented material on-line (Longo, Brown and Orcutt, 2002; Freeman-Longo, 2000).

There is no way to accurately assess the number of children and teens who go on-line daily and access adult-orientated materials. Studies on the use of the Internet by young people with sexual behaviour problems for sexual purposes are rare. However, in one study by Phil Rich (2002a, 2002b) a self-report survey conducted at Stetson School in Massachusetts of

---

1. For purposes of this paper, adult-oriented web sites refers to web sites or services that include pornography, sexually-oriented materials, adult dating services, and chat rooms that focus on explicit sexual conversation and 'cyber-sex' activities.

young people with sexual behaviour problems revealed that 65% of adolescent clients reported using Internet pornography.

Young people with sexual behaviour problems who go on-line have access to tens of thousands of web sites that are adult-oriented and readily accessible to on-line users by simply typing in the word 'sex' in one of the many search engines available to Internet users. In fact, the word 'sex' is one of the most frequently typed words in search engines (Freeman-Longo, 2000). On-line chat rooms also pose a potential problem and threat to youth.

The extent of the problem

There are few studies in the literature that address young people with sexual behaviour problems and their self-reported use of pornography (OJJDP, 2002). From the few studies that exist, the general indication is that a significant number of young people who sexually abuse have a history of using pornography. This may be changing as more programmes begin to do more in-depth inquiry as to their use of the Internet. An informal survey by this author, on a professional list-serve,[2] resulted in a response by ten programmes and professionals treating young people with sexual behaviour problems and found that between 10-100% of young people being treated self-report and/or have documentation in their clinical records indicating they use the Internet for sexual purposes, and the mean for the ten reporting programmes was 55%.

At the same time, the inquiry into Internet use by young people with sexual behaviour problems for sexual purposes prompted many questions, concerns, and comments from professionals who treat this population. One concern is how to differentiate the use of the Internet for sexual purposes by young people with sexual behaviour problems, for the same use by a population of normal functioning adolescents who have no involvement with the

legal system. A second concern is to further understand the purpose for accessing these materials. A third concern was to address what if anything makes use of the Internet any different than acquiring and reviewing printed matter of a pornographic nature.

Many young people explore the Internet to address curiosity about human sexuality, curiosity about pornography, curiosity about sexual lifestyles, and so forth. Such activity does not always lead to sexual behaviour problems. A range of comments below from professionals who treat young people with sexual behaviour problems are an indicator of the need to further address the problem.

Marsha Ring of Asheville, North Carolina writes:

> *Whether 'normal' kids are using the same pornography [as young people with sexual behaviour problems] becomes irrelevant. The process by which the clients we treat acted out after viewing pornography and why the son of a colleague did not act out (after viewing pornography), intrigues me. There are obviously some barriers that are not in place and not working with clients in treatment.*
>
> *About 30% of the clients we treat who go on-line, and after being barred from their own access (computer source), will use public library terminals, parent's work terminals, etc., to gain access. I had one client tell me that once when he was in the library he got busted by library staff because he had about 40 sites (pornography sites) open on the desktop, and he couldn't clear them fast enough to evade detection. We think it is a much bigger problem than other types of pornography, and much more accessible in our computer savvy society.*

Scott Zankman of Everett, Washington notes:

> *I would rather talk to the youth about how pornography played into their sexual offenses, and talk about the insatiable and escalating quality of pornography. In some ways, the deviance is in this process rather than in what they are actually looking at. When a youth looks at pornography,*

---

2. The Association for the Treatment of Sexual Abusers (ATSA) provides a professional list-serve for ATSA members.

they don't do it once. For many, it becomes what they look forward to, what they think about and so on...and to top it off, it is only a temporary distraction from their issues. Isn't this conversation more important in most situations than what is normal and what is not? Isn't this the deviance? Many of the opportunistic juvenile sexual offenders that I have seen acted out with the child who was available after an escalation in pornography use, mostly via the Internet.

Asking about Internet pornography use is a standard question both during pre-sentencing evaluation and also as an aspect in treatment. They are asked to sign a list of treatment guidelines that specifically spells out not to use the Internet this way. I frequently ask parents or the youth if they have Internet access at home. For many youth, I ask that the Internet use be supervised.

Tom Tobin from California notes:

What do we know about normative youthful behavior with regard to Internet sexual and pornographic activity. One source claims that more than 60% of all the activity on the Internet has a sexual purpose. Internet pornography is certainly an issue for youthful sex offenders in treatment for an offense, but perhaps the larger context is their membership in a generation socialized into a new way to satisfy their sexual curiosity and interests.

Perhaps the best we can do is to keep reminding people that we all participate in a culture/society that actually supports and enables sexual and other violence – despite our efforts to frame all identified sex offenders as incomprehensible monsters.

Kara Cornelisse, MSW from Michigan states:

Our program noted a 21% increase in exposure to pornography in just over two years, as well as learning that close to half of those used the Internet to do so. It is necessary to emphasize that continued research, not only within our program but across this very specialized field, is essential to undoubtedly identify pornography as an important operant variable in the sexual acting out of our community's youth.

Kerry Lindorfer of Idaho reports:

Since I've been in private practice...37 adolescents have been in sex-offense specific treatment. Of those, 19 had used pornography to the point that it was a significant part of the development of assaultive behavior and/or triggered the offense of record. Five of these used magazines only, 14 used the Internet and often used videos, and two used video only.

Additionally, 23 clients had histories of sexual victimization which contributed significantly to development of assaultive behaviour. 11 of the 37 came from 2 parent (bio) homes at the time of offense. Leaving 26 with single parent, foster parent, grandparent, etc...

Some of these youths identified pornography as a major precipitator to their offending behavior. For a smaller percentage, perhaps 10%, stopping their use of pornography was extremely difficult and required parental restrictions. Many of the adolescents/young adults who transition from residential programs start to view pornography within two months. They often state it is normal and should be no problem, yet they return to compulsive masturbation when viewing such.

Denise Carlton of Michigan reports:

We just did an informal survey among our group members and found that 100% had accessed pornography on the Internet. We informally surveyed our groups three years ago and found that 67% had used the Internet for pornography. So quite a jump in three years.

And finally, Judy Holt, a US Probation Officer in Missouri notes:

Being with the federal system, we don't discriminate with age and we get some juvenile offenders. In the past two to three months, we have sentenced two teens for possession of child pornography. While these guys were in their late teens, based on their statements and the evidence, it appears they began their collection some time ago.

As we have only a few studies on young people who sexually abuse regarding their use of pornography, and no studies on young people who use the Internet for sexual purposes, we do not fully understand why young people use pornography, on the Internet or otherwise. Studies on adults, however, may shed some light as to why young people may use pornography and therefore why they may turn to the Internet for access to pornography. Erick Janssen, PhD, an associate scientist at The Kinsey Institute for Research in Sex, Gender, and Reproduction at Indiana University in his paper *Why People Use Pornography*[3] writes:

> *Pornography as we know it is used predominantly by men. That is not to say that women do not use it, but simply that men are the main consumers of this 'pleasure technology'. Why men? It may not come as a surprise, but research suggests that most men are more interested in sex than most women are. More men than women masturbate, and they do so more frequently. More men experience orgasms, and do so more consistently.*
>
> *In his landmark interview studies in the 1940s and 1950s, conducted with nearly 17,000 men and women, Alfred Kinsey and his colleagues found that 54 percent of men and only 12 percent of women reported being erotically aroused by seeing photographs, drawings, or paintings of nude people.*

There are a few studies that have addressed the issue of pornography use and subsequent impact on the lives of users. In 1997, Elizabeth Oddone-Paolucci and colleagues published a study that was a meta-analysis of published research on the effects of pornography use (Oddone-Paolucci, Genuis, and Violato, 1997). The study of over 12,000 adult men and women found that there was an increased risk for negative development when individuals are exposed to pornography. Oddone-Paolucci and Genuis (2002) found that views of pornography were more likely to have 'deviant' attitudes towards sexuality and in particular intimate relationships. Perceptions of sexual dominance, submissiveness, sex-role

stereotyping or viewing persons as sexual objects were common among viewers. The authors propose that the rise in sexual crimes, sexual dysfunction, and family breakdown may be linked to the increased availability and use of pornography, and conclude that exposure to pornography puts viewers at increased risk for developing sexually deviant tendencies, committing sexual offences, and experiencing problems in intimate relationships. While the above study was conducted with an adult sample, the fact remains that exposure and use of pornography by young people may have similar impact. In this case, the use of the Internet for sexual purposes cannot be ignored.

In a study by Wilson and Abelson (1973) 84% of men and 69% of women reported exposure to one or more pictorial or textual modes of pornography, with the majority of the subjects reporting that they were first exposed to sexually explicit materials before the age of 21.

As clinicians and professionals in the field of treating young people with sexual behaviour problems, we may be left with more questions than answers regarding why young people use pornography and in particular why young people with sexual behaviour problems use such and particularly the Internet. However, we must be cognisant of the fact that we will be seeing a growing number of young people with histories of using the Internet specifically for sexual purposes as the brief case examples below illustrate.

The following cases were provided to this author for purposes of inclusion in this chapter. Some are from our facilities at New Hope Treatment Centers in South Carolina. To protect the confidentiality of patients and clients, no names are used and the programmes and therapists are not identified in the cases below.

> *I have had one patient, 17-years-old at referral, who began accessing pornography from the Internet from school. He quickly became*

---

3. http://www.pbs.org/wgbh/pages/frontline/shows/pornography/special/why.html

interested in some sites devoted to sexual spanking, and used these sights enough that he developed a fetish around spanking small children. He disclosed several offenses that involved this behavior. He still uses the Internet at home, but is supervised directly. He no longer has privileges at school to use the Internet.

I have two patients who describe extensive use of the Internet for pornography. One was looking up girlie stuff, normal pornography if you will, but the other patient's father found that his son was heavily into gay and transvestite web sites. The first patient, who is almost through treatment, states that pornography on the Internet was definitely one of the factors that put him on the path to offending. The second patient has just been admitted and is not yet giving me honest accounts of his use of the Internet or of anything else for that matter.

I have one 12-year-old male patient who reportedly disguised himself as a 22-year-old male to visit gay chat rooms. He would visit these sites to talk with other adult participants.

We had a 12-year-old female at our agency who was sexually reactive, and we didn't know she had a pre-occupation with Internet pornography. We allowed this 12-year-old child to look at what we thought were innocuous web sites and it turned out she found her way to www.pink.com. The fact is, she picked this information up at school without assistance of anyone other than classmates. So, it's a problem. We installed a filter and that seems to have helped her.

There was one kid I did an evaluation on a while ago, and he accessed child pornography on the Internet. No charges, or legal action were taken with this boy who was turning 18 within a very short time. He made no apologies for his behavior, and stated he enjoyed this.

I just evaluated an 18-year-old young man who was referred by Juvenile Probation after he had sex with a minor who was three years and one month younger than he was when he was 17¹/₂ years old. When they searched his home he had

child pornography stored on some discs that were reportedly from 2000. He was convicted of the Child Molest charge, however, they were still undecided on the Child Pornography issue.

Last night in a session with a newer client we were discussing this very issue. I was able to meet his father for the first time who, when asked, informed me that my client had a significant amount of pornography on their 'old' computer. My client admits that he was using the computer for his own fantasy base, however in addition (because he has a fairly sophisticated computer set up and printer), he would print up the pornography and sell it at school. What is even more interesting is that he was presenting this as his 'defense'. When questioned about the pornography he answered, 'It's not what you think. I am just selling it that's why there was so much on the computer.'

I recently began treating a 12-year-old boy who was referred after it was discovered that he had touched the genitals of eight boys in his class. During the intake he acknowledged downloading thousands of pictures of naked boys and engaging in a variety of sexual acts with a 14-year-old male cousin.

As a result of an increased number of cases presenting themselves to clinicians and therapists, a growing awareness of professionals regarding this issue, and a lack of literature regarding the problem, an ever increasing number of programmes are now beginning to include the use of the Internet for sexual purposes as a part of their assessment, and some programmes are now looking to research the area closer.

Kathe Dellacecca, Associate Director at Mille Lacs Academy states:

I run a large (94 beds) adolescent male [sex] offender residential program in Minnesota and I have also been laboring with this question [the use of the Internet by juvenile sex offenders for sexual purposes]. A colleague and I recently created a demographic data collection form and devoted the 8th page specifically to use of pornography and also the Internet by juvenile offenders. My goal is to collect a fair amount of *data over the next 12 months to begin to answer this question. We will be getting the data from both out patient and inpatient juveniles.*

Our facility has four sexuality therapists and four family therapists that routinely ask specific questions around this issue during assessment, and continue asking throughout treatment. We have only seen two residents with formal charges and those were for possession of Internet child pornography.

Professional response

It is not prudent to prohibit young people or young people with sexual behaviour problems from using the Internet as it provides unparalleled opportunities for young people to learn about the world and to learn about almost any topic they choose to explore, including human sexuality. However, we must be cognisant of the potential hazards. Cooper et al. (1999) describe the Internet as a triple 'A' engine because the Internet is accessible, affordable, and provides anonymity. The Internet is also a double edged sword. It is capable of bringing a world of information to its user within seconds without having to go to the library or leave one's home. Yet, as demonstrated in numerous articles and studies (Cooper, 2002), it can have tremendous impact on individuals and organisations by damaging relationships, creating a variety of sexual problems, or negatively effecting families and communities.

Internet use by children and young people provides them with enormous positive opportunities and equally devastating potential problems (Longo et al., 2002). This can be the case when a young person goes beyond the normal curiosity of their peers regarding use of the Internet for sexual purposes. When young people with sexual behaviour problems present us with histories that include unhealthy sexual practices, abusive or aggressive sexual behaviours, and sexual problems when on-line, we must be cautious to not simply adhere to the traditional relapse prevention strategies of escape and avoidance. We live in the age of computers and

communications technology that will guide these young persons through the rest of their lives, and we need to look at each case individually. Additionally, we need to avoid the trickle down phenomenon of using adult sex-offender based treatment strategies with children and young people with sexual behaviour, and not forget the many advantages the Internet may bring to young people with sexual behaviour problems (Longo et al., 2002; Longo, 2003).

Longo, Brown, and Orcutt (2002) note:

Assessing what is healthy and what is not when it comes to teen sexuality is often difficult to do. This is due, in large part, to the narrow research and public discussion about adolescent sexuality which focuses solely on what is unhealthy about adolescent sexuality (unplanned pregnancy, out-of-wedlock birth, sexually transmitted diseases including AIDS and sexual abuse) rather than what is sexually healthy for teenagers. Moreover, professionals doing the assessing have little empirical guidance from research and therefore often fall back on viewing adolescent sexual behavior through the lens of their own personal backgrounds and values.

Our belief is that when evaluating the sexual behaviors of adolescents it is critical to avoid dichotomous thinking and view them on a continuum from healthy to problematic. It is also critical to view adolescent sexual behaviors not as isolated behaviors, but in the context of the whole person. There is clearly a big difference between a 15-year-old who has initiated sexual intercourse with a partner and is functioning well in other realms of his life (family, peers, academics, etc.), and a 15-year-old doing the same behavior whose parents recently divorced, is cut off from his family, and is abusing alcohol. Similarly, we believe it is important to assess the function that the sexual behavior serves for the particular teen. All people engage in sexual behavior for complex reasons and to meet a variety of needs, both sexual and non-sexual. However, an important indicator of sexual health for teenagers is the degree to which the sexual behavior is in the service of developmentally appropriate sexual needs as opposed to primarily non-sexual needs. A 16-year-old gay boy from a rural community who is experimenting with cyber sex on-line may be quite healthy if he has had little opportunity to explore or express his sexuality in other ways. Contrast this with a 16-year-old boy who is engaging in cyber-sex because he has few friends and it momentarily helps him to escape his painful depression.

They go on to say:

Distinguishing fact from fiction about sexuality. Adolescents who are sexually healthy are able to seek out accurate information about sexuality when they need it and can distinguish between realistic and distorted media messages about sexuality (Facing Facts, 1995). Teens with a positive sense of self who have internalized positive modeling about sexual values, gender roles and developmentally appropriate sexual behavior are somewhat inoculated from the impact of the media, including the Internet, which so often portrays sex in an extreme stereotypical manner. Teenagers who are less sexually healthy tend to have few positive and realistic role models to help them learn about sexuality. They are more vulnerable to adopting as fact misinformation and distorted media messages about, for example, how men and women are supposed to act, what is a healthy relationship, and what is involved in a mutually pleasurable sexual relationship, areas seldom addressed in sexually explicit materials on the Internet.

In regard to young people and sexual behaviour in general, another professional, Nike Delson from Trinidad, California notes:

We are discussing the issue without really exploring who we (the current cultural climate) are in the matter. How do we research sexual health in a sexually unhealthy culture. Children routinely talk about sexual abuse, but not sexual health. The media explodes with sexual messages – essentially telling youth (and all of us) that sex is something you should always want, always try to get, and you never have enough…Daytime television presents sex as drama, and sensationalism. The popular culture

is titillated by the notion of 'sexy' children, but unwilling to talk about those feelings and so they are expressed as outrage.

I asked my granddaughter (age 9) where she learns about sex – other than school programs and family. Her quick reply was 'On the school bus.' Children age 5 to high school ride the same bus. I asked for an example about 'learning about sex.' She told me that an 11-year-old girl brought a chocolate flavored condom on the bus. A 5-year-old boy asked what you do with it, and she demonstrated to all by putting it on her thumb and saying 'you just put it on a weenie and suck'.

Warning signs that young people may be moving into sexual problems on the Internet

Freeman-Longo (2000) suggests there are potential indicators that a young person may be experiencing problems on the Internet. In the absence of scientifically validated studies on young people that pinpoint potential warning signs for on-line sexual behaviour problems, the following are offered:

- Young people spend excessive time on the Internet at the expense of personal relationships.
- Young people may display acute or chronic depression.
- Young people may display withdrawal and isolation from peers and personal relationships.
- Young people may seek repeated mood-altering experiences on-line.
- Young people may display a sense of pseudo-intimacy with others on-line.
- The Internet may serve as an outlet for unresolved sexual difficulties and unfocused sexual energy.
- Children and young people with histories of sexual behaviour problems may be more prone to engage in these activities.
- Young people begin to spend less time engaging in peer related social activities.

- Young people found downloading pornography including adult oriented and child pornography.
- Young people spend extended periods of time in chat rooms on the Internet.

Young and Rogers (1998), report that with adults there appears to be a correlation between time on-line and negative consequences. When a young person with sexual behaviour problems spends more than one or two hours at a time on-line, we should consider this behaviour as a potential red flag. There are several directions clinicians and others can take in working with young people with sexual behaviour problems that demonstrate problematic histories of using the Internet for sexual purposes.

Working with and managing young people with sexual behaviour problems and Internet use

It is strongly encouraged that clinicians, caregivers and others work with youth in order to help them manage how the Internet will be used. Prohibiting young people with sexual behaviour problems from using the Internet is not realistic except in those extreme cases when the patient refuses to comply with established Internet use guidelines as set forth by the family and/or clinician. Internet Service Providers (ISP) and software companies have devised a variety of programmes and tools that limit youth's access to materials that parents or those in positions of authority determine are inappropriate. Freeman-Longo (2000) notes:

> Unfortunately, many children are now more skilled than their caretakers and overseers in the use of computers and technology. With such knowledge, skills and abilities, these young people can more easily work around software and other devices that attempt to limit their access to material on the Internet. Once done, they can easily share their secrets with peers.

One of the problems with ISP programming and software providing blocks to certain materials on the Internet, is that in some cases the blocks filter so thoroughly that some non-sexual materials can end up being blocked as well. In this case, a more realistic response is to use software that tracks usage and visited web sites. There is no blocking, but one can easily track the usage. This teaches the young person self-control, and thus the potential to impart responsible behaviour, versus the use of external controls. Of course when software of this type is used, a responsible adult needs to check daily to see if the young person has gone onto the Internet, the length of time spend on-line, and the various web sites the young person has visited while on-line.

Professionals and others working with young people with sexual behaviour problems have resources and several options in working with this clinical population. The most important role is providing education to patients and others about the hazards and potential consequences for engaging in on-line sexual activities. Many young people get involved in this activity without recognising the problems and potential legal consequences for downloading sexually explicit materials.

Treating young people with sexual behaviour problems requires that we educate them about age appropriate on-line web sites and materials that are factual and honest and about the many hazards associated with going on-line. We cannot assume that all young people with sexual behaviour problems understand the illegality of:

- Child pornography.
- Downloading illegal materials.
- The potential harm of using pornography and other adult-oriented materials.
- The potential problems associated with meeting people on-line.
- The dangers of meeting them in person.

Young people with sexual behaviour problems need to be informed that everything on the Internet is not factual and correct especially those materials and web sites that pertain to sexual matters and human sexual behaviour. In most cases, young people with sexual behaviour problems will need supervision when going on-line.

Children and young people are naturally curious about sex and will seek out sexual information and stimuli. Parents, educators, professionals, and caregivers should not panic when they discover a child or teen's natural curiosity and exploration. Instead we can use such times as 'teachable moments,' and then guide the young person to age appropriate materials, books, or sites on the Internet.

Anyone with time and experience of going on-line can speak of the honest accidents that occur when using search engines to look up even the most common information. For example, typing in simple non-sexual words such as whitehouse, puppies, pussy cat, and girls into a search engine can bring up web sites that are sexually oriented. Simply typing in the word 'sex' will bring up over 185,000,000 sites.

Once we understand a young person's interest and purpose for going on-line to access sexual and non-sexual material we can educate them and when feasible, provide web sites of an appropriate nature that are both educational and developmentally appropriate. Additionally, there are basic guidelines one might use in working with young people with sexual behaviour problems who will continue to have access to computers and going on-line (Freeman-Longo, 2000). These include:

- Don't put computers with Internet access in a young person's room. Instead keep the computer with Internet access in a public place with lots of activity at home and where the individual's use can be easily monitored by parents. Some of the best places are in the family room or kitchen.

- Test ISP and software that claims to block young people's access to adult-oriented materials on the Internet, before using them. Try to navigate around the software and see if you can beat it. If you can, the child can.

- Provide young people with age-appropriate alternatives. Help them explore what is out there in cyber space. If together you come upon inappropriate web sites, take the time to talk with them about why certain sites are inappropriate.

- If need be, limit use to certain time frames and durations. For example, 'You can go on-line between 7–8pm and only for the hour. If you need more time on-line, we will work on projects together'.

- Be careful about the 'chat rooms' young people visit. Some are designed for certain age groups and are monitored, but most are open for anyone to go into. Public chat rooms are the place kids will meet people who will lie, be sexual, and may offer to meet them in person.

- If a young person has downloaded any pornography or sexual materials, they should be erased from the hard drive. Young people who download sexual materials will initially need to be monitored every time they go on-line. ISP restrictions / parental controls may need to be applied.

A creative approach to helping young people with the Internet has been developed in New Zealand. McCarthy (2002) notes:

It's certainly been the topic of much discussion down here over the past little while. You might be interested in the fact that a multi-agency Internet Safety Group has been formed in Auckland. The Group has produced kits and other materials for parents and young people about on-line safety, and developed a website – http://www.netsafe.org.nz or http:// www.netsafe.org.nz/home/home_default.asp.

Young people who have engaged in spending large blocks of time on-line, downloaded pornography or other sexual materials, frequent public or adult chat rooms frequently, should be banned from using chat rooms and may need to be restricted from going on-line unless they are in the presence of a responsible adult.

If the young person has a history of both sexual offending and going on-line for sexual purposes, the young person should be entered into sex-offender specific treatment. Issues about the use of the Internet, etc., should be explored during the course of treatment. A part of treatment should include why the young person with sexual behaviour problems went to sex-related web sites, what he did with materials he learned or obtained, and the programme should explore if the youth used or downloaded sexual materials for purposes of fantasy or masturbation.

As noted above, for some youth, sex-offender specific treatment will not be necessary. Young people who go on-line to explore sexuality, but have not been charged with a sexual offence or have not engaged in sexually abusive or aggressive behaviour, may not need sex-offence specific treatment. These young people are probably best suited to taking a comprehensive course on human sexuality and working on sexuality issues, problems, with a professional who specialises in treating children and young people.

In either case young people who are abusing sexuality on-line or engaging in age-inappropriate on-line activities, and/or engaging in on-line sexual practice/behaviours should be assessed by a professional who specialised in assessing and treating young people with sexual behaviour problems. The assessment should be performed in order to determine what treatment modality is most appropriate for the young person given their specific circumstances.

Summary

We are just beginning to understand the problem of young people with sexual behaviour problems and Internet use for sexual purposes. A growing number of cases appear to be presenting themselves in general mental health clinics as well as in sex-offence specific treatment programmes. As a result, standard assessments should include questioning young people about Internet use and interests, including visiting adult-oriented or sex-oriented web sites, chat rooms, and downloading sexual materials.

Currently there is a lack of scientific research, general literature, and information regarding children, young people and sexual activity on the Internet. It has only been in the past two years that we have seen a few articles written about young people and sexual activity and practices on the Internet.

We are uncertain about the potential for young people to become sexual compulsives or even sexually addicted if they engage in these on-line behaviours. The American Psychological Association has determined that exposure to TV violence is impacting children and their aggressive behaviours in negative ways. We should be equally as cautious about children's exposure to sexual materials on the Internet, and through other forms of media. This is especially true given recent research on domestic violence and its impact on children. There is growing evidence to support the idea that children who live in families in which partner violence takes place are at high risk for being abused physically, sexually, and psychologically (Williams, 2002).

Because the short and long term impact of children engaging in these activities is not known, we must be cautious about how we proceed in gathering this information and think about the presumed current risks associated with this behaviour. The risks as we understand them now include:

- Exposure to incorrect information about human sexual behaviour.
- Exposure to age inappropriate sexual materials.
- The potential to develop sexually compulsive behaviour.
- The potential to develop sexual addiction.
- The potential to use internet materials of a sexual nature to enhance deviant (inappropriate) sexual fantasies.
- The potential to masturbate to materials viewed on or downloaded from the internet.

Few young people should be altogether banned from using the Internet. Conditions for prohibiting them access to the Internet may include:

- Young people in denial of the problem.
- Young people refusing to enter treatment.

- Young people failing in treatment.

- Young people dropping out of treatment.

- Young people who have been unsuccessfully terminated from treatment.

- Young people who display continued violation of established rules for going on-line.

There are several methods of working with young people with sexual behaviour problems who have abused the Internet for sexual purposes. Much of what we can do is to offer these young people guidance in Internet use and supervision when necessary. While many youth have encountered problems while on-line and engaged in inappropriate use of the Internet, we should not automatically ban them from using the technology and communications systems of today and their future.

References

Carich, M.S. and Calder, M.C. (2003) *Contemporary Treatment of Adult Male Sex Offenders.* Lyme Regis: Russell House Publishing.

Carlton, D. Personal communication. E-mail dated 9/4/02.

Cornelisse, K. Personal communication. E-mail dated 9/5/02.

Cooper, A. et al. (1999) Online Sexual Compulsivity: Sexual Addiction and Compulsivity. *The Journal of Treatment and Prevention,* 6: 2, 79–104.

Cooper, A. (Ed.) (2002) *Sex and the Internet: A Guidebook for Clinicians.* New York: Brunner-Routledge.

Dellacecca, K. Personal communication. E-mail dated 9/4/02.

Delson, N. Personal communication. E-mail dated 9/4/06.

Freeman-Longo, R.E. (2000) Children, Teens, and Sex on the Internet. *Sexual Addiction and Compulsivity,* 7: 75–90.

Holt, J. Personal communication. E-mail dated 11/26/02.

Lindorfer, K. Personal communication. E-mails dated 9/4/02 and 11/25/02.

Longo, R.E. (2003 under review) *Emerging Issues, Policy Changes, and the Future of Treating Children with Sexual Behavior Problems.* NYAS.

Longo, R.E., Brown, S.M. and Orcutt, D.P. (2002) Effects of Internet Sexuality on Children and Adolescents. In Cooper, A. (Ed.) *Sex and The Internet: A Guidebook for Clinicians.* New York: Brunner-Routledge.

McCarthy, J. Personal communication. E-mail dated 12/2/2002.

Oddone-Paulucci, E. and Genuis, M.L. (2002) *The Effects of Pornography on Attitudes and Behaviors in Sexual and Intimate Relationships.* http://www.culture-of-life.org/pornography_nffe.htm

Oddone-Paolucci, E., Genuis, M. and Violato, C. (1997) A Meta-Analysis of the Published Research on the Effects of Pornography. *Medicine, Mind, and Adolescence,* 12: 1–2.

OJJDP Report (2002) *Juveniles Who Have Sexually Offended: Executive Summary.* http://www.ncjrs.org/html/ojjdp/report_juvsex_offend/sum.html

Rich, P. Personal communication. E-mail dated 9/4/2002.

Rich, P. (2002) *Survey Results: Student Self Reports of Sexually Aggressive Behaviors, 2002.* (Available from Stetson School, Inc., 455 South Street, Barre, MA 01005).

Ring, M. Personal communication. E-mail dated 9/4/02.

Tobin, T. Personal communication. E-mail dated 9/4/02.

Williams, L.M. (2002) *Children's Exposure to Violence in Families: Implications for Child Outcomes.* Presentation to SCPSAC annual Conference. Charleston, SC 2/21/02.

Young, K.S. and Rogers, R.C. (1998) The Relationship Between Depression and Internet Addiction. *CyberPsychology and Behavior,* 1: 1, 25–8.

Zankman, S. Personal communication. E-mail dated 9/4/02.

Chapter Five

Assessing Internet Sex Offenders

Joe Sullivan and Anthony Beech

Introduction

Pornography plays an important part in contributing to sexual violence.

(Itzin, 1992).

While far from the only activity sex offenders engage in on the Internet, the accessing, collection and distribution of pornography is what most people imagine when they think of sexual offending on the Internet. As much of the pornography on the Internet involves adults and is not illegal in this country, sexual offending on the Internet has become synonymous with the trade in indecent images of children and child sexual abuse.

Since 1995 when the first man was prosecuted in Britain for possessing indecent images of children the perception of the Internet sex offender was that of a career paedophile who joined an underworld of like-minded people trading in sexual images of children across continents. This perception was reinforced by law enforcement operations like 'Cathedral' which was a worldwide police investigation into the Wonderland Club culminating in 135 arrests and prosecutions in 13 countries. The group comprised collectors and producers of indecent images of children who communicated through chat rooms.

More recent developments in the Internet have led to the creation of pay-per-view sites like the 'landslide' web site that was initially uncovered by the US Postal Services. This investigation identified a database of global customers purchasing indecent images of children (as well as other pornography) and led to the identification of over 1,300 people in the UK who could be proven to have accessed indecent images of children from the landslide website. The scale of the subsequent police operation, codenamed 'Ore', has impacted upon the courts, police, probation and social services and has raised one major question for all those involved in the risk assessment of sex offenders: Are people who view indecent images of children likely to commit contact offences against children?

The people dealt with thus far under Operation Ore have challenged the previous perception of the Internet sex offender. While some do fit the stereotype of the 'organised paedophile' who conspires with others to distribute indecent images of children as part of a wider pattern of sexual offending against children, others do not. Interrogation of hard drives has suggested that some offenders have had limited or in some cases only one visit to a 'child pornography' web site. While inevitably there are some who are forensically aware and have managed to cover their tracks it seems reasonable to assume that some offenders will be caught in the early developmental stages of their sexual interest in children and others will have looked at indecent images of children out of curiosity and did not develop the interest further. Figure 1 suggests three potential motivation typologies.

Figure 1: Motivation Typologies

- Collecting as part of a larger pattern of sexual offending possibly including contact sex offending.
- Collecting to feed a developing sexual interest in children.
- Accessing indecent images of children out of curiosity.

Clinicians' observations of sex offenders who acknowledge a pre-existing sexual interest in children prior to using the Internet suggest that they similar to other sex offenders (Burke et al., 2001; Sullivan and Sheehan, 2002). Those who deny a sexual interest in children may well be lying but it is conceivable that some will not have a sexual interest in children.

The problem for the professional assessing risk is to determine which type of motivation is involved in any specific case as most offenders on initial detection are likely to claim theirs was a curiosity rather than a sexual arousal to children. From an assessing clinicians point of view assumption of curiosity rather than a possible sexual interest in children is a dangerous perspective which is inconsistent with child protection.

The aim of this chapter is to offer an overview of the various assessment techniques employed and outline some additional tools which might assist practitioners to understand and intervene in the fantasy world of the Internet sex offenders.

Who assesses sex offenders?

Risk assessment of sex offenders has traditionally been the domain of specially trained probation officers or psychologists. In recent years, and particularly since the Sex Offender Act, 1997, more agencies are becoming involved in the process of risk assessment. Multi-agency Public Protection Panels (MAPPP) now oversee the management of sex offenders in the community, adding police, social services, housing and education officers to the probation and prison staff who have until now been responsible for risk assessment.

The nature of the assessments undertaken by each of these professionals will differ depending on the focus of the respective organisation they represent. For example a probation officer in a Public Protection Unit who is preparing a report for a criminal court will consider the perpetrators account of the offences and reflect on the dynamic factors in the individuals life which might increase or decrease risk. A housing officer will also be concerned to protect children but will assess the suitability for housing an offender in a particular area. The philosophy upon which these assessments are based should be the same and it is critical therefore that the training provided to these professionals is undertaken, at least in part, together with the other agencies to ensure consistency.

Assessment tools

Although central to the process of assessment, an evaluation of the risk of re-offending is only part of the task. Effective practitioners with a responsibility for assessing a sex offender's risk will use a variety of tools in determining risk. These will include actuarial, psychometric and clinical approaches.

Actuarial assessment approaches

Actuarial assessment seeks to identify a risk categorisation for an individual offender based upon the characteristics they have in common with re-offending sex offenders. Actuarial tools such as the SACJ (Grubin, 1998), RRASOR (Hanson, 1998), Static-99 (Hanson and Thornton,1999), and more recently the Risk Matrix 2000 (Thornton, 2000) are static risk assessment tools which identify the common characteristics of sex offenders and the simple objective features present in the personal histories of those who re-offend. Often based upon study groups of convicted sex offenders these tools have limitations, particularly when applied to the first time offender. Nevertheless, they are considerably more accurate than many of the clinical approaches in determining those who are most likely to re-offend and particularly in identifying the more high-risk offenders. For a fuller discussion of this the reader is referred to Calder (2000).

As the majority of Internet sex offenders, to date, do not have previous convictions (Burke et al., 2001) the more popular actuarial tools are of limited use.

Psychometric evaluation

The primary focus of psychometric assessment is to examine the key aspects of a perpetrator's personality, which research has shown contributes to sexual offending. This is achieved through an examination of their stated attitudes and responses to self-report questionnaires. These psychometric measures have collated data from convicted or admitted sex offenders and 'normal samples' of people who are not identified as sex offenders thereby allowing analysis of how far an individual's scores deviates from the normal (Fisher, Beech and Brown, 1999).

Research has shown that sex offenders will typically have problems in a number of key areas: empathy (Beckett and Fisher, 1994; Davis, 1980; Marshall, Hudson, Jones and Fernandez, 1995); self-esteem (Marshall, Anderson and Champagne, 1996); sexual deviance, admittance, sexual desirability and sexual obsession (Nichols and Molinder, 1984); emotional loneliness (Russell, Peplau and Cutrona, 1980); attachments and intimacy (Marshall, 1989); and locus of control (Nowicki, 1976).

In the United Kingdom, prison, probation and specialist assessment and treatment organisations like the Lucy Faithfull Foundation and the Wolvercote Clinic use the standardised battery of psychometric tests compiled by the Home Office commissioned STEP (Sex Offender Treatment Evaluation Project) to assess sexual offenders (Beech, Fisher and Beckett, 1998). Factor analysis of these measures suggested that these scales measured three main areas:

- Denial or admittance of offending behaviours.
- Distorted thoughts or justifications about offending.
- Level of social competence and accountability that might predispose to offending in the presence of pro-offending attitudes.

The disadvantage is that they rely upon self-report which increases the chances that the subject will second-guess the measures and 'fake good' by answering in a more socially acceptable manner. Psychometrics can, however, be used to offer insight into the potential treatment needs of the offender. It is important to have these measures scored and interpreted by a psychologist or someone specially trained to do so as, in common with all tools reliant upon self-report, they have limitations.

Clinical assessment

The aim of clinical risk assessment is to determine the nature of any risk posed by the offender and highlight the treatment needs specific to that individual. The cognitive behavioural approach to sex offender treatment is generally regarded as the most effective (Beech, Fisher and Beckett, 1998; Marshall, Anderson and Fernandez, 1999). Clinical assessments tend to follow the same principles and will generally incorporate the actuarial and psychometric perspectives.

Central to the process of clinical risk assessment is an understanding of the perpetrator. Practitioners use models such as Wolf's (1988) 'cycle of sexual offending', Finkelhor's (1984) 'preconditions to sexual offending' and Sullivan's (2002) 'spiral of sexual abuse' to provide themselves with a framework for understanding how sex offending works. Among the key principles of cognitive behavioural therapy is the concept that a person can only change that which they acknowledge and understand. Therefore the clinical assessment while gathering information on the offender will also seek to provide information about the nature of sexual offending and the change process.

Most people when asked to explain their socially unacceptable behaviour will give an account which either spreads the blame or dilutes their responsibility. Consequently the clinical assessment process is less a 'voyage of discovery' and more an 'excavation of a more honest account'. The approach to the assessment is therefore critical requiring integrity, clear boundaries, humanity and respect on the part of the professionals concerned.

Clinical assessments of sex offenders tend to be structured and target three specific areas in an attempt to understand the nature of the offending and decide upon the suitability for treatment:

- An offence analysis leading to exploration of offending pattern.
- An investigation of the level of victim awareness or empathy.
- An exploration of the role of fantasy in their offending.

Offence analysis

The most common start-point for an assessment is to offer the offender the opportunity to give his account of the offences. If the assessment is undertaken in a group, as is the more common approach (Beech, Fisher and Beckett, 1998), the other participants and the professional involved will then examine the account identifying justifications, distortions and manner in which the victim is portrayed. In the case of the Internet sex offender a basic level of computer knowledge is required so that accounts which are wrapped in a technical disguise can be unravelled. One of the benefits of group work is that other participants will often know what is technically possible and what is not. In any event it is unwise to allow the discussion to become a technical joust as the focus will be quickly lost, much as it does if you allow a sex offender who is a religious fanatic to engage in a theological debate about the issues.

Examining their offence account can facilitate a better understanding of the evolution of their sexual interest in children and will allow for initial exploration of the importance of the on-line community, collecting or trading and the degree to which Internet offending was used to avoid or escape other difficulties in their 'real' world.

Victim existence, awareness and empathy

Particularly relevant to the Internet sex offender is the concept of 'victim existence' (Burke et al., 2000; Sullivan and Sheehan, 2002). Many Internet sex offenders will deny they have sexually abused anyone by looking at images which have been created and uploaded by others. It is important to explore this concept during the assessment phase as it may clarify the degree to which victim awareness work might succeed in assisting the participant to develop victim empathy in treatment.

The role of fantasy in sexual offending

Not only sex offenders fantasise about deviant sex. There is evidence that men and women who are not believed to be sex offenders fantasise about deviant sexual acts as well as those who do sexually offend (Gold and Clegg, 1990; Greendlinger and Byrne, 1987; Hurlburt and Apt, 1993; Kinsey, Pomeroy and Martin, 1948; Kinsey, Pomeroy, Martin and Gebhard, 1953; and Laan Everaerd, Van Aanhold, and Rebel, 1993). From the early work on sexual deviance by behaviourists, fantasy has been regarded as one of the central concepts determining and reinforcing a desire to sexually offend (McGuire, Carlisle, and Young, 1965).

The classical Pavlovian perspective of this process would suggest that if an individual repeatedly masturbates to images of children, whether they are indecent or not, they will eventually generate or condition a response of becoming sexually aroused to children. Laws and Marshall (1990) and Marshall and Eccles (1993) argued that a Pavlovian explanation of the process of linking fantasy and masturbation was too simplistic and did not explain why people developed a sexual interest in children or other deviant sexual acts. They suggest that social learning theory and a process of operant conditioning combined to develop deviant sexual behaviour. What is clear is that the process of conditioning does have a part to play in the creation and maintaining of deviant sexual arousal (Marshall, Anderson and Fernandez, 1999).

Other assessment tools

Polygraph

Often referred to as a 'lie detector' the polygraph has just begun to feature in assessment of sex offenders in Britain. In the USA polygraphy has become a mainstream tool in the ongoing assessment of sex offenders before, during and after treatment. The process involves a skilled polygrapher interviewing an offender prior to and after the actual polygraph test. During the test the offender has sensors attached to measure physiological reactions. They are asked neutral questions to obtain a baseline reading of their reactions and then the subject is asked a series of questions some of which are neutral and some of which are targeted at the aspects of their offending behaviour requiring scrutiny. The reactions are recorded and subsequently analysed to identify the questions where the physiological response suggest the person was lying.

Screening

There are a number of computer based assessment programmes which seek to explore the sexual interests of sex offenders. For the most part these programmes are based on the research findings that, when presented with a series of images, men spend longer looking at images they find more sexually attractive, (Landolt et al., 1995; Lang et al., 1980; Quinsey et al., 1993, 1996). Examples of these screens include the Abel Assessment (Abel et al., 1998) Affinity versions 1 and 2 (Glasgow, 2003) and a screen which is being devised specifically for Internet sex offenders by Sean Hammond as part of the COPINE project (see Chapter 6).

Penile plethysmography

A somewhat more controversial approach to assessing the sexual interests of sex offenders is the penile plethysmograph. This approach involves the attachment of sensors which measure changes in penis size during exposure to various categories of image. For a fuller review of the procedure, refer to Calder (1999).

What are sex offenders doing on the net?

Sex is one of the Internet's biggest industries. Indeed the term 'sex' is the most searched for topic on the 'World Wide Web', (Cooper, Scherer, Boeis, and Gordon, 1999). In order to accurately assess any sex offender's behaviour it is necessary to have some understanding of the behaviours they may engage in on the Internet. The following section contains extracts from a series of semi-structured interviews undertaken with 14 offenders from the Wolvercote Clinic who admitted using the Internet in order to sexually offend. The group contained convicted contact offenders as well as some offenders who denied contact offences.

Indecent images of children

The accessing, downloading, uploading, collection and distribution of indecent images of children is a common behaviour disclosed by Internet sex offenders (Quayle et al., 2000; Quayle and Taylor, 2001). Some offenders with a developed sexual interest in children buy a computer simply to access the images they knew were on the Internet.

> *It started off the very first day I go on the PC. I had heard about newsgroups, I had read about newsgroups. I did a search on keywords and came across newsgroups that contained illegal pictures [of children] and I started to download immediately.*

Not all sex offenders are interested in indecent images and some will prefer images of children partially clad or in uniforms:

> *I also downloaded what I might describe as ordinary pictures of children, not pictures of sexual abuse but just pictures of children, to use in fantasy.*

As these images may not be illegal it is important to clarify the purpose for which they were accessed or collected. If the motivation was to gain sexual gratification then they are clearly relevant to the assessment.

A number of offenders have spoken about their fantasy developing and evolving through exposure to almost unlimited deviant material. This 'fantasy escalation effect' (Sullivan and Sheehan, 2002) has been described by offenders as a process of becoming bored with one type of image and moving on to gradually more and more explicit material:

> By the end I had seen so much of the stuff that it had lost its uniqueness, it's enjoyment factor. I moved on from pictures to Mpegs, movie clips. I was trying to download movies rather than still pictures, because that was even more real. And again having seen quite a few of those, that tailed off in terms of excitement. I still used it to masturbate to but I was actually getting more from being around other offenders and pretending to be young myself, to live out a fantasy through cyber sex. But it had become quite addictive.

Stories

Not all sex offenders prefer the medium of pictures for enhancing their fantasy. Some offenders will access, download or collect stories as they prefer the written word to images:

> I would download a lot of stories, which was for me the big thing really. The pictures I would use almost to supplement the stories. And the stories were there to fuel my fantasies.

For others who collect these stories rather than images the motivation is more pragmatic. They know that the written word is not illegal and so they cannot be prosecuted for having a collection of stories about children having sex with adults.

Research

Some offenders spoke of researching the topic of sex with children. This would include academic articles about the assessment and treatment of sexual offenders and the so-called

intellectual paedophile material which argued the case for adults to have sex with children.

> I went round looking at various web sites dealing with paedophile issues both for and against. And I read those and downloaded some articles from those.

Role-play

A more interactive extension of the stories is role-play. Offenders will meet in a chat room and designate a role to each other and then:

> It was very much like building up a story. We'd create the story plot and put various scenes into it. You'd say you play a child of 10 and I'll play an adult and there would be some other adults there as well and we'd just do two halves of the story, I would do half and then some else did and that's the sort of form it would take. Who played what didn't really matter much. It was just creating the story. And sometimes there would be masturbation to it, but often each person would just pretend to do it because it was the thought of creating enjoyment was almost better than that fact of what you were doing itself.

Web cams

One participant who had been an administrator of the Wonderland Club spoke of how a sub-group of the club used web cams to facilitate the sexual abuse of children in front of an invited Internet audience:

> If you had a camera and the correct software, you could do a live video conference call. And something called the orchid club, actually got busted because of it. They were doing basically a live sex show, that people on one end of the link would request what they wanted this guy to do with, I think it was his daughter or grand-daughter and they would do it at the other end.

Networking

The reinforcement of deviant attitudes through contact with other offenders can be a powerful aspect to the Internet sex offender's world

(O'Connell, 2001). Some offenders referred to going on-line for the first time as, discovering a new world where they were able to speak openly about their thoughts and feelings towards children for the first time:

> *The sense of being on the net was that, unlike when I was at work or anywhere else, I didn't have to wear the mask. I could actually be myself. It was an incredible feeling like you know what gay people say it's great to like to come out of the closet, they don't have to pretend anymore. It was exactly like that. It must be. I could be myself and people wouldn't tell you to act your age. You could lark about and people, well sometimes they snapped but a lot of the time people tolerated that and they loved you for it...Well they loved me for it. That was the thing with these people, I could be me, I didn't have to hide. And that really was...oh I can't describe the feeling, to be able to talk about children in that way.*

They were able to get their views validated and reinforced by others and in some cases they were able to use their connections with other sex offenders to gain access to children who were already being abused. One offender spoke of co-working with another offender he had met on the net to target and sexually manipulate children in chat rooms.

Assessments of the Internet sex offender need to take into account the power of this community and the degree to which distortions have had external reinforcement as well as the internal reinforcement offered by ejaculation to fantasies of sex with children.

Grooming

There are a variety of different ways sex offenders can groom on the Internet. Perpetrators can pretend to be a child in order to lure a child into sexual discussion or ultimately to meet. Figure 2 below illustrates how one offender typically groomed in a chat room. He is using the screen name Tom (11) to suggest that he is a young boy and he engages a person in the children's chat room, quickly establishing where the person lives to eliminate any who did

not live within easy access. He then explores whether the child is in fact 'a child' by asking questions about school which most adults might not know and then establishes rapport through discussion about mutual interests. Finally within a few minutes of starting to chat to this boy he introduces a sexual agenda.

Other offenders we spoke to said that they targeted vulnerable parents in order to gain access to their children while some did not attempt to disguise the fact they were adults and used their candour to gain the trust of the young people they were communicating with.

Figure 2: Chat room grooming

Tom (11)	Zoro U busy? age / sex ???
Zoro	No. 11/male
Tom (11)	Cool, where u from? I'm in UK
Zoro	I'm in London
Tom (11)	Way cool, I'm not far from there. What year u in at school?
Zoro	Year 7.
Tom (11)	Me too :-) Do you like school? ...Whats your fav subject?
Zoro	Schools ok – But only enjoy PE
Tom (11)	Whats your fav sport...mines cricket
Zoro	Cricket...Yawn I like football
Tom (11)	Who do you support.
Zoro	West Ham U?
Tom (11)	Promise you won't laugh
Zoro	Ok
Tom (11)	Forrest
Zoro	LOL
Tom (11)	I know u would laugh...U got a GF yet?
Zoro	GF?
Tom (11)	Girlfriend
Zoro	No
Tom (11)	BF?
Zoro	??
Tom (11)	Boyfriend?
Zoro	No
Tom (11)	Me neither yet

Exploring deviant sexual fantasy – some new tools

As fantasy is often the most difficult area for clinicians to address in assessment the remainder of this chapter will focus on some new methodologies for understanding and exploring deviant sexual fantasy. While these tools will be of particular interest to clinicians assessing Internet sex offenders they are applicable to all perpetrators.

While it is generally understood that sexual fantasy reinforces and develops the desire to sexually abuse children, practitioners have long struggled with how to address the issue of fantasy both in assessment and treatment. This section seeks to offer practitioners a framework for understanding fantasy and assisting perpetrators to explore their arousal and fantasy. The work is derived from the therapeutic interventions used by The Lucy Faithfull Foundation staff at the Wolvercote Clinic between August 1995 and August 2002.

Most practitioners are able to use the models of sexual offending mentioned earlier (Finkelhor, 1996; Sullivan, 2002; and Wolf, 1998) to demonstrate the importance of understanding the role of fantasy. Specifically, that continuing to masturbate and ejaculate to deviant sexual fantasies will increase rather than decease the possibility of progressing to a contact sexual offence, (Sandberg and Marlatt; Sullivan and Beech, 2003) and that deviant fantasy will serve to overcome inhibitors, (Marshall et al., 1999) and for some will be both a motivator to sexually offend and a method of rehearsing future behaviour, (Ward and Hudson, 2000).

Beyond this it is important to explore the nature of the Internet sex offender's fantasy, to gain an understanding of his motivation, to understand what he derives from the experience and what needs are being met. These are all necessary to adequately identify the specific treatment needs of each offender. To assist in achieving this goal it is important to have a common understanding of what is meant by the terms used. It is important for

practitioners to remind themselves and the offender that these concepts are broad and flexible frameworks which can be used to guide discussion rather than rigid models which must apply to everyone. Some key terms are:

- sexual arousal
- appropriate or inappropriate fantasy
- fantasy types
- fantasy themes
- the spectrum of control in fantasy
- the imagined self in fantasy

It is important for all participants to invest in the definitions of these concepts and terms to avoid the manipulations and backsliding often associated with this module. Therefore, time spent revisiting this material at the beginning of each module is well invested. Some of the most common problems associated with each term are explored below.

Key Terms

Sexual arousal

It is important that participants understand the process of sexual arousal and that while it is possible to control what you do with arousal when it happens it is not possible to stop arousal occurring altogether. Figure 3 provides a conceptual framework for understanding how sexual arousal occurs and how it develops. Perhaps most importantly it identifies the point at which it becomes possible to control the arousal and prevent it from developing further. The understanding which comes from exploring this process can often come as a relief to the participant who may have felt for years that there was no way of stopping the process of sexual arousal from developing into fantasy.

Research has shown that sexual preferences once established cannot be changed (Laws and Marshall 1991). Behavioural treatment techniques such as 'aversion therapy' (Laws and Marshall, 1990; McConaghy, 1975) and

Figure 3: Sexual arousal

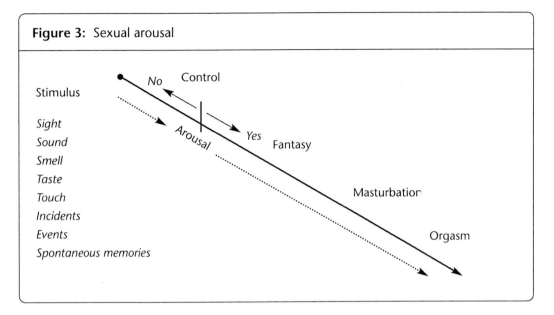

'orgasmic reconditioning' (Conrad and Wincze, 1976) have been shown to be of little use in altering states of sexual arousal. However, the behaviour arising out of deviant sexual arousal can be controlled. The cognitive behavioural perspective suggests that if a sex offender changes the way they think about children that this will have an effect upon their patterns of arousal. Arousal patterns don't change magically: changing them requires a participant to do something about them. Some people experience times when they don't feel aroused by offence-linked images and they imagine that they are 'cured'. In reality though, if a participant has built their sexual fantasies around satisfying thoughts of offending, they may be vulnerable to running similar fantasies and feeling aroused to them again, especially in certain mood states. It's important to have ways of managing offence-related sexual arousal in order to maintain an offence-free lifestyle.

Sometimes a participant may feel he wants to experience old offence-related fantasies and may actually want to look for children in order to do that. At other times, it can be something as simple as a sight, a sound or a smell that stimulates old arousal patterns. Control needs to take account of both. The impact of the feeling of arousal can be reduced by the level

of control exercised, the extent of change in beliefs and desire to have an offence-free life.

Appropriate or inappropriate fantasy

It is important to develop the participants thinking on the issue of acceptable fantasy. In the early stages of the assessment process it may be more straightforward to focus on the terms 'legal' and 'illegal' fantasy. It is important however to expand this concept to include an exploration of 'appropriate' and 'inappropriate' fantasy. Figure 4 shows how these concepts can be easily illustrated. Referring to the area between legal and illegal and appropriate and inappropriate as the grey zone can be helpful when considering aspects of legal fantasy which might be inappropriate for a specific offender to use. Using the analogy of stopping distance in a car can help in this illustration i.e. if you are too close to the danger when you need to stop, you may not be able to stop in time.

Fantasy types

Sex offenders generally report having a selection of fantasies which they use for different purposes. Listed below are some

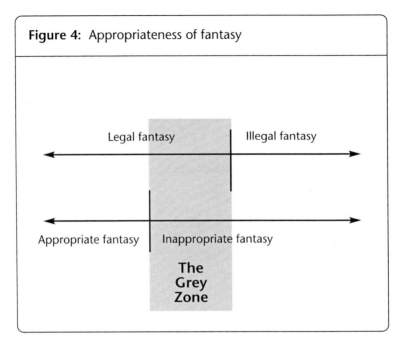

Figure 4: Appropriateness of fantasy

typologies which can be helpful in structuring the exploration of the different fantasies.

- imagined non-contact
- imagined consenting contact
- imagined consenting contact becoming non-consenting
- imagined non-consenting becoming consenting contact
- imagined non-consenting contact throughout

Sometimes a participant may feel that their fantasy does not fit into the five categories. This may be the case although the categories are deliberately broad to attempt to accommodate most fantasies. However the terms and definitions are not set in stone and it is a worthwhile exercise to explore what ways the participant's fantasy may not fit.

Fantasy themes

Sex offenders tend to have a variety of themes occurring within their fantasy life. For example someone who uses non-contact 'fantasy types' may have a variety of 'fantasy themes' within this type. Perhaps one fantasy would focus on secretly watching children while another

would involve exposing to children. Both fantasies are non-contact types but have different content or 'fantasy themes'.

Themes can be diverse and often participants will report a large number of different themes within their fantasy world. For others there will be less. What is important is that the therapist presents the concept as a relatively straightforward human process. If a participant picks up a reticence or hesitancy on the part of the therapist around any of these areas, it is likely to be interpreted as a criticism or indication of greater perceived risk. Throughout this work it is important to humanise the fantasy process to make it easier for participants to explore the true nature of their fantasy.

The spectrum of control in fantasy

How the perpetrator sees himself in the fantasy is of central importance in understanding his potential motivation for using deviant sexual fantasy. Fantasy themes will generally vary in the degree to which each person in the fantasy will be in control of the sexual interaction. A helpful way of analysing the issue of control in fantasy is to imagine a continuum between the two extremes of, others being in total control and to the offender being in total control at the other (see Figure 5). The mid-point between these two extremes can be the point where they see themselves and the other person in the fantasy as having sex by mutual consent. As offenders often have several fantasy types and themes they may move the point of control. For example a person who regularly runs a fantasy involving them exerting high levels of control over others may also at other times use fantasy where they are being controlled by others. An exploration of the spectrum of control is important to any clinical assessment.

Start by describing the two extremes of the model and the notional mid-point of imagined mutual consent. At this point it is necessary to clarify who is in control either side of the mid-point by including the next segment.

Next explore the sub-divisions within each segment. It is best that this is undertaken with the participant by asking questions such as 'what are the most extreme ways of exerting your control over a victim' or by pointing at a place along the line as 'how would someone who was here exert control'. This will allow you to establish titles for the sub-divisions as outlined below. Finally add in the scale as a means of assisting the participant to locate the extremes to which their fantasy ranges. As the discussion on this conceptual framework develops be aware of the possibility that the participant may not have a continuous range. This often occurs for those participants who do not have arousal to consenting contact but who might have fantasy at both extremes; i.e. fantasising about themselves being controlled by others or them controlling others.

Once completed, this task will provide the material for much discussion. Remember, as with any exercise the task is not complete until the participant has been enabled to 'create relevance' for themselves. Hence they will need to have given actual examples of the fantasy they have had which relates to the range they have identified. Without this it will be easy for the participant to slip back therapeutically.

The imagined self in fantasy

It is important to recognise the actual nature of the deviant sexual arousal which the participant is reinforcing through fantasy and masturbation and orgasm. Perhaps the most

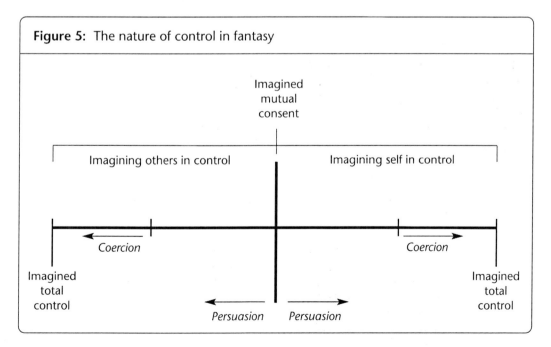

Figure 5: The nature of control in fantasy

Imagined mutual consent

Imagining others in control   Imagining self in control

Coercion   Coercion

Imagined total control   Imagined total control

Persuasion   Persuasion

difficult area for participants to acknowledge and discuss is the issue of arousal to distress of the victim. Some offenders assume that it is better to fantasise about being caring towards a child while having sex with them. This is simply a distortion as any sexual contact between an adult and a child is abusive and damaging towards the child. Hence it is not a 'better' way of abusing a child, it is simply a different way of sexually abusing a child which is pseudo-caring or pretending to be caring.

Other people who sexually abuse children say they are aroused to distress either on their own part or on the part of the victim in fantasy. This callous or sadistic arousal is often difficult for people to talk about, as it is perceived as a worse way of sexually abusing. Again, it is not a question of being better or worse, simply different.

Humanising the process of sadistic sexual arousal is more likely to facilitate an acknowledgement of these fantasies on the part of the offender.

Figure 6 below illustrates the concept of 'imagined self' in fantasy and assists the professionals engaged in assessment to introduce the issue of arousal to distress or sadism in fantasy. It is important for the offender to recognise the actual nature of the arousal that is made stronger through reinforcing fantasy with masturbation/orgasm.

Explaining the above concepts can be an important skill for professionals engaged in clinical assessment to learn. Rather than draw the diagrams before the session, try to draw it as you explain the concept. This will encourage you to break down the description into small sections, which should make the process easier to follow, rather than bombarding the participant with a complex conceptual framework in its entirety. This process will also allow the therapist to check out whether the participant following the presentation makes it more likely they will internalise the material. People generally have a greater investment in something that they feel they contributed in developing, so approach the presentation as a puzzle that you will solve together.

The Internet sex offender: some unanswered questions

As the technology evolves to facilitate law enforcements scrutiny of the offender's hard-drive(s) new questions are being posed which research has yet to answer. What does the nature of an offender's collection tell us about his potential risk of future offending? Does the size of a collection, or the spread of deviant sexual interest contained within it, have any relation to seriousness or risk of contact sexual offending?

It would be simple if there was a direct correlation between the nature of the material which a person has accessed and the actual behaviour they are likely to engage in. Perhaps because of the complex relationship between the conditioning process and the influence of other social and personal development factors it would appear that it is not as straightforward as early behaviourists would have argued (Laws and Marshall, 1990).

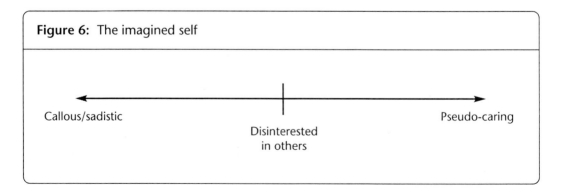

Figure 6: The imagined self

Callous/sadistic ← — — — — — — — — → Pseudo-caring

Disinterested
in others

Evidence obtained from our semi-structured interviews with Internet sex offenders appears not to support the assertion that the offender will eventually do whatever he fantasises and masturbates about. Some of the non-contact sex offenders we interviewed disclosed a highly sadistic Internet based fantasy world including the collection of extreme images of sexual violence and a pattern of role-playing abduction, torture and murder scenarios with contacts. There was no evidence that these individuals were likely to offend in this way although they did report that the process did disinhibit them, and in their opinions, this led eventually to their directly seeking sexual contact with children.

Marshall and Eccles (1993) found that actual experiences of deviant sex were more likely to influence future behaviour than fantasies about the acts. This raises a question about the nature of the Internet. How far will the significantly more 'real' fantasy world of the Internet influence the future behaviours of adults and the inquisitive children whose first sexual explorations are on the boundary-less virtual world of the Internet?

As the research into Internet sex offending evolves it should become possible to establish whether existing approaches are sufficient to inform the assessment and adequately meet the treatment needs of the Internet sex offender. In turn greater clarity should be achieved about whether it is necessary for all Internet sex offenders to receive the same treatment or whether programmes need to develop a flexibility to respond more directly to specific treatment needs of some sex offenders whose sexual interest in children are at their early stages of development.

References

Abel, G.G., Hoffman, J., Warberg, B. and Holland, C.L. (1998) Visual Reaction Time and Plethysmography as a Measure of Sexual Interest in Child Molesters. *Sexual Abuse: Journal of Research and Treatment*, 10: 2, 389–94.

Beckett, R.C. et al. (1994) *Community-based Treatment for Sex Offenders: An Evaluation of Seven Treatment Programmes*. Home Office Occasional Report. HMSO.

Beckett, R.C., Fisher, D. (1994) *Assessing Victim Empathy: A New Measure*. Paper presented to the 13th Annual Conference of ATSA (The Association for the Treatment of Sexual Abusers) San Francisco, USA.

Beech, A., Fisher, D. and Beckett, R.C. (1998) *An Evaluation of the Prison Sex Offender Treatment Programme*. HMSO.

Burke, A., Sowerbutts, S., Blundell, B. and Sherry, M. (2001) *Child Pornography and the Internet: Policing and Treatment Issues*. Paper presented to the ANZAPPL Conference, Melbourne.

Calder, M.C. (1999) *Assessing Risk in Adult Male Sex Offenders: A Practitioner's Guide*. Lyme Regis: Russell House Publishing.

Calder, M.C. (2000) *Assessing Risk in Adult Male Sex Offenders*. Lyme Regis: Russell House Publishing.

Conrad, S.R. and Wincze, J.P. (1976) Orgasmic Reconditioning: A Controlled Study of Its Effects Upon The Sexual Arousal and Behaviour of Adult Male Homosexuals. *Behaviour Therapy*, 7: 155–66.

Cooper, A. et al. (1999) Sexuality on the Internet: From Sexual Exploration to Pathological Expression. *Professional Psychology: Research and Practice*, 30: 154–64.

Davis, M. (1980) A Multi-dimensional Approach to Individual Differences in Empathy. *JSAS Catalogue of Selected Documents in Psychology*, 10: 85.

Eldridge, H. (1998) *Therapist Guide for Maintaining Change: Relapse Prevention for Adult Male Perpetrators of Child Sexual Abuse*. London: Sage Publications.

Finkelhor, D. (1984) *Child Sexual Abuse: New Theory and Research*. NY: The Free Press.

Finkelhor, D. (1986) *A Sourcebook on Child Sexual Abuse*. Newbury Park: Sage Publications.

Fisher, D., Beech, T. and Brown, K. (1999) Comparison of Sex Offenders to Non-Offenders on Selected Psychological Measures. *International Journal of Offender Therapy and Comparative Criminology*, 43: 4, 473–91.

Greendlinger, V. and Byrne, D. (1987) Coercive Sexual Fantasies of College Men as Predictors of Self-Reported Likelihood to Rape and Overt Sexual Aggression. *The Journal of Sexual Research*, 23: 1–11.

Gold, S.R. and Clegg, C.L. (1990) Sexual Fantasies of College Students With Coercive Experiences and Coercive Attitudes. *Journal of Interpersonal Violence*, 5: 464–73.

Grubin, D. (1998) *Sex Offending Against Children: Understanding the Risk*. London: Home Office Research, Development and Statistics Directorate.

Hanson, K. and Bussière, M.T. (1998) Predicting Relapse: A Meta-analysis of Sexual Offender Recidivism Studies. *Journal of Consulting and Clinical Psychology*, 66: 348–62.

Hanson, K. and Thornton, D. (1999) *STSTIC-99: Improving Actuarial Risk Assessments for Sex Offenders*. Ottawa: Department of the Solicitor General of Canada.

Hurlburt, D.F. and Apt, C. (1993) Female Sexuality: A Comparative Study Between Women in Homosexual and Heterosexual Relationships. *Journal of Sex and Marital Therapy*, 19: 315–27.

Itzin, C. (1992) *Pornography: Women Violence and Civil Liberties, A Radical New View.* New York: Oxford University Press.

Kinsey, A.C., Pomeroy, W.B. and Martin, C.E. (1948) *Sexual Behaviour in the Human Male.* Philadelphia: W.B. Saunders.

Kinsey, A.C. et al. (1953) *Sexual Behaviour in the Human Female.* Philadelphia: W.B. Saunders.

Laan, E. et al. (1993) Performance Demand and Sexual Arousal in Women. Behaviour Research and *Therapy,* 31: 25–35.

Landolt, M.A., Lalumiere, M.L. and Quinsey, V.L. (1995) Sex Differences and Intra-Sex Variations in Human Mating Tactics: An Evolutionary Approach. *Ethology and Sociobiology*, 16: 3–23.

Lang, A.R. et al. (1980) Expectancy, Alcohol and Sex-Guilt as Determinants of Interest in and Reaction Time to Sexual Stimuli. *Journal of Abnormal Psychology*, 89: 644–53.

Langevin, R., Lang, R.A. and Curnoe, S. (1998) The Prevalence of Sexual Offenders With Deviant Fantasies. *The Journal of Interpersonal Violence*, 13: 3, 315–27.

Laws, D.R. and Marshall, W.L. (1990) A Conditioning Theory of the Etiology and Maintenance of Deviant Sexual Preferences and Behaviour. In Marshall, W.L., Laws, D.R. and Barbaree, H.E. (Eds.) *Handbook of Sexual Assault: Issues Theories and Treatment of the Offender.* New York: Plenum Press.

Laws, D.R. and Marshall, W.L. (1991) Masturbatory Reconditioning With Sexual Deviates: An Evaluative Review. *Advances in Behaviour Research and Therapy*, 13: 13–25.

Marshall, W.L. (1989) Intimacy, Loneliness and Sexual Offending. *Behavioural Research and Therapy*, 17: 491–503.

Marshall, W.L. (1989) Intimacy, Loneliness and Sexual Offenders. *Behavioural Research and Therapy*, 27: 491–503.

Marshall, W.L. et al. (1995) Empathy in Sex Offenders. *Clinical Psychology Review*, 15: 99–113.

Marshall, W.L., Anderson, D. and Champagne, F. (1996) Self-esteem and its Relationship to Sexual Offending. *Psychology, Crime and the Law*, 3: 81-106.

Marshall, W.L., Anderson, D. and Fernandez, Y. (1999) *Cognitive Behavioural Treatment of Sex Offenders.* Chichester: John Wiley and Sons.

Marshall, W.L. and Eccles, A. (1993) Issues in Clinical Practice with Sex Offenders. *Journal of Interpersonal Violence*, 6: 68–93.

McConaghy, N. (1975) Aversive and Positive Conditioning Treatments of Homosexuality. *Behaviour, Research and Therapy*, 13: 309–19.

McGuire, R.J., Carlisle, J.M. and Young, B.G. (1965) Sexual Deviations as Conditioned Behaviour: A Hypothesis. *Behaviour, Research and Therapy*, 2: 185-90.

Nowicki, S. (1976) *Adult Nowicki-Strickland Internal-External Locus of Control Scale.* Department of Psychology, Emory University, Atlanta.

Nichols, H.R. and Molinder, L. (1984) *The Multiphasic Sex Inventory.* Tocomo, WA: self-published.

O'Connell, R. (2001) Paedophiles Networking on the Internet. in Arnaldo, C.A. (Ed.) *Child Abuse on the Internet: Ending the Silence.* Paris: UNESCO.

Quayle, E. et al. (2000) The Internet and Offending Behaviour: A Case Study. *Journal of Sexual Aggression*, 6: 1/2, 78–96.

Quayle, E. and Taylor, M. (2001) Child Seduction and Self-representation on the Internet. *CyberPsychology and Behavior*, 4: 5, 597–608.

Quinsey, V.L. et al. (1993) The Phylogenetic and Ontogenetic Development of Sexual Age Preference in Males: Conceptual and Measurement Issues. In Barbaree, H.E. and Marshall, W.L. (Eds.) *The Juvenile Sex Offender.* NY: Guilford.

Quinsey, V.L. et al. (1996) Viewing Time as a Measure of Sexual Interest. *Ethology and Sociobiology*, 17: 341–54.

Russell, D., Peplou, L.A. and Cutrola, C.E. (1980) The Revised UCLA Loneliness Scale. *Journal of Personality and Social Psychology*, 39: 472-80.

Sandberg, G.G. and Marlett, G.A. (1989) Relapse Fantasies. In Laws, D.R. (Ed.) *Relapse Prevention With Sex Offenders.* NY: Guilford Press.

Sullivan, J. (2002) The Spiral of Sexual Abuse: A Conceptual Framework for Understanding Child Sexual Abuse. *NOTA News*, April.

Sullivan, J. and Sheehan, V. (2002) *The Internet Sex Offender: Understanding the Behaviour and Engaging the Assessment and Treatment Issues.* Paper presented to the 21st Annual Conference of ATSA (The Association for the Treatment of Sexual Abusers) Montreal, Canada.

Sullivan, J. and Beech, A. (in press) Are Collectors of Child Pornography a Risk to Children? In McVean, A. and Lowe, D. (Eds.) *Policing the Internet.* London.

Thornton, D. (2000) *Matrix 2000.* Unpublished manuscript.

Ward, T. and Hudson, S.M. (2000) A Self-Regulation Model of Relapse Prevention. In Laws, D.R., Hudson, S.M. and Ward, T. (Eds.) *Remaking Relapse Prevention With Sex Offenders: A Sourcebook.* London: Sage Publications.

Wolf, S.C. (1988) A Model of Sexual Aggression/Addiction. *Journal of Social Work and Human Sexuality*, 7: 1, 131–48.

Chapter Six

The Challenge of Sex Offender Assessment: The Case of Internet Offenders

Sean Hammond

Introduction

In this chapter we are concerned with the psychometric assessment of Internet sex offenders. I intend to show how the process of sex offender assessment presents a number of complex challenges and is far more involved than simply reaching for the nearest questionnaire or interview schedule. However, before we proceed further it may be necessary to define a few terms. Psychometry means literally the 'measurement of the mind'. Typically, when practitioners talk of psychometric tests they are actually referring to self-report questionnaires or intelligence tests. This is a very limited use of the term as psychometrics actually refers to a body of theory that supports a huge range of strategies and procedures. The purpose of these strategies is to obtain and collate information in order to measure and extrapolate to mental processes and behaviours. Thus psychometrics applied to sex offender assessment should involve a range of strategies and techniques and there is no inherent limitation to the use of questionnaires. Such strategies may include clinical interview and collation of offence histories as well as the use of questionnaires, repertory grids, penile plethysmography, preference scaling and timed response tasks.

When we refer to Internet sex offenders, we are talking about those individuals who have been apprehended for illegal sexual activity over the Internet. This is a wide definition since it may include, for example, individuals who make financial gain by generating or dispensing sexually abusive images of children as well as those who have downloaded such images for sexual gratification. In other words the motive or function of the offending may vary from acquisitive to sexually purposeful. However, the term Internet sex offender is typically applied to the sexually motivated individual and this is the meaning we will apply here. Chapter 2 by Ethel Quayle (in this book) provides a more detailed account of this group of offenders.

Issues in the assessment of Internet sex offenders

The assessment of sexual offenders is a complex exercise and throws up a number of difficulties and uncertainties. The Internet sex offender presents the clinician with a number of challenges that may be summarised under three general headings:

1. The absence of a coherent body of knowledge.
2. The particular nature of the client group.
3. The parlous state of psychometric practice.

The absence of a coherent body of knowledge

There has been much work on sex offenders and there is now a rich body of knowledge in the area (Beech, Fisher and Beckett, 1999; Fisher and Beech, 1999; Hanson and Bussiere, 1996; Hollin and Howells, 1991; Howitt, 1995; Laws and O'Donohue, 1997; Perkins, Hammond, Coles and Bishopp, 2000). This has informed a variety of treatment programmes and assessment procedures. That is not to say that there are no controversies in the area but what debate there is tends to be fuelled by a fairly rich knowledge base.

However, in the case of Internet offenders there has been very little coherent work. Recent celebrated police operations have highlighted the potentially high prevalence rate of this kind of offending but it has only been recently that

much interest has been shown by psychologists (Quayle and Taylor, 2002). The furtive and relatively solitary nature of the behaviour coupled with its recency appear to have conspired to keep Internet offenders 'off the map' for researchers in sexual offending. As a result there is very little specifically designed for Internet sex offenders either in treatment and management terms or in assessment methods. The COPINE project based at University College, Cork is one of very few that is currently attempting to adjust this shortfall.

The nature of the client group

Sex offenders are a particularly challenging group to assess (Happel and Auffrey, 1995; Salter, 1988). Like many offenders, sex offenders are not generally compliant at initial contact. Issues of denial and minimisation are an enormous challenge to the clinician working with sex offenders. Assessment under such circumstances with its typical reliance on self-report can at best, provide only an approximate initial profile of the person. The problem may be ameliorated if the client enters a treatment programme and the practitioner is then able to observe him over time. In this case assessment may be seen as an ongoing process alongside and integrated with the treatment or intervention. A potential pitfall here is that the client may learn to 'talk the talk'. In such a case the treatment process provides the client with the vocabulary and insights necessary to present as low risk while his cognitions, motivation and behaviour is unaffected.

So it is that the non-compliant or manipulative client may undermine the accuracy of the assessment. All forms of assessment are affected but clinical interviews and self-report questionnaires are particularly prone to this form of bias. Thus, there is a great need for corroborative evidence with sexual offenders and a multi-modal approach to assessment in which a variety of different methods are used to collect information (Blanchette, 1996). Collaborative evidence may be obtained from victim statements, forensic

and/or psychiatric histories and third party observations such as family, prison officers, police, GP etc. Of course, the assumption here is that such sources are available and this is typically not the case (O'Rourke and Hammond, 2000)

Certain clinicians may take exception to the observation that clinical interviews are particularly prone to error with non-compliant clients. It might be argued that a highly trained clinician will be able to see signs of dissembling during the interview. This may be true but there is another side to this particular coin. The highly trained clinician will learn during training that sex offenders are highly defended and typically engage in both factual and psychological denial and minimisation. Therefore s/he will expect the client to dissemble and the danger is that a negative halo effect may then operate. The importance of this point is not so much for the typical child molester for whom there is a large body of research data informing our expectations and against which our assessments may be mapped, but rather for the type of offender that we know less about. The Internet offender is one such type. It is tempting to apply what we know about child molesters to Internet offenders, it lessens our cognitive load and simplifies the practical management of these people. However, in doing so we make assumptions and while these assumptions may be appropriate it should be remembered that we currently have very little empirical data to support or reject them.

The state of psychometric practice

It should always be born in mind that the basic statistical edifice, upon which classical test theory stands, was pioneered by Charles Spearman in the early part of the 20th century as a means of providing a theoretical framework for the measurement of intelligence (Spearman, 1904; 1927). Since that time Classical Test Theory has become the prevailing model informing measurement and testing in a wide range of areas from attitudes to personality to psychological health and risk appraisal. Rarely have the practitioners using this measurement model seriously questioned its appropriateness for sex offender assessment.

Practitioners do need to ask themselves whether the assumptions of Classical Test Theory are really appropriate in the particular context and settings in which it is applied. For example, the assumption of the randomness of measurement error might be quite appropriate in the assessment of intelligence tests but in a forensic setting it should be quite apparent that the context of the assessment plays a major role in the nature of the information elicited. In other words, we might expect high levels of systematic error in our measurements.

In fact, many psychometric alternatives to Classical Test Theory do exist. These include Generalisability Theory (Shavelson and Webb, 1991), an extension of Classical Test Theory to take account of systematic error, Item Response Theory (Hambleton, Swaminathan and Rogers, 1991), a radical model-based departure with some extremely valuable implications for forensic assessment, and Idiographic Strategies including repertory grids and multiple card sorting (Houston, 1998; Canter, Brown and Groat, 1985).

Occasionally, an original and highly promising technique for assessment is developed but it is hindered by the fact that it has been developed around a sub-optimal psychometric model. An example is Abel's viewing time paradigm that offers a potentially useful and accessible alternative to penile plethysmography (Abel et al., 1998; 2001) but the use of the classical test model to collate and score the procedure means that the technique is essentially flawed in measurement terms (Fischer and Smith, 1999; Hammond and Crowder, 1998). This has led David Glasgow, the developer of AFFINITY, a UK equivalent of Abel's task, to argue that the method should be utilised primarily as an idiographic technique.

It is beyond the brief of this chapter to go into detail on the variety of alternative measurement models but the interested reader is referred to the following texts (Embretson and Hershberger, 1995; Nunnally and Bernstein, 1993). The author is currently preparing a book with Paul Barrett that attempts to describe the practical application of a range of psychometric models in the forensic context.

The three facets of forensic assessment

In developing an assessment strategy for a patient or a client group the practitioner needs to keep three aspects of the enterprise foremost in their mind. We have always thought of these as the fundamental facets of assessment in that they are overlapping but discrete elements of assessment planning. The first relates to the purpose of the assessment, the second concerns what specific characteristic is to be assessed and the third involves the method chosen to collect and collate the relevant information. Thus, purpose, focus and method are the fundamental facets of all psychological assessments and may be reduced to three questions 'Why assess?', 'What to assess?' and 'How to assess it?' We will now look at each facet in turn, bearing in mind their interrelated nature.

Facet A. The purpose of assessment

The practitioner should always be aware of the purpose of their assessments since this will to a great extent dictate the focus and the method. I will consider four reasons for assessment that are common in sex offender work and we will look at their place in the assessment of Internet offenders. The four reasons I will examine are research, treatability, change and risk management.

A1. The research purpose

Very little is known about Internet sex offenders as a group. Therefore one primary aim of those working in the area is to gather information to provide the basis for a working profile or typology of such individuals. The use of assessment tools is vital to enable us to build a picture of this particular client group. For the purpose of sex offender treatment programmes it has been assumed that Internet offenders do not differ appreciably from contact offenders and the management of such people should be essentially similar. However, although the nature of the offence may imply a common paedophilic orientation, the behaviour exhibited by contact and Internet offenders may be quite different. Murray (2000) for example distinguishes between paedophiles and child molesters and it may be plausible to argue that Internet offenders should be similarly distinguished from contact offenders. This does not imply that there is not an overlap between the two as many Internet offenders may well also be contact offenders but we cannot assume that for all offenders.

Of course, we cannot take this differential argument too far because there are clearly many cases where the two types of offending overlap and ultimately the Internet offender is, at the very least, colluding in the emotional and physical abuse of young children. The question of whether one can make clear distinctions between Internet offenders and contact offenders is an empirical one. Unfortunately, at present, there is insufficient data available to support such distinctions although there is some relevant work now being carried out in the area. What does appear to be the case is that different types of offender present different needs and risk profiles (Furby, Weinrott and Blackshaw, 1989).

Due to the lack of work in this area there is very little information on what might distinguish Internet offenders from other groups of people. Of course, this would be easier to do if these individuals constituted a clear homogenous group. However, apart from some level of sexual interest in children and access to the Internet there is no obvious profile for the 'average' Internet offender. Clearly, it is helpful when considering treatment and management of such offenders to be able to think in general terms in order to inform the treatment strategies that meet the needs of the

particular group. However, if no coherent group can be said to exist then the justification for a programmatic treatment approach is weakened.

This leads us to the question of whether there may be multiple types of Internet offender each presenting with different therapeutic needs. For example, the individual who is apprehended for downloading abusive images of children and who also has a long predatory history of physical and sexual abuse of young children may present very different treatment needs to another person arrested for the same offence who has an obsessional and solitary interest in collecting and cataloguing images and yet little or no interest in physical contact with young children.

A2. The case management purpose

In the previous section I looked at assessment from a normative perspective but one central function of clinical assessment for intervention is to provide the basis upon which individual case management decisions might be made. Thus, the specific needs and characteristics of an individual are identified. These may either inform the treatment goals and methods to be applied for a particular client in an individualised treatment, or they may inform on the suitability of the client to a pre-existing treatment programme.

It is also important to assess individuals to identify any characteristics that might exclude them from particular forms of treatment and this may involve tapping into aspects that are not directly related to the offending behaviour and specific treatment needs. For example, psychopathy may be assessed since there is some evidence that it may be counterproductive to offer a standard groupwork programme to a marked psychopathic individual. Equally, the level of cognitive functioning may need to be assessed if some of the treatment work involved intellectually challenging material. Other, general measures might include compliance or readiness to engage in treatment as well as self-esteem and affective state.

In the case of Internet offenders there is very little work to inform appropriate treatability assessment. However, the usual caveats regarding psychopathy, cognitive functioning, self-esteem and affective state would apply. It is quite likely that Internet offenders will be drawn from relatively high functioning individuals when we take into account the cognitive skill required to access the problematic material as well as the fact that the necessary equipment is not cheap to buy.

The main challenge for the clinician who wishes to assess an Internet offender in order to target treatment is that not a lot is known about the group in general so a well-structured battery of assessment tools is not available. This implies that the clinician relies heavily upon batteries developed for a more general clientele or that s/he places a greater emphasis on a more qualitative and idiographic assessment of each Internet offending client.

A3. The evaluation of change purpose

There are no accredited treatment programmes for Internet sex offenders and our knowledge is still pretty rudimentary on the kinds of needs that they may present. Therefore, it is important that the treatments applied to such offenders are properly evaluated. Ideally, this will take a dynamic form so that programmes may be modified and developed in light of emerging evidence. Of course, it is impractical to use outcome measures such as re-convictions in this context because of the timescales involved. Individual assessments taken before, during and after treatment, providing the tools are appropriately chosen, offers a useful strategy for evaluating the impact of an intervention programme 'on the fly'. While it is unlikely that such a short-term strategy will offer much on the analysis of behavioural change it may provide insights into changes in cognition and affect.

I alluded to the fact that assessment devices in this context must be appropriately chosen.

What is meant here is that they should have robust psychometric properties as well as being valid measures of those specific characteristics for which change is anticipated. One of the psychometric properties at a premium when assessing change is temporal stability (usually indexed by the test-retest reliability coefficient). Unfortunately, clinical psychology in general has not produced much of a wealth of psychometrically strong measurement tools.

The burden is upon the practitioner to identify measures that have high reported stability of test-retest reliability. Only in this way can they be confident that any changes in the scores over time are due to psychological changes and not to random fluctuation of an inconsistent measurement device. A range of techniques exist for evaluating change and not all of them are dependent upon the classical test theory. The interested reader is referred to Mellenbergh and Van den Brink (1998) for a good practical account of some of the most widely used procedures.

A4. The risk management purpose

A major motive for assessment is to provide a basis for decisions concerning risk prediction and management. Typically, risk assessment utilises checklists of factors that are known, from previous prospective studies, to predict the future behaviour under scrutiny. The list of factors one utilises for a risk assessment, of course, depends upon the specific behaviours to be predicted. Most widely used risk assessment devices in the forensic setting are oriented to offending behaviours resulting in reconviction and this reflects the needs of the prison and probation service. However, there are many other risks that might also be of interest to the practitioner with the responsibility of clinical case management.

Risk of self-harm, mental instability and vulnerability to victimisation or manipulation are also vital considerations. With Internet offenders the likelihood that the nature of the index offence may change (for example, potential for escalation to contact crime) is also a central concern. In the case of Internet offenders there is very little data enabling the user to build a definitive checklist of risk factors, thus risk assessment for this group is currently based upon rational and logical judgement rather than empirical criteria.

By definition, risk assessment is about assessing potential. Having identified that potential for harm, the practitioner acts to mitigate the risk. Thus, risk assessment is not simply about risk prediction because a good risk management procedure, in mitigating the risk, removes the predictive validity of the assessment. This suggests that a defensible strategy for risk assessment with Internet offenders may be to adopt a protocol such as the Risk Assessment Management and Audit System (RAMAS) designed specifically for the purpose of containing risk within good case management (O'Rourke, Hammond and Davies, 1997; O'Rourke and Hammond, 2002).

Facet B. Focus of assessment (domain facet)

Psychometric assessment ranges over a vast area and the practitioner is often confronted with a bewildering array of devices purporting to measure an almost infinite number of characteristics. In designing an assessment protocol it is vital that the focus of the assessment is clearly defined along with its purpose such that the assessments are direct and appropriate for their purpose.

Thus, if the purpose of the assessment is to evaluate the change produced by some form of intervention, it is vital to clearly identify the characteristics that are targeted by the treatment. These characteristics may be very broad or very narrow but they need to be precisely defined before selecting or developing a psychometric procedure. Due to the need for brevity we will briefly describe just three elements of this facet, 'personality functioning', 'interpersonal functioning' and 'sexual interest'.

B1. Personality functioning

Here we define personality as an enduring predisposition to respond and behave in a certain manner. Thus, the extravert may have a predisposition to behave in a gregarious and impulsive manner. An important point to emphasise here is the use of the word *'enduring'*. Personality is generally defined as a fairly fixed aspect of an individual. The most widely used measures for normal personality are probably those tapping the so-called 'Big-5' factors (extraversion, anxiety, agreeableness, conscientiousness and openness). However, other models exist such as the Eysenkian and Cattell's trait models or the Jungian typology approach and measures are available for them all (Briggs-Myers and McCaulley, 1985; Cattell and Cattell, 1995; Costa and MacCrae, 1985; Eysenck and Eysenck, 1985).

One aspect of personality functioning which is of fundamental importance in the forensic context is that of personality disorder. For example, the degree of antisocial or borderline personality disorder that an individual manifests can have a significant relationship to treatment compliance and risk. In this way personality functioning overlaps to some extent with mental health functioning.

B2. Interpersonal functioning

The manner in which an offender behaves interpersonally is important. Two models for interpersonal functioning that are in current use are the circumplex and octagon. These identify interpersonal behaviours as an inter-related network that may be represented spatially. It is tempting to surmise that the 'passive' Internet offender operates differently in this regard than the predatory contact offender. This would be empirically verifiable by obtaining interpersonal profiles of the two types of offender. The two measures most commonly used for circumplex and octagon assessments are the Circle (Blackburn, 1998) and the PROQ (Birtchnell, 1994).

B3. Sexual interest

An obvious target for assessment with sexual offenders is their sexual interest and the degree to which there may be a deviant pattern underlying their behaviour. The DSM-4 psychiatric classification for paraphilias, particularly paedophilia, may be useful here in that the symptomatic features are clearly stated. However, in order to utilise these criteria it is necessary to delve deeply into the offender's most private self. Singer (1984) provides a useful model of erotic response in the form of three sequential stages. First is the triggering response that Singer labels 'aesthetic'. This response is triggered by an attractive stimulus and results in attention being diverted towards the object. This results in the second response, 'approach' which involves a physical orientation and approach to the object. Finally, the physiological response occurs and this may entail genital vasocongestion. Singer labels this the genital response although there may be a number of non-genital physiological signs such as pupil dilation, blood pressure changes etc.

Typically, sexual interest is measured by bio-signal techniques such as the penile plethysmograph and this will be discussed later. However, according to Singer's response model such techniques only work if the sexual response is quite marked. Also, it should be clear that relying upon self-report in this area is highly unrealistic. It is apparent (Hanson and Bussiere, 1998) that deviant sexual interest is one of the best predictors of contact sexual offence recidivism and so the latest developments in sex offender assessments appear to be concentrating very much on this area. Clearly, the sexual interest of Internet sex offenders is of central interest since the identification of their sexual interest patterns should provide some indication of risk potential as well as giving insights into the heterogeneity or otherwise of this offender group.

In the space available for this chapter I cannot cover the vast array of potential foci for the assessment of sex offenders. However, we cannot move on without very briefly touching on some specific domains of interest. Readers are referred to Briggs et al. (1998) and Calder (1999; 2000; Carich and Calder, 2003) for an accessible practical guide on sex offender assessment that looks at a variety of focal areas. Briefly, other important elements for Internet sex offenders might include:

- Self-concept: and self-esteem (Beckett et al., 1994).
- Attitudes and beliefs (Murphy, 1990; Proctor, 1994).
- Mental health status (Farmer, McGuffin and Williams, 2002).
- Sexual history (Maletsky, 1991).
- Relapse prevention strategies (Laws, 1989).

Facet C. Methods of assessment (method facet)

We have already alluded to the fact that there are a variety of potential strategies and techniques available to the clinician when assessing a sex offender. However, the vast majority of sex offender assessments are carried out using self-report questionnaires or face-to-face interviews. As we have seen, this poses problems when we wish to assess defensive and non-compliant clients. The fact that there are a plethora of such tools available 'off the shelf' and that the alternatives often involve an added burden of research and training, pushes the practitioner towards the, often less suitable, option of self-report. It is the responsibility of academics and researchers in the area of sexual offending to provide accessible alternatives to the practitioner and happily this is increasingly happening, albeit slowly (Glasgow, 2001; Gray et al., 2003). Below we will briefly comment upon some of the elements of this 'methods' facet of sex offender assessment.

C1. Self report methods

The most common strategy for eliciting information for an assessment is through self-report, usually through the medium of a questionnaire or interview. The questionnaire has the distinct advantage of being highly structured and relatively cheap to administer and this is particularly useful if the purpose of assessment is to gather large amounts of information in order to research and profile the client group. One great advantage of self-report is that the range of characteristics available for assessment is almost infinite and may include self-concept, readiness for change, attitudes and sexual interest.

Batteries of questionnaires are also commonly compiled for assessment within the context of case management and treatment evaluation. A good example of the way in which such assessments have been integrated into treatment programmes is the Sex Offender Assessment Package (SOAP) which is part of the STEP Programme (Beech and Fisher, 2000).

However, a major drawback of this strategy of data collection is that it cannot protect against the vagaries of denial and mendacity. We have already stated that sex offenders are a notoriously highly defended client group. We have no guarantees that the responses to our questionnaires will be accurate and truthful. Indeed, depending on the characteristic being assessed, we might anticipate high levels of dissembling. In psychometric terms we anticipate a high degree of systematic error that severely limits the validity of our measurements.

A number of self-report devices include so-called validity scales designed to trap the mendacious respondent. However, these are usually quite simplistic and transparent to the intelligent respondent. Thus, while self-report methods have certain advantages they should always be used with caution. Their use with sex offenders is problematic and it is certainly unwise to base the whole formulation for such a client on such information.

C2. Rating methods

Another strategy for gathering information is to ask others to provide data. This is best done

in the form of highly specific checklists of behaviour to be filled in by someone who knows the client well. Typically, the person doing the rating will be a professional such as a prison officer or key worker. The advantage of this method is that the data lacks the subjectivity of self-report. However, this advantage may be more apparent than real unless certain safeguards are met. The assessor needs to be very aware of the possibility of the halo effect where certain irrelevant characteristics of the client might unduly sway the rater in their judgements.

The characteristics to be measured must be manifest in behavioural terms. It is not reasonable to expect raters to have sufficient insight into the feelings and cognitions of the client in question for the purpose of measurement. On the other hand observable behaviours provide an objective basis upon which raters can supply information for assessment purposes.

It is important to emphasise that the raters must always use the same judgement criteria and this implies that either these criteria are extremely simple or that there must be a period of training built into the assessment. The reliability of rating procedures need to be evaluated by ascertaining consistency between raters on common assesses (inter-judge reliability).

These techniques are most applicable in situations where there is a degree of control over the client's environment which places certain limits upon his or her repertoire of possible behaviours. Thus, they are most widely used in hospital or prison settings. A widely used example of such a device is Blackburn's (1998) CIRCLE test which is used to assess interpersonal behaviour.

C3. Corroborative history taking

Where there are available records such as those drawn from a criminal or mental health history, a valuable source of corroborative evidence exists. Collation of such records is time consuming and often frustrating. The information is often in an unstructured form and needs to be sifted through to obtain relevant nuggets of information. It is very important that the assessor knows what they are looking for before they begin the process. To this end it is useful to develop an 'a-priori' list of the relevant features being searched for before reading the clients notes. In this way the assessment procedure resembles a content analysis using an a-priori coding scheme.

A number of assessment devices include provision for corroborative note searches and these are particularly important in risk assessment. One very common measure of psychopathy utilises an interview and a corroborative note search (Hare, 1991) and a number of clinicians have made use of the notes alone.

Clearly, a major drawback in the use of patient notes is their lack of availability and also the fact that they will vary in detail between clients. In the case of many if not most Internet offenders there may be no prior criminal activity and no psychiatric history. However, where such information does exist it is a very useful source of corroboration of self-report assessments.

C4. Idiographic methods

Idiographic methods are techniques for eliciting personal information that is unique to the client being assessed. Thus, assessment of a client's family and social networks would involve an idiosyncratic set of data because no client has the same family and friends. This form of assessment is not commonly used but can be particularly useful in an individualised functional assessment of the offending behaviour.

Idiographic methods vary considerably and may include an open-ended analysis of diaries or the highly structured method known as repertory grid analysis. The latter has the advantage of providing a clear and mathematically objective basis for assessing change. Idiographic methods of assessment are ideally suited for assessing individuals in the context of treatment. The focus is on a single case and the identification of personal thoughts, feelings and cognitions. The repertory grid is closely associated with Personal Construct Theory (PCT) although the technique is more general than this implies. An excellent introduction to this approach is Huston's book (1998). A simpler yet more general approach that keeps the mathematical advantages of the repertory grid without the basis in PCT is multiple card sorting (Canter, Brown and Groat, 1985).

Idiographic methods are single case methods. They provide a useful insight into the cognitions of the individual offender and, as such, they are a very useful adjunct to normative assessment in the context of treatment. However, they are time consuming and although there are a number of automated systems to simplify the process, the idiosyncratic nature of the assessment means that it is never possible to predict the amount of time that will be required.

C5. Biosignal methods

Biosignal methods employ the use of physiological techniques to measure bodily changes. These bodily changes are viewed as somatic manifestations of an underlying psychological state (Wormith, 1986). The assessment of male sexual arousal patterns is typically facilitated by the use of a penile plethysmograph (PPG). This is a device that detects changes in the penis (circumference or volume) when the client is presented with stimuli of varying kinds. Thus a paedophile when presented with images of young children may show signs of tumescence that are absent when images of young adults are presented. In this way very specific paraphilias may be examined (Laws et al., 2000; Seto, 2001). This technique is, on the surface, a direct and objective way of detecting the presence of paedophilic tendencies.

Unfortunately, there are a number of drawbacks to the use of the PPG and the most critical is its availability. The PPG is a complex and costly piece of equipment. It requires a dedicated space to perform and a properly trained technically proficient assessor. There are few places outside hospitals and prison settings where the requisite equipment and skill can be found. There are other difficulties with the use of the PPG. First, the legality and ethical status of the stimuli used to elicit a response may be problematic. While the stimuli do not need to be visual it is common to use photographic images or video. Clearly, if the purpose is to detect a paedophilic orientation then images of children may be required and this may produce intractable ethical concerns. Second, the scientific nature of the assessment does not imply that the PPG cannot be faked, it is quite possible for men to produce measurable levels of tumescence to images they do not find attractive at will (Mahoney and Strassberg, 1991). Finally, the erection response is notoriously prone to the inhibitory and activating effects of emotional states that may have little to do with the stimuli in question.

There are procedures and techniques available that mitigate many of these difficulties and the careful assessor will be well aware of such pitfalls. Nevertheless, there are always cases where the PPG fails to provide a reliable and valid profile (Marshall and Fernandez, 2001).

C6. Latency methods

A promising approach to the assessment of defensive clients is the use of procedures that record response times in a variety of situations and under specific conditions. A particularly interesting approach is that proposed by Abel and his colleagues (Abel et al., 2001; Kruger, Blandford and Glancy, 1998). This procedure presents clothed images of people of all ages and both sexes on a computer screen one at a time. The person being assessed is asked to rate each in terms of attractiveness. As well as recording the rating the computer records the amount of time that the offender spends considering each image. Abel has found people

with a sexual interest in children spend significantly longer considering the images of children than those of adults. They are able to demonstrate clear group differences between child molesters and non-paedophile offenders.

The great advantage of this procedure over the PPG is the fact that it does not require sexually explicit or provocative images to be used. However, attractive as this procedure is there is one serious caveat to its widespread use. It is an ipsative measure since the scores obtained are the *relative* amounts of time spent on images within various categories (e.g. male-child, female-child, male-adult, female-adult). For a detailed account of the ipsativity problem the reader is referred to Hammond and Barrett, 1996; Hicks, 1970; Johnson, Wood and Blinkhorn, 1988) but the upshot is that comparisons between individuals are not meaningful and thus aggregated data, such as group means, are highly problematic.

This has led Glasgow (2003), who has developed a computerised system for carrying out the procedure named Affinity (Glasgow, 2001) to advocate it as an idiographic rather than a normative tool. A number of other latency procedures may be appropriate for the assessment of sexual offenders. For example Wright and Adams (1994) were able to discriminate between homosexual and heterosexual individuals by using a simple reaction time paradigm involving the presentation of images. Other current developments include variations of the Implicit Association Task (COPINE, 2002; Grey et al., 2003) while Beech and Kalmus (In submission) discuss a technique involving Rapid Serial Visual Presentation. However, while these methods are showing very positive results they should be considered experimental at this stage.

Conclusions

This chapter has attempted to show that the assessment of sexual offenders is a complex challenge and where Internet sex offenders are concerned it is exacerbated by a large number of unknowns. Current psychometric practice in sex offender assessment is typically naive and not well thought out despite the fact that more appropriate models and methods exist to aid the practitioner in this area. Some of the fault lies in the fact that until recently these advances have not been widely disseminated although this is now changing as the psychometrics curriculum in undergraduate training courses is beginning to catch up with developments (Embretson and Harshmann, 1999). On the other hand, researchers have been slow to develop new strategies that have immediate and practical benefits for the practitioner. Again the outlook is optimistic as increasing numbers of psychology graduates are drawn to forensic work and this means that research in the forensic assessment area has seen a recent upsurge.

In the area of Internet sex offenders, reliability and breadth of assessment is vital because we are still in a stage of discovery. The fundamental question of whether such offenders may be qualitatively distinct from contact offenders, and the degree of overlap there is between them, depends upon the collection and collation of data. This in turn relies upon appropriate assessments to provide the requisite reliable information. As with most complex areas it is helpful to break the domain down into interrelated facets. We have attempted to do this by suggesting a three facet approach to sex offender assessment, A. Purpose, B. Focus and C. Method. We make no great claims for novelty here but this way of organising the issue of assessment provides us with a clearer picture of the task ahead.

References

Abel, G.G. et al. (1998) Visual Reaction Time and Plethysmography as Measures of Sexual Interest in Child Molesters. *Sexual Abuse: A Journal of Research and Treatment*, 10: 81–95.

Abel, G.G. et al. (2001) Classification Models of Child Molesters Utilizing the Abel Assessment for Sexual Interest. *Child Abuse and Neglect*, 25: 703–18.

Beckett, R.C. et al. (1994) *Community-Based Treatment for Sex Offenders: An Evaluation of Seven Treatment Programmes*. Occasional Report 1-216. London: Home Office.

Beech, A.R. (1998) A Psychometric Typology of Child Abusers. *International Journal of Offender Therapy and Comparative Criminology*, 42: 319–39.

Beech, A.R. and Fisher, D. (2000) Maintaining Relapse Prevention Skills and Strategies in Treated Child Abusers. In Laws, R., Hudson, S. and Ward, T. (Eds.) *Remaking Relapse Prevention With Sex Offenders*. London: Sage.

Beech, A.R., Fisher, D. and Beckett, R.C. (1999) *An Evaluation of the Prison Sex Offender Treatment Programme*. Home Office Occasional Report. Home Office Publications Unit.

Beech, A.R. and Kalmus, E. (in submission) *Developing a Computer-based Assessment Using Rapid Serial Visual Presentation and Attentional Phenomena: A New Means of Measuring Sexual Interest?*

Birtchnell, J. (1994) The Interpersonal Octagon: An Alternative to the Interpersonal Circle. *Human Relations*, 47: 511–27.

Blackburn, R. (1998) Criminality and The Interpersonal Circle in Forensic Psychiatric Patients. *Criminal Justice and Behavior*, 25: 155–76.

Blanchette, K. (1996) *Sex Offender Assessment Treatment and Recidivism: A Literature Review. Research Report R-48*. Ottowa: Correctional Service of Canada.

Briggs, D. et al. (1998) *Assessing Men Who Sexually Abuse*. London: Jessica Kingsley.

Briggs-Myers, I. and McCaulley, M.H. (1985) *A Guide to The Development and Use of The Myers Briggs Type Indicator*. Consulting Psychologists Press.

Calder, M.C. (1999) *Assessing Risk in Adult Male Sex Offenders: A Practitioner's Guide*. Lyme Regis: Russell House Publishing.

Calder, M.C. (2000) *Complete Guide to Sexual Abuse Assessments*. Lyme Regis: Russell House Publishing.

Canter, D., Brown, J.M. and Groat, L.A. (1985) Multiple Sorting Procedure for Studying Conceptual Systems. In Brenner, M., Brown, J.M. and Canter, D. (Eds.) *The Research Interview*. London: Academic Press.

Cattell, R.B. and Cattell, H.E. (1995) Personality Structure and The New Fifth Edition of The 16PF. *Educational and Psychological Measurement*, 6: 926–37.

COPINE (2002) The COPINE Project Assessment and Treatment Package. Http://Copine.Ucc.Ie

Carich, M.S. and Calder, M.C. (2003) *Contemporary Treatment of Adult Male Sex Offenders*. Lyme Regis: Russell House Publishing.

Costa, P. and McCrae, R. (1985) *The NEO Personality Inventory*. Odessa, FL: Psychological Assessment Resources.

Embretson, S.E. and Hershberger, S.L. (1995) *The New Rules of Measurement*. London: Lawrence Erlbaum.

Eysenck, H.J. and Eysenck, S.B. (1985) *Eysenck Personality Questionnaire-Revised (EPQ-R) and Short-Scale (EPQ-RS).* London: Hooder and Stoughton.

Farmer, A., McGuffin, P. and Williams, J. (2002) *Measuring Psychopathology.* Oxford: Oxford University Press.

Fisher, D.D. and Beech, A.R. (1999) Current Practice in Britain With Sexual Offenders. *Journal of Interpersonal Violence,* 14: 233–49.

Fischer, L. and Smith, G.M. (1999) Statistical Adequacy of The Abel Assessment for Interest in Paraphilias. *Sexual Abuse: A Journal of Research and Treatment,* 11: 195–205.

Furby, L., Weinrott, M.R. and Blackshow, L. (1989) Sex Offender Recidivism: A Review. *Psychological Bulletin,* 105: 3–30.

Glasgow, D. (2001) *Affinity* (Available From Glasgow, D., Email-Dvglasgow@Aol.Com)

Glasgow, D. (2003) *The Affinity Program. New Developments.* Paper Presented at The Tools to Take Home 2 Conference, April, Birmingham.

Grey, N.S. et al. (2003) Violence Viewed by Psychopathic Murderers. *Nature,* 423.

Hambleton, R.K., Swaminathan, H. and Rogers, H.J. (1991) *Fundamentals of Item Response Theory.* Beverly Hills, CA: Sage Publications.

Hammond, S.M. and Barrett, P.T. (1996) The Psychometric and Practical Implications of The Use of Ipsative, Forced Choice Formal Questionnaires. *Proceedings of The BPS Occupational Psychology Conference,* 1: 135–44.

Hammond, S.M. and Crowder, M. (1999) A Psychometric Rasch-Type Model for the Viewing Time Assessment Paradigm: Work in Progress. www.ramas.co.uk/abelmodel.pdf -

Hanson, R.K. and Bussiere, M.T. (1998) Predicting Relapse: A Meta-Analysis of Sexual Offender Recidivism Studies. *Journal of Consulting and Clinical Psychology,* 66: 348–62.

Happel, R.M. and Auffrey, J.J. (1995) Sex Offender Assessment: Interrupting The Dance of Denial. *American Journal of Forensic Psychology,* 13: 2, 5–22.

Hare, R.D. (1991) *The Hare Psychopathy Checklist-Revised.* Toronto: Multi-Health Systems.

Hicks, L.E. (1970) Some Properties of Ipsative, Normative and Forced-Choice Normative Measures. *Psychological Bulletin,* 74: 3, 167–84.

Hollin, C. and Howells, K. (1991) *Clinical Approaches to Sex Offenders and Their Victims.* Chichester: Wiley.

Houston, J. (1998) *Making Sense With Offenders: Personal Constructs, Therapy and Change.* Chichester: Wiley.

Howitt, D. (1995) *Paedophiles and Sexual Offences Against Children.* Chichester: Wiley.

Johnson, C.E., Wood, R. and Blinkhorn, S.F. (1988)

Spuriouser and Spuriouser: The Use of Ipsative Personality Tests. *J. Occupational Psychol,* 61: 153–62.

Kruger, R.B., Bradford, J.M. and Glancy, G.D. (1998) Report From the Committee on Sex Offenders: The Abel Assessment for Sexual Interest: A Brief Description. *Journal of the American Academy of Psychiatry and The Law,* 26: 277–80.

Laws, D.R. (1989) *Relapse Prevention With Sex Offenders.* New York: Guildford Press.

Laws, D. and O'Donohue, W. (1997) *Sexual Deviance: Theory, Assessment and Treatment.* New York: Guildford Press.

Laws, D.R. et al. (2000) Classification of Child Molesters by Plethysmographic Assessment of Sexual Arousal and A Self-Report Measure of Sexual Preference. *Journal of Interpersonal Violence,* 15: 1297–312.

Mahoney, J.M. and Strassberg, D.S. (1991) Voluntary Control of Male Sexual Arousal. *Archives of Sexual Behavior,* 20: 1–16.

Maletsky, B.M. (1991) *Treating The Sexual Offender.* London: Sage.

Marshall, W.L. and Fernandez, Y.M. (2000) Phallometric Testing With Sexual Offenders Limits to its Value. *Clinical Psychology Review,* 20: 807–22.

Mellenbergh, G.J. and Van Den Brink, W.P. (1998) The Measurement of Individual Change. *Psychological Methods,* 3: 470–85.

Murphy, W.D. (1990) Assessment and Modification of Cognitive Distortions. in Marshal, W.L., Laws, D.R. and Barbaree, H.E. (Eds.) *Handbook of Sexual Assault.* New York: Plenum.

Nunnally, J.C. and Bernstein, I. (1993) *Psychometric Theory.* New York: Mcgraw-Hill.

O'Rourke, M. and Hammond, S.M. (2003) *Multi-Agency Risk Management: Safeguarding Public Safety and Individual Care.* Cork: RAMAS.

O'Rourke, M.M. and Hammond, S.M. (2000) *Risk Management: Towards Safe and Effective Practice.* Guilford: SHB.

O'Rourke, M.M., Hammond, S.M. and Davies, J. (1997) Risk Assessment and Risk Management: The Way Forward. *Psychiatric Care,* 103–7.

Perkins, D. et al. (1999) *An Evaluation of Sex Offender Treatment Programmes.* High Security Commissioning Board. Department of Health.

Proctor, E. (1994) *The Sex Offence Attitudes Questionnaire.* Oxford: Oxford Probation Service.

Quayle, E. and Taylor, M. (2002) Paedophiles, Pornography and The Internet: Assessment Issues. *British Journal of Social Work.* 32: 863–75.

Salter, A. (1988) *Treating Child Sex Offenders and Victims.* Newbury Park, CA: Sage Publications.

Seto, M.C. (2001) The Value of Phallometry in the Assessment of Male Sex Offenders. *Journal of Forensic Psychology Practice*, 1: 65–75.

Shavelson, R.M. and Webb, N.M. (1991) *Generalizability Theory*. Newbury Park CA: Sage.

Singer, B. (1984) Conceptualising Sexual Arousal and Attraction. *Journal of Sex Research*, 20: 230–40.

Spearman, C. (1904) General Intelligence Objectively Determined and Measured. *American Journal of Psychology*, 15: 201–93.

Spearman, C.E. (1927) *The Abilities of Man, Their Nature and Measurement*. New York: Macmillan.

Wormith, J.S. (1986) Assessing Deviant Sexual Arousal: Physiological and Cognitive Aspects. *Advances in Behaviour Research and Therapy*, 8: 101–37.

Wright, L.W. and Adams, H.E. (1994) Assessment of Sexual Preference Using a Choice Reaction Time Task. *Journal of Psychopathology and Behavioral Assessment*, 16: 221–31.

Chapter Seven

Current Treatment Approaches

David Middleton

Introduction

It's not that pornography causes you to commit crime. I've never blamed pornography for what I've done...but it's like a snowball at the top of a mountain and as it rolls down it gets bigger and faster until it is out of control, that's how pornography fuels your fantasy.

(Barry, convicted of indecent assault against children).

This chapter will examine our current understanding of successful approaches to treatment, the aims of treatment and a consideration of therapist characteristics and treatment style. It is acknowledged at the outset that much of what is known about successful treatment approaches with Internet users who sexually abuse derives from work with other forms of sexual offence behaviour. Whilst the growth of problematic Internet use has been meteoric, the collection of research data and evaluation of treatment outcomes has trailed far behind in both volume and pace.

Marshall (1996) and Marshall et al. (1999) provide a succinct summary of the development of psychological treatment approaches for problematic behaviour including deviant sexual behaviour. He charts the move from Freudian psychoanalysis in the 1930s through to the emergence of behavioural interventions in the 1960s. Marshall identifies in particular the emergence of the 'sexual motivational' account for the development of deviant sexual interest, principally from the work of McGuire et al. (1965). In this analysis great importance was attached to the early sexual experiences of inexperienced children (or adolescents). These early sexual experiences were deemed to become associated with sexual arousal. They were accompanied by masturbation to the remembered experience. The hypothesis was used to explain the development of deviant sexual arousal in

adults for, if these early experiences were with a young child, and reinforced through fantasy and masturbation then sex with children would thereafter be entrenched as the primary sexual preference. Marshall comments:

This hypothesis, although neither then nor now supported by more than anecdotal evidence proved to be so appealing that it quickly came to be accepted as doctrine and persists to this day.

(p16).

Whatever the validity of the hypothesis, it is clear that it was extraordinarily influential in shaping subsequent treatment programmes. These programmes were to focus on eliminating deviant sexual preferences or re-conditioning the subject to non-deviant sexual arousal. The techniques used were almost exclusively behavioural, including aversion therapy. The treatment was designed to change, suppress or eliminate deviant sexual preferences. It is not the purpose here to rehearse the arguments, either positively or negatively concerning this approach. What is clear however is that the idea of addressing problematic sexual behaviour, solely by attempting to change sexual preference, is considered too narrow a focus by current treatment providers. This applies even more strongly to addressing the needs of individuals who access indecent images of children through the Internet.

In order to sustain change over the longer term a more holistic approach is taken. Thus whilst current treatment programmes still contain elements designed to assist offenders to understand and control how the use of deviant fantasy contributes to subsequent offence behaviour, programmes will also ensure that work is undertaken to address personality characteristics associated with sexual offending. In addition work is undertaken to address the cognitive process which underpins the abuse behaviour and increase the offender's understanding of how situational factors may need to be controlled to reduce the occurrence of the behaviour. These programmes therefore are based on a mixture of cognitive and behavioural therapeutic techniques (Bakker et al., 1998; Barbaree and Seto, 1997)

Current approaches to sex offender treatment in the UK

The widespread implementation of cognitive-behavioural techniques in the treatment of sex offenders has reflected the move towards offence-focused work in dealing with criminal populations. Meta-analyses of treatment outcomes have shown that the most successful programmes are those which target the specific criminogenic behaviours involved (Andrews et al., 1990; Antonowicz and Ross, 1994; Andrews, 1995; Lipsey, 1995; Losel, 1995). However, such implementation also reflects the development of multi-factorial models to explain the existence and diversity of sexually abusive behaviour and a move away from the assumption that psychopathology can account for all such behaviour. Multi-factorial models of sexual offending stress the importance of both individual and socio-cultural factors in sexual abuse, where such factors are seen as complementary rather than in opposition to one another. In addition, these models have the empirical support lacking in more traditional, single factor theories (Finkelhor, 1984; Marshall and Barbaree, 1990).

By the late 1990s the largest treatment provider in the UK for sexual offenders in the community was the Probation Service of England and Wales (Fisher and Beech, 1999; Findlater and Ford, 1999). In a move to apply research evidence of effectiveness in a consistent manner, the Probation Service took the strategic decision that each Area of the Service would run one of three programmes which had been accredited as conforming to standards of design, range of methods used,

appropriate targeting, sequencing, motivation and evaluation (Home Office, 2001).

The treatment model

The treatment model for the accredited Sex Offender Programmes in England and Wales is adapted from the model presented by Fisher and Beech (1998). It addresses four components namely denial, offence specific behaviours, social adequacy and relapse prevention skills.

Research indicates that 87% of sex offenders will deny or minimise their offending at first interview (Maletzky, 1991). Perhaps surprisingly denial of offence behaviour is not correlated with an increased risk of re-conviction (Hanson and Bussiere, 1998), however it seems logical that if we require offenders to control and change their behaviour, a first step in this process is that they should accept responsibility for their offending (Marshall et al., 1999). Therefore initial work on denial is an important feature of the programme.

Secondly, treatment programmes need to focus on offence specific problems known to be associated with sexual offending such as cognitive distortions, deviant sexual arousal, lack of victim empathy etc. (Allam, 2000; Beech et al., 1998; Hanson and Bussiere, 1998; Marshall and Serran, 2000; Rice et al., 1994).

The third component is attending to problems of social adequacy experienced by many, but not all sexual offenders. These problems may be in the area of poor problem recognition, poor problem solving, lack of consequential thinking, issues around self management especially impulsivity and anger control (Fisher and Beech, 1998; Fisher and Howells, 1993; Hanson and Scott, 1995). Further problem areas may be associated with low self-esteem, lack of assertiveness and an inability to achieve or sustain intimacy in relationships (Bumby and Hanson, 1997; Garlick et al., 1996; Hudson and Ward, 1997; Marshall, Anderson and Fernandez, 1999; Smallbone and Dadds, 1998). It should be noted that offenders of all kinds exhibit characteristics of poor self-management and often poor social adequacy. However, it is the combination of these characteristics together with the offence specific problems, which distinguish sexual offenders.

Finally, offenders will need to be aware of their own high risk situations, mood states and behaviours, and acquire new strategies and skills to avoid or deal with them appropriately in order to lead an offence-free lifestyle (Pithers et al., 1983; Pithers et al., 1988; Ward et al., 1995). Since offenders are not an homogeneous group it follows that the treatment programme will have a varying impact on offenders according to their degree of motivation to change, their view of their own ability to control events and how they respond to those events (locus of control) and finally by the degree to which their sexual and emotional behaviour is fixated.

Applying this model to sexual offenders who use the Internet

As stated earlier there is an absence of research concerning the specific characteristics of this offender group. However, early analysis of psychometric testing suggests evidence that these offenders have similar characteristics to those who commit other forms of sexual offending (Beech, personal communication). Therefore whilst an assessment will be required to determine the appropriate treatment targets in each individual case, the above model which is designed to address the specific criminogenic needs of sexual offenders, is applicable to sexual offenders who use the Internet.

Similarly the evidence from other forms of sexual offending suggests that differing lengths of treatment (dosage) may be applicable to achieve a 'treated profile'. Allam (2000) and Beech et al. (1998) were able to identify that low deviance offenders reached a treated profile after approximately 100 hours of intervention. However, high deviance offenders required at least 200 hours of intervention to reach the same profile. Clinical

experience suggests that offenders who use the Internet present along a similar spectrum of high treatment need through to relative low treatment need and practitioners will need to take account of these needs in determining the length of treatment intervention. It should be borne in mind that these dosage levels were based on offenders taking part in a group programme.

It is possible that a treatment intervention which works with offenders on an individual basis may be effective over a reduced number of hours. Clearly group programmes generally incorporate a range of possible treatment targets, not all of which will apply to each group member. The content of programmes delivered to individuals can be specific to the needs of the individual which may reduce the number of sessions involved, however, sufficient time between sessions should be planned to allow for assimilation of the learning and the practice of new skills.

Additional treatment targets for sexual offenders who use the Internet: issues of compulsivity, community and collecting

Whilst it is argued that this treatment model has general applicability, an assessment of the individual may identify additional treatment targets. These may include the degree to which the offender has exhibited compulsive or obsessive behaviour in pursuing the on-line activity. Carnes et al. (2001) propose that on-line sexual activity is indicated as problematic for the individual in three areas:

- **Compulsivity:** indicated by entrenched habits and routines.

- **Continuation despite consequences:** e.g. effect on relationships, fear of discovery.

- **Obsession:** preoccupied to the exclusion of other parts of life.

In work with the offender the therapist will need to identify whether the indications of on-line compulsivity are different from those of sexual pre-occupation which feature in accounts from other sexual offenders. In addressing this issue the therapist will seek evidence that the compulsive behaviour may be a symptom of other linked problematic behaviour, namely depression, low self-esteem, an ability to make or sustain relationships.

Similarly, some sex offenders who use the Internet may have particular attractions to the sense of community gained through the pursuance of sexual interests. Taylor and Quayle (2003) suggest that the sense of community gained through the Internet has a distinctive quality. Unlike living in a physical community the Internet offers a virtual community. It offers superficiality in relationships, which may be characterised by a particular and limited form of social skills. It meets the need for intimacy without the possibility of threat or criticism. Finally it allows for the reinforcement and normalisation of distorted cognitions that justify offence behaviour. In the course of treatment intervention therefore the therapist will need to explore the needs that the offender met through pursuance of acting in a virtual community and how these needs may be met through more appropriate means.

A further dimension may be the degree to which the offender is obsessive about collecting. Taylor and Quayle (2003) differentiate between accumulating, hoarding and collecting. The latter infers a deliberate act of selection and choice where items are acquired beyond a level appropriate to necessity or need. Offenders who already have 10,000 images each which is unlikely to have been viewed regularly, seek further images. There appears to be a thrill derived from seeking out and extending the collection regardless of the utility derived from the images. Furthermore a related feature of the collector's behaviour appears to be constant cataloguing, organising and filing in an organised process which increases the engagement with the collection. Understanding the needs which are met by such behaviour may be a further focus of treatment intervention.

In summary the initial aims of treatment will include:

- Recognition of a pattern of behaviour.
- Recognition of negative consequences of the behaviour: on inter-personal relationships, life balance, work etc.
- Recognition of risk of escalation.
- Recognition that images are scenes of abuse to real victims.

The Process of Treatment

Dealing with denial

It is rare to encounter an offender charged with sexual offences who is fully admitting the extent and nature of their behaviour. Even those caught 'red-handed' in possession of child pornography by police 'sting' operations for example, will seek to minimise the extent of their intention, degree of previous use of pornography and the gratification derived from use of the material. Such denial is to be expected. Mann (2000) refers to a reframing of such denial as 'client resistance' and furthermore suggests the degree of resistance can be influenced by the approach taken by the therapist:

> *The underlying principle is that resistance to treatment is a product of the interaction between the client, the therapist, and the treatment goals. If treatment and its goals can be made appealing and the therapist can adopt a treatment style that facilitates change, then client resistance can be significantly minimized'.*
>
> (p187).

In dealing with such resistance it is useful to apply a cognitive therapy model (see for example Beck, 1995) to analyse the interaction between offender and therapist. For example the therapist may wish to speculate on the cognitions which lay behind the verbal statement of the offender. What for example may be the cognitions behind an offender who states, 'I did not get aroused to those images'? The self-talk may be, 'I am not the sort of person who is aroused by this'(which relates to his self-image) 'I cannot risk being seen to be the sort of person who is aroused to this' 'I will lose everything if I admit to the full extent of what I have done' (which relates to possible negative consequences) 'If I can get away with this I can always stop myself in future' (which may relate to poor problem recognition and rationalisation).

Equally important is to recognise the feelings that the offender may be experiencing during the course of this exchange. In the above example the offender may be feeling shame (self image) fear (negative consequences) and confusion (poor problem recognition).

If this interaction is to progress it will be necessary for the therapist to make explicit that these self-talk statements and feelings are recognised. Equally important will be the need for the therapist to consider an appropriate response to help someone come to terms with feelings of shame, fear and confusion. In the course of training workers to approach interviews from this perspective they have often realised that their own self-talk statements and feelings need to be examined before being able to assist the offender. Many have described that their approach to dealing with denial would previously have involved, or led to, some form of confrontational exchange. However, viewed from the above perspective it is apparent that such an approach is not appropriate. Inviting workers to deal with the presenting problems of the offender by responding to his/her feelings of shame, fear and confusion produces a different, and more productive, dynamic within the intervention. For more information on effective therapeutic styles which should be adopted in work with this offender group see Jenkins (1990; forthcoming a and b), and Miller and Rollnick (2002).

Dealing with offence-specific problems

The second element of the model of change focuses on offence-specific problems. These are critical to the commission of the offence and without them a sexual offence would not have

occurred. Frequently these problems will include cognitive distortions, lack of victim empathy and deviant sexual arousal. Therapists may find it useful at this stage to discuss with the offender how the commission of the offence formed a pattern of behaviour, which became reinforced by distorted cognitions, deviant fantasy and masturbation.

A number of theoretical models can be used to help offenders identify these processes including the Sexual Assault Cycle (Eldridge, 1998; Wolf, 1988); Four Preconditions for Sexual Assault (Finkelhor, 1984) and the Sexual Abuse Spiral (Sullivan, 2002). All of these models require some modification to make them relevant for sexual abuse involving the Internet, since they were originally developed to explain the pattern of behaviour involved in 'hands-on' child abuse.

Using the Finkelhor model (Figure 1, overleaf) for example the four stages normally refer to 'Motivation', 'Overcoming internal inhibitors'; 'Overcoming external inhibitors' and 'Overcoming victim resistance' (for a detailed discussion see Calder, 1999; Carich and Calder, 2003). For the purposes of applying this model with Internet users the 'Overcoming external inhibitors' stage could be adapted to ask 'What steps did you take to make sure no one close to you (or at work) knew what you were looking at? The stage of 'Overcoming victim resistance' could be adapted to 'What needed to happen to make the child participate in the image?'

Experience in working with offenders suggests that they have great difficulty in identifying or admitting, being motivated to sexually abuse, or their motivation to view sexual abuse images. In discussion the therapist may find it useful to explore with them the factors identified from the Finkelhor model. In this model motivation may feature some or all of three components:

- **Emotional congruence.** This refers to the way the offender feels a special affinity with children and seeks to achieve emotional intimacy with children rather than with age appropriate partners. Exploring this factor may involve

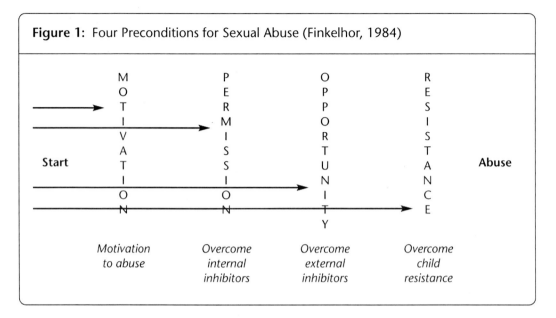

Figure 1: Four Preconditions for Sexual Abuse (Finkelhor, 1984)

examining the role of low self-esteem and feelings of social inadequacy in accounting for interactions with children which give feelings of power and control.

- **Deviant sexual arousal.** Despite initial denial from offenders it is evident that arousal to the images presented in pornography or developed through fantasy form a key component to sexually abuse.

- **Blockage.** This may refer to an inability, perhaps for developmental reasons, to relate appropriately to peers for reasons of poor social skills, sexual anxieties or maladaptive attachment styles. Situational blockage may also relate to abusers with adult sexual interests whose normal sexual outlets are lost because of a transitory crisis or loss of a relationship.

Identifying patterns of behaviour and cognitive distortions

To take the case of Barry, who opened this chapter, the pattern of offending was identified through introducing the Finkelhor Pre-conditions Model. He was able to identify his motivation as sexual interest in both adults and children. He had a history of viewing pornography initially of adults and admitting 'curiosity' concerning seeing children in sexual activities. He was reluctant to acknowledge this as a sexual interest but admitting becoming aroused to such images. Asking questions concerning the particular mood states in which he was more likely to seek out such images enabled him to identify times of increased personal stress from which he sought 'relief'. Some support for this pattern of behaviour can be found in the literature. Marshall, Cripps et al. (1999) for example, found that sex offenders were more likely to resort to deviant fantasy and masturbation as a coping mechanism for non-sexual problems, than non-offenders. Barry also described a deterioration in the relationship, including sexual, with his wife although it was difficult for him to identify at the initial stage the reasons for this deterioration.

Finkelhor describes two ways in which internal inhibitors to offending are overcome. First the offender can make use of dis-inhibiting substances such as drugs and alcohol. Alcohol misuse in particular is a common precursor to sexual offending. Support for this is found in Pithers et al. (1988) study which found that alcohol use prior to offending was reported by 42% of rapists and

23% of child molesters. Rada (1978) reported alcohol use prior to offending in 50% of rapists, and Amir (1971) found rates higher than 60%.

In relation to the use of the Internet, practitioners should consider the role that 'logging on' may play in dis-inhibition. Taylor and Quayle (2003) comment on the quick and easy access to a whole range of pornography through logging on to the Internet and the rapid way in which such interaction can induce mood change. The question can be posed therefore that the process of 'logging on' performs the same function as opening a bottle of alcohol for those seeking to 'give themselves a lift' from negative mood states. In this respect 'logging on' becomes a substitute for addressing the underlying causes of negative mood, and like abuse of alcohol, in providing a means of temporary escape from problems, gives rise to the possibility of dependency .

The second strategy Finkelhor identified as used to overcome internal inhibitors is to give permission through self talk or cognitive distortions (Murphy, 1990; Ward et al., 1997). In applying the Finkelhor Model further, Barry was able to examine dis-inhibiting factors. In this respect Barry told himself that in viewing such material he was 'not harming anyone' and that the images 'were there whether he looked at them or not'. Over time he began to rationalise accessing the images as something he 'deserved' and no different from viewing adult pornography. He was able to admit that he began to masturbate to fantasies involving the images he was viewing and that his behaviour in this regard began to escalate. He did not think of the pictures as abusive, and believed that the children taking part in the pictures were doing so willingly and 'probably got paid to do so'. The process of challenging such distortions involves using open-ended Socratic questioning techniques. Asking, for example, 'what other explanations might there be for the children taking part in the scenes?', 'what evidence is there that it is normal for children to willingly take part in sexual activities with adults?'

This brings into focus the role played by pornography in supporting the development

of these distortions. Clearly a process of regularly viewing abusive images may give rise to the offender habituating to any initial 'shock', often a phrased used by offenders, until viewing such images becomes codified as accepting that the images are 'normal'. Once this position has been reached it allows the offender to give himself permission to view the material. Barry also used self-talk statements which reflected sexual entitlement beliefs such as 'I deserve this, it's my only way of getting sexual satisfaction'.

Developing empathy

Crucial to effective work with offenders who view sexual images of children is developing awareness that the children are victims of abuse. For sadistic offenders of course such awareness is not only present but forms part of the arousal. For most offenders, however, their arousal is dependent on fantasies in which the child is a willing and active partner. Marshall, Hudson et al. (1995) have suggested that empathy is an unfolding four-stage process that involves:

- Emotional recognition: the process of recognising the signs of distress.
- Perspective taking: the ability to predict what emotion a person will feel if something happens to them.
- The experience of a compassionate emotional response.
- Taking action to comfort or reduce suffering.

Clearly in producing effective change with offenders it is insufficient for them to understand the feelings of another or understand how their behaviour will affect the other. They must also act in accordance with the needs of the other person. In discussion with sex offenders this multi-component model of empathy is seen as a helpful tool to identify empathy deficits particularly when the stages are simplified as *See, Think, Feel and Do*.

Many offenders will feel that they do have the ability to empathise with others, but are able to recognise that they have ignored or overridden these indicators. During discussion it is possible to gain recognition that they have blocked or distorted their ability to empathise in order to get their own needs met. By seeing that all four stages of empathy are important, offenders can be helped to see the necessity of moving beyond their sense of being helpless victims of their own needs, and into a state of being where they can completely control whether or not they choose to harm others. Offenders viewing sexual images of children can be helped by hearing survivor accounts of adults who were coerced into taking part in the production of child pornography. Such accounts also serve to express the feelings of betrayal and powerlessness from having their images in the public domain and being unable to ever have them removed. In addition survivor accounts may help to dispel notions that they entered into the activity on a voluntary or consensual basis. Fundamentally there needs to be recognition that such images are images of sexual abuse. The therapist may be assisted in this process by drawing on research detailing the psychological and physiological effects of being used in pornography and prostitution such as Silbert (1989).

Addressing deviant sexual fantasy

Deviant sexual preference is the single biggest predictor of sexual recidivism (Hanson and Bussiere, 1998). In working on offence-specific problems therefore it is necessary to explore with the offender the extent of this preference and whether it is capable, if not of being changed, then of being controlled. The therapist will need to explore the range of sexual fantasy used by the offender and the events which trigger the lapse into abusive fantasy.

Leitenberg and Henning (1995) define sexual fantasy as 'almost any mental imagery that is sexually arousing or erotic to the individual'. They emphasise that 'fantasy' and 'daydream' are interchangeable concepts which refer more generally to any thought

activity that is not orientated towards solving a problem or working on a task. A fantasy therefore can be an elaborate imaginary sequence, a replaying of a memory or a fleeting thought.

Clearly therapists are interested in the type of images which are most frequently viewed by, and incorporated in to fantasy, by the offender and how entrenched these images have become embedded in masturbatory behaviour. Efforts should also be made to identify how frequently, and in what circumstances the offender is lapsing into abusive sexual fantasy when off-line. Finally the therapist will seek to explore the incorporation into abusive sexual fantasy of children to whom s/he has access or is in a position to commence a grooming relationship, which may signal the beginning of the process of turning a fantasy into a 'hands-on' abusive sexual contact.

Offenders may be helped to change the content of abusive sexual fantasies through a variety of behavioural modification techniques such as:

● **Aversion therapy:** in which the viewing of an abusive image is linked with an unpleasant consequence such as inhaling of noxious substances.

● **Covert sensitisation:** in which the offender incorporates into the sexual fantasy an imagined unpleasant consequence which destroys the enjoyment of the fantasy.

● **Masturbatory reconditioning techniques:** which involve attempts to disrupt the process of physical arousal to deviant images. These techniques may include directing the offender to introduce non-deviant imagery into fantasy whilst masturbating, masturbating to deviant fantasy beyond the point of ejaculation, and repeated verbalisation of the deviant fantasy to reduce arousal.

It has to be said that the evidence for effectiveness of these techniques rests on small scale studies and it is likely that this form of intervention, on its own, is unlikely to induce a long term change in deviant sexual preference.

It may also be necessary to link the decease in use of the deviant fantasy with increasing arousal to appropriate sexual images to achieve the greatest benefit from these techniques.

Dealing with factors associated with social adequacy

The approach so far has been to identify the pattern of behaviour and associated distorted cognitions, the development and escalation of abusive sexual fantasy and helping the offender to develop victim empathy. However, effective treatment will also need to address the underlying reasons that drive the offender into problematic Internet use.

If the premise is that use of the Internet is a means of altering mood or avoiding negative emotional states such as boredom, depression or anxiety (in much the same way that individuals may resort to instrumental use of alcohol or drugs) then it is clear that any strategies so far discussed will have limited impact unless the individual is able to gain insight into the causes of the behaviour and helped to generate alternative coping strategies. Similarly if the problematic use of the Internet is driven by the need to avoid negative emotional states or personal distress then the practice of downloading and masturbating to child pornography provides a highly rewarding or reinforcing context for further avoidance.

Further, the use of the Internet to obtain gratifying emotional experiences such as a sense of community and reinforcement through shared values (for example through communicating in chat rooms) provides a compensatory positive stimulus. Any combination of these factors may provide an explanation why such rewards become 'addictive' for the individual concerned. Support for this hypothesis comes from the research of Cortoni et al. (1996); Proulx et al. (1996) who examined various coping strategies and found that the typical response of sexual offenders to stress, emotional difficulties, or other sources of problems, was

to seek out sexual contacts or engage in sexual fantasies of both a deviant and non-deviant nature.

A further factor to be addressed in treatment will be the effect on inter-personal relationships. Schneider (2000) reports the effects of compulsive use of the Internet for sexual purposes through a survey of the partners of users. The variety of detrimental effects on relationships range from hurt, betrayal, rejection, abandonment, humiliation, anger and loss of self-esteem. Among 68 per cent of couples in this study, one or both partners had lost interest in relational sex. Some couples had no relational sex in months or years. Clearly it is difficult to determine whether the relationship breakdown occurs prior to the offender spending increasing time alone on their computer, or whether the breakdown of intimacy within the relationship makes the opportunity to achieve sexual gratification through Internet activity more appealing. This will need to be a focus of discussion with the offender and if appropriate, their partner.

In 1997 the West Midlands Area of the probation service collaborated with the West Midlands Police in an operation to assess offenders using child pornography, apprehended through a 'sting' operation. The assessment involved making a judgement on the likelihood that the offender had already been involved in contact offences against children, or whether their offence pattern was such that an escalation of their behaviour, and instigation of contact offences, was likely. Furthermore offenders were assessed to determine if early treatment intervention could divert them from such escalation. The potential outcomes of assessment were that the offender could be prosecuted in the normal way or be subject to a formal caution at the end of their participation in the treatment programme. The caution also made them liable for registration under the Sex Offender Act 1997 and allowed for DNA samples to be held. An analysis of 15 of these cases who were dealt with through this process is shown in Figure 2.

Figure 2: Sample of cases arrested for child pornography offences dealt with by West Midlands Police and Probation Service 1997–1998

Age

average   44 yrs

range 26–73 yrs

Relationships

In relationship at time of arrest   66%

Self report no sexual relationship at time of arrest   80%

Health

Sexual dysfunction – self report   50%

General health problems – self report   75%

Risk

Admit fantasy/admit risk of escalation to hands on   25%

Admit fantasy/deny risk   50%

Deny fantasy/deny risk   25%

Despite being caught in possession of child pornography 25 per cent of these offenders denied they had sexual fantasies concerning sex with children and also denied there was a risk of their behaviour escalating to contact offending. Of the 75 per cent who did acknowledge fantasising about sex with children, 25 per cent considered there was a risk that they could pursue their interest in seeking contact offences with children.

These cases consisted of offenders who possessed a variety of different forms of pornography including pornography downloaded from the Internet. What was striking was the number of offenders (80 per cent) who described loss of intimacy in their relationships as a causal factor for their interest in pornography. However, when this was explored further with them, in almost all cases they admitted to an interest in viewing pornography which predated the deterioration in their intimate relationships, although this interest may have escalated as

the sexual relationship declined. It was difficult for these offenders to untangle cause and effect even with treatment intervention. Furthermore the sample showed a high incidence of self-report health problems and sexual dysfunction. Again it was apparent that these problems were held by the offender to explain the deterioration in their sexual relationships, although none had sought medical assistance with their sexual dysfunction. For some it also appeared that they had accepted that pursuing their sexual gratification through the use of pornography was an easier route to take than addressing the difficulties of an unsatisfactory relationship.

In conclusion therefore it is clear that an exploration will need to be conducted with the offender to help them identify how their behaviour was contributing to emotional avoidance or was used to deal with negative mood and emotional states. Furthermore the offender may need help to identify how more appropriate strategies of dealing with these problems can be developed.

Knowledge of relapse prevention

Relapse prevention has its roots in the field of addictive behaviour concerning drugs or alcohol (Marlatt and Gordon, 1985). It suggests that apparently successful treatment gains are unlikely to be sustained unless the client is able to develop strategies to maintain these gains. Laws et al. (2000) summarise the premise as:

> *Following treatment, the thinking went, the client would inevitably find himself or herself in risky situations or in the presence of factors associated with various risks. If the client learnt self-management strategies to deal with these threats to abstinence, then the effects of the cessation-oriented treatment should be maintained.*

In applying this model to sexual offending Marques et al. (1989) and Pithers et al. (1983) sought to examine past offences in order to define the characteristic steps taken which led to the offence. In addition it requires the identification of high risk factors, situations and mood states which make the offender vulnerable to relapse into offence behaviour. Although these models have been subject to modification (Ward and Hudson, 1995) they remain one of the most popular components of sex offender treatment programmes (Hanson, 2000).

Applying relapse prevention to offenders who use the Internet to access sexually abusive images involves drawing on the insight gained from work on offence-specific behaviours and on recognising deficits in social adequacy. These will of course vary from each offender and reflect the heterogenic nature of sexual offending. However, relapse prevention would demand that these insights are complimented by the learning of new skills or strategies which enable the offender to deal more appropriately with the underlying casual factors. For example, the ability to generate alternate coping strategies to deal with

negative emotional affect, training in problem recognition and problem solving skills. Such strategies may assist with adjusting the motivation to continue, and increasing the ability to self-regulate over the abusive behaviour. These strategies can be enhanced by physical restrictions on access to computers, by placing the computer in open communal areas which allow for the screen to be viewed by others, or by blocking software to prevent access to sites from which abusive images can be viewed.

However Mann (2000) argues that such avoidance goals in themselves are insufficient as a goal for offenders in treatment. She argues that relapse prevention could be made more attractive for offenders if they are helped to define goals which reflect positive approach goals. The focus changes to things that can be achieved rather than things that must be avoided. In short the offender is helped to acquire new lifestyle goals and the skills which may be required to achieve these goals:

> *A rephrased approach version of the goal of sex offender treatment might be for the client 'to become someone who lives a satisfying life that is always respectful of others'.*
>
> (p194).

For Internet offenders this may involve learning skills to enter and sustain intimate relations outside of the pseudo-intimacy and anonymity afforded by on-line relationships.

Conclusion

Treatment for offenders who use the Internet to access abusive images of children are currently dependent on adapting generic treatment programmes for sexual offenders which have been developed over the last thirty years. These programmes target a number of dynamic risk factors which appear to be as relevant for Internet offenders as other forms of sexual offending. Research to examine the efficacy of these intervention programmes is continuing and may well highlight areas for further development. At the very least the treatment needs to be based on a specific assessment of the individual including the context in which the behaviour was developed and sustained. Most human behaviour can be understood as meeting needs for the individual and, in order to be effective, treatment will help the individual to meet these needs in a more appropriate manner.

References

Allam, J. (2000) *Community Based Treatment for Child Sex Offenders*. Unpublished Doctoral Thesis. University of Birmingham.

Amir, M. (1971) *Patterns of Forcible Rape*. Chicago: University of Chicago.

Andrews, D.A. (1995) The Psychology of Criminal Conduct and Effective Treatment. In McGuire, J. (Ed.) *What Works: Reducing Reoffending: Guidelines From Research and Practice*. Chichester: John Wiley.

Andrews, D.A. et al. (1990) Does Correctional Treatment Work? A Clinically Relevant and Psychologically Informed Meta-Analysis. *Criminology*, 28: 3, 369–404.

Antonowicz, D. and Ross, R.R. (1994) Essential Components of Successful Rehabilitation Programmes for Offenders. *International Journal of Offender Therapy and Comparative Criminology*, 38: 97–104.

Bakker, L. et al. (1998) *An Evaluation of the Kia Marama Treatment Programme for Child Molesters*. Christchurch: New Zealand Department of Justice.

Barbaree, H.E. and Seto, M.C. (1997) Pedophilia: Assessment and Treatment. In Laws, D.R. et al. (Eds.) *Sexual Deviance: Theory, Assessment and Treatment*. New York: Guilford Press.

Beck, J.S. (1995) *Cognitive Therapy: Basics and Beyond*. New York: Guilford Press.

Beech, A., Fisher, D. and Beckett, R. (1998) *STEP 3: An Evaluation of The Prison Sex Offender Treatment Programme*. London: Home Office Research, Development and Statistics Directorate.

Bumby, K.M. and Hanson, D.J. (1997) Intimacy Deficits, Fear of Intimacy, and Loneliness Among Sexual Offenders. *Criminal Justice and Behavior*, 24: 3, 315–31.

Calder, M.C. (1999) *Assessing Risk in Adult Male Sex Offenders: A Practitioner's Guide*. Lyme Regis: Russell House Publishing.

Carich, M.S. and Calder, M.C. (2003) *Contemporary Treatment of Adult Male Sex Offenders*. Lyme Regis: Russell House Publishing.

Carnes, P., Delmonico, D.L. and Griffin, E. (2001) *In the Shadows of the Net*. Minnesota: Hazeldine.

Cortoni, F., Heil, P. and Marshall, W.L. (1996) *Sex as a Coping Mechanism and its Relationship to Loneliness and Intimacy Deficits in Sexual Offending*. Paper Presented to 15th Annual Research and Treatment Conference of the Association for the Treatment of Sexual Offenders, Chicago.

Eldridge, H. (1998) *Therapist's Guide for Maintaining Change*. London: Sage.

Findlater, D. and Ford, H. (1999) *Community Based Interventions With Sex Offenders Organised by The Probation Service: A Survey of Current Practice*. London: Association of Chief Officers of Probation.

Finkelhor, D. (1984) *Child Sexual Abuse: New Theory and Research*. New York: Free Press.

Fisher, D. and Beech, A. (1998) Reconstituting Families After Sexual Abuse: The Offender's Perspective. *Child Abuse Review*, 7: 420–34.

Fisher, D. and Beech, A.T. (1999) Current Practice in Britain With Sexual Offenders. *Journal of Interpersonal Violence*, 14: 3, 240–56.

Fisher, D. and Howells, K. (1993) Social Relationships in Sexual Offenders. *Sexual and Marital Therapy*, 8: 2, 123–35.

Garlick, Y., Marshall, W.L. and Thornton, D. (1996) Intimacy Deficits and Attribution of Blame Among Sexual Offenders. *Legal and Criminological Psychology*, 1: 2, 251–8.

Hanson, R.K. (2000) What Is So Special About Relapse Prevention? In Laws, D.R., Hudson, S.M. and Ward, T. (Eds.) *Remaking Relapse Prevention With Sex Offenders: A Sourcebook*. London: Sage.

Hanson, R.K. and Bussiere, M.T. (1998) Predicting Relapse: A Meta-Analysis of Sexual Offending Recidivism Studies. *Journal of Consultancy and Clinical Psychology*, 66: 348–62.

Hanson, R.K. and Scott, H. (1995) Assessing Perspective-Taking Among Sexual Offenders and Non-Sexual Criminals: Risk Predictors and Long-Term Recidivism. *Sexual Abuse: A Journal of Research and Treatment*, 7: 259–77.

Home Office (2001) *What Works Implementation 3*. Probation Circular 92/2001. London: National Probation Directorate.

Hudson, S.M. and Ward, T. (1997) Intimacy, Loneliness, and Attachment Style in Sex Offenders. *Journal of Interpersonal Violence*, 12: 325–39.

Jenkins, A. (1990) *Invitations to Responsibility*. Adelaide: Dulwich Centre Publications.

Jenkins, A. (forthcoming a) Making it Fair: Creating A Context for Just Intervention With Disadvantaged

Young People Who Have Sexually Abused. In Calder, M.C. (Ed.) *Children and Young People Who Sexually Abuse: New Theory, Research and Practice Developments.* Lyme Regis: Russell House Publishing.

Jenkins, A. (forthcoming b) Knocking on Shame's Door: Facing Shame Without Shaming Young People Who Sexually Abuse. In Calder, M.C. (Ed.) *Children and Young People Who Sexually Abuse: New Theory, Research and Practice Developments.* Lyme Regis: Russell House Publishing.

Laws, D.R., Hudson, S.M. and Ward, T. (2000) The Original Model of Relapse Prevention With Sex Offenders: Promises Unfulfilled. In Laws, D.R., Hudson, S.M. and Ward, T. (Eds.) *Remaking Relapse Prevention With Sex Offenders: A Sourcebook.* London: Sage.

Leitenberg, H. and Henning, K. (1995) Sexual Fantasy. *Psychological Bulletin,* 117: 469–96.

Lipsey, M.W. (1995) What Do We Learn From 400 Research Studies on the Effectiveness of Treatment With Juvenile Delinquents? In McGuire, J. (Ed.) *What Works: Reducing Reoffending: Guidelines From Research and Practice.* Chichester: John Wiley.

Losel, F. (1995) The Efficacy of Correctional Treatment: A Review and Synthesis of Meta-Evaluations. In McGuire, J. (Ed.) *What Works: Reducing Reoffending: Guidelines From Research and Practice.* Chichester: Wiley.

Maletzky, B.M. (1991) *Treating The Sexual Offender.* California: Sage Publications.

Mann, R.E. (2000) Managing Resistance and Rebellion in Relapse Prevention. In Laws, D.R., Hudson, S.M. and Ward, T. (Eds.) *Remaking Relapse Prevention With Sex Offenders: A Sourcebook.* London: Sage.

Marlatt, G. and Gordan, J.R. (Eds.) (1985) *Relapse Prevention.* New York: Guilford.

Marques, J.K. et al. (1989) The Sex Offender Treatment and Evaluation Project: California's Relapse Prevention Program. In Laws, D.R. (Ed.) *Relapse Prevention With Sex Offenders.* New York: Guilford.

Marshall, W.L. (1996) Assessment, Treatment, and Theorizing About Sex Offenders: Developments During The Past Twenty Years and Future Directions. *Criminal Justice and Behavior,* 23: 1, 162–99.

Marshall, W.L., Anderson, D. and Fernandez, Y. (1999) *Cognitive Behavioural Treatment of Sexual Offenders.* Chichester: Wiley.

Marshall, W.L. and Barbaree, H.E. (1990) An Integrated Theory of Sexual Offending. In Marshall, W.L., Laws, D.R. and Barbaree, H.E. (Eds.) *Handbook of Sexual Assault: Issues, Theories and The Treatment of The Offender.* New York: Plenum Press.

Marshall, W.L. et al. (1999) Self-Esteem and Coping

Strategies in Child Molesters. *Journal of Interpersonal Violence,* 14: 9, 995–62.

Marshall, W.L., Hudson, S.M. and Ward, T. (1995) Empathy in Sex Offenders. *Clinical Psychology Review,* 15: 99–113.

Marshall, W.L. and Serran, G.A. (2000) Improving the Effectiveness of Sexual Offender Treatment. *Trauma, Violence and Abuse,* 1: 3, 203–22.

McGuire, R.J., Carlisle, J.M. and Young, B.G. (1965) Sexual Deviations as Conditioned Behaviour: A Hypothesis. *Behaviour Research and Therapy,* 32: 571–5.

Miller, W.R. and Rollnick, S. (2002) *Motivational Interviewing: Preparing People for Change,* 2nd edn. New York: Guilford Press.

Murphy, W.D. (1990) Assessment and Modification of Cognitive Distortions in Sex Offenders. In Marshall, W.L., Laws, D.R. and Barbaree, H.E. (Eds.) *Handbook of Sexual Assault: Issues, Theories and The Treatment of the Offender.* New York: Plenum Press.

Pithers, W.D. et al. (1983) Relapse Prevention With Sexual Aggressives: A Self-Control Model of Treatment and Maintenance of Change. In Greer, J.G. and Stuart, I.R. (Eds.) *The Sexual Aggressor: Current Perspectives on Treatment.* New York: Van Nostrand Reinhold.

Pithers, W.D. et al. (1988) Relapse Prevention of Sexual Aggression. In Prentky, R.A. and Quinsey, V.L. (Eds.) Human Sexual Aggression: Current Perspectives. *Annals of New York Academy of Sciences,* 528.

Proulx, J., Mckibben, A. and Lusignan, R. (1996). Relationships Between Affective Components and Sexual Behaviors in Sexual Aggressors. *Sexual Abuse: A Journal of Research and Treatment,* 8: 279–89.

Rada, R.T. (Ed) (1978) *Clinical Aspects of The Rapist.* New York: Grune and Stratton.

Rice, M.E. et al. (1994) Empathy for The Victim and Sexual Arousal Among Rapists and Non-Rapists. *Journal of Interpersonal Violence,* 9: 4, 435–49.

Schneider, J.P. (2000) Effects of Cybersex Addiction on the Family: Results of a Survey. *Sexual Addiction and Compulsivity,* 7: 1, 31–58.

Silbert, M.H. (1989) The Effects on Juveniles of Being Used for Pornography and Prostitution. In Zillman, D. and Bryant, C. (Eds.) *Pornography: Research Advances and Policy Considerations.* Hillside NJ: Lawrence Erlbaum.

Smallbone, S.W. and Dadds, M.R. (1998) Childhood Attachment and Adult Attachment Incarcerated Adult Male Sex Offenders. *Journal of Interpersonal Violence,* 13: 555–73.

Sullivan, J. (2002) The Spiral of Sexual Abuse: A Conceptual Framework for Understanding Child Sexual Abuse. *NOTA News,* April.

Taylor, M. and Quayle, E. (2003) *Child Pornography: An Internet Crime.* Hove: Brunner-Routledge.

Ward, T., Hudson, S.M. and Siegert, R.J. (1995) A Critical Comment on Pithers' Relapse Prevention Model. *Sexual Abuse: A Journal of Research and Treatment*, 7: 167–75.

Ward, T. et al. (1997) Cognitive Distortions in Sex Offenders: An Integrative Review. *Clinical Psychology Review*, 17: 479–507.

Ward, T. et al. (1995) A Descriptive Model of the Offense Chain for Child Molesters. *Journal of Interpersonal Violence*, 10: 4, 452–72.

Wolf, S.C. (1988) A Model of Sexual Aggression / Addiction. *Journal of Social Work and Human Sexuality*, 7: 1, 131–48.

Chapter Eight

Virtual Offenders: The Other Side of Internet Allegations

Dr Bill Thompson and Andy Williams

Introduction

It's very difficult to tell whether abuse of children is increasing…But there certainly has been big growth for the past five years in child abuse on the Internet. And that's where the big future growth will be.

(Deputy Assistant Commissioner Carole Howlett, *Guardian*, 15.01.03: 15).

It is important that we do not finger small groups of people, without evidence being produced.

(David Blunkett, UK Home Secretary, *Guardian*, 15.01.03: 7).

Although our research preferences include ethnography, we had no idea we would be forced into that method while researching this article. Just as we were completing an initial draft, the potential threat we were discussing became all too real: on 5th March, 2002, Thames Valley Police officers smashed their way into Dr Thompson's house; while others entered the University and seized Dr Williams files on the Paulsgrove 'Riots', and a PhD student's computer, despite not having warrants for this material. Eighteen months on, no interviews, no arrests, and no charges have occurred; nor will they. However, apart from losing our computers, files of research data and drafts, and teaching materials for over a year, Dr Thompson suffered erroneous media reports, was attacked in the street, could not complete several legal cases, missed publication deadlines and lost a £250,000 research grant.

The magistrate had issued warrants believing that the police had 'reliable witnesses' who had actually seen Dr Thompson downloading child pornography. They did not. The police were acting solely on the basis of a malicious phone call, merely the latest in a decade long harassment campaign by someone who objected to his work. The police also failed to inform the court of: Dr Thompson's expert status; his history of successfully overturning false convictions, including the *AJE -v- HMA* Appeal only three weeks before when he was complimented by three Law Lords; that several Thames Valley Police officers had attended his lectures on problematic allegations and convictions, including the legal anomalies which place experts at risk; and that he was shortly to give evidence to the Home Affairs Committee regarding investigative malpractice by the authorities in some 90 operations. Despite the police finding no pictures at all, let alone any of children, on any of his computers, numerous inaccurate stories were fed to the UK media, including the ridiculous claim that despite arrest he had fled to Hong Kong. Only one report covered the illegal seizure of privileged legal files, PhD files, or the fact that a PhD student had been so traumatised by the raid that he could not continue his studies. Given that 30 of Operation Ore suspects lived in Reading (*Sunday Times*, 26.01.03) why so much police time was wasted on a malicious call remains a mystery. Consequently, while we were to address some of the issues raised by such raids within a wider discussion of the law, comparing our finding with Redden's American cases (2000), we have subsequently prioritised this issue because of the lack of publicity given to the damage caused by false allegations and how they actually hinder child protection.

Fighting evil

When fighting evils like child sexploitation it is easy to adopt a 'by any means necessary' approach. Sir William Utting, former Chief Inspector of Social Services, was quite blatant about his priorities:

*It may be that innocent people are being
convicted but we ought to be more worried
about the guilty who may get away.*
(Newsnight, BBC 1, 15.02.00).

As if the time, effort, and resources wasted
targeting the innocent does not help guilty
people 'get away'. The police, regrettably,
adopt the same attitude. When initially
justifying exaggerated claims about sexual
assaults in care homes, exposed as false three
years later, the police asserted that any
'distress' caused to innocents by malicious
allegations was an acceptable price to pay
(*Daily Mail*, 25.02.00). We do not agree,
especially when this 'distress' may include
being shot (*The Sun*, 21.02.00) or invoke suicide
(*Scotsman*, 04.05.01) or lose your job despite
being innocent. Then there is the living hell.

Derek Collins was left with more than a
huge legal bill when he attempted to correct a
'clerical error' by Hampshire County Council,
which branded him a paedophile. Being
banned from premises used by children, he lost
employment as a security guard. The High
Court then ruled that redress would not be in
'the public interest' because the mistake
occurred in the course of protecting the public!
The Council were 'delighted' (*This is Gosport*,
09.07.01) but where does that leave Mr Collins
and others like him who have never committed
an offence in their lives?

False allegations of, and false convictions
for, child sexual assault are far more common
than many want to believe, as the teacher's
union NASUWT can testify. Knowing what
will happen to the accused, a false allegation is
the easiest way to destroy anyone you do not
like, as the Taylor family discovered when a
neighbour made malicious allegations of intra-
familial assaults. Despite the neighbour's
vexatious history, the Taylors were subject to
extensive investigations, ended up on anti-
depressants, and had to place one of their
children on a suicide watch (*Daily Record*,
11.03.03). Leading and suggestive questioning
of children, which produces convincing but
confabulated allegations is not confined to the
high profile scandals like Cleveland or Satanic

Cases (Bell, 1988; Ceci and Bruck, 1995).
Incredibly, the Courts frequently ignore the
chronic transgressions of interview protocols;
claiming, as in *R -v- Monkford* (2003) that it is a
matter for the jury to assess the viability of
interviews, despite their ignorance of the
guidelines, let alone how to assess whether
they have been followed or broken. That many
Best Evidence interviews are no guide to
reality was demonstrated in *Reg -v- Clarke*,
when one of the four children volunteered in
court that the whole story was concocted after
seeing media publicity about paedophiles; yet
their accounts had easily fooled the uncritical
interviewers, the investigating officers, and the
CPS, which then made an incredible
admission:

*We make our decisions to prosecute on the basis
of written statements. The people making
allegations are not cross examined before they
come to court...Neither ourselves nor the police
can know that the allegations are false just from
interviews.*
(EDP24, 31.01.03).

Of course not; that's why one should not
rely upon allegations, but investigate; and if
one is incapable of doing so, then it's about
time the authorities employed people who can,
especially as so many UK cases are based
solely upon the alleged victims' claims. Real
investigations are rare; but interviewers do not
even review interview transcripts; they are
incapable of making viable assessments of
validity (Home Affairs Committee, 2002:
Ev139) and the Thames Valley force are
certainly not the only force with a history of
generating unreliable testimony (*Times*,
22.03.01). Thankfully, since the *AJE -v- HMA*
Judgment, Scottish courts should be more alert
to this problem, as well as the ability of some
paediatricians to find medical 'evidence' where
it does not exist (*The Times*, 01.08.02).

The current dispute over tainted interview
practices is the latest in a long line of dubious
practices which have generated or supported
false allegations and convictions in the name of
child protection: Satanic Ritual Abuse,
Recovered Memory, Care Home trawling; and

Shieldfield, the UK's answer to the McMartin Preschool disaster, suggest convictions rather than uncovering reality is the priority. The latter case also demonstrates that many child protection personnel are still ignoring the lessons of Cleveland and Orkney (see *Lillie & Reed -v- NCC*). Yet, if one thinks that there could be no chance of replicating such errors when it comes to child pornography, especially downloaded material – either the evidence is there or it is not – one will have to think again.

Candymen

No one can deny the serious threat posed by the Internet. Given that it has become the major means to distribute child pornography, transcending what was once a 'cottage industry' and a by-product of contact offences, it has rightly become a law enforcement preoccupation (Jenkins, 2001). For those deliberately obtaining material available on the Web, such actions may have several overlapping functions beyond sexual arousal or entrapping children, including: validation, collectability, networking, 'avoiding' real life problems, and anonymity (Quayle and Taylor, 2002) even though collections do not always provide an exact guide to their 'owners' fantasies and preferences as some believe (Unit Chief Heimbach, CJHR, 2002: 10). Although 'rings' still produce their own material (*Yorkshire Today*, 06.03.03) and most material is traded through News Groups and Bulletin Boards (Jenkins, 2001) commercial sites like Landslide Inc. and Internet Relay Chat (*icNewcastle*, 14.09.02) drastically increases the numbers of those intentionally involved, but also the possibility of accidental exposure to material or collectors. Children have been targeted while chatting using library computers (*This is Staffordshire*, 11.03.03) and adults have stumbled across sites while seeking accommodation on a well known search engine (*icCheshire*, 14.02.03). Apart from the large number of sites, demonstrated by a Wiltshire case involving no fewer than 1400 (*icWiltshire*, 20.01.03) and Operation Landmark's review of 1500 newsgroups

(Manchester Online, 29.03.02) we believe the most alarming feature of Internet exploitation is the large number of video clips of assaults available for sale or 'trade' found in contemporary cases (*This is Bristol*, 23.03.02). A growing percentage of still pictures also appears to involve clear acts of force on very young children (e.g. *Yorkshire Today*, 06.03.03) and the size of collections is growing: 75,000 in one case (*icBirmingham*, 07.03.03) 120,000 in another (*This is Nottingham*, 27.04.02). Ironically, using the web thankfully increases the chances of exposure, especially when using a works computer, or being monitored by SurfControl in chat rooms (*icLiverpool*, 25.04.02). Terry Jones' Manchester squad even managed to track down a group of contact offenders by the location clues found in photographs (*Manchester Online*, 06.04.02). And although only a minority of those caught by Operation Ore were contact offenders (*icBirmingham*, 26.02.03) its corollary, the large number of those who had never come to the attention of the authorities before, finally provides convincing evidence that sexual interest in children is more extensive than imagined; but then, so is the number of falsely accused people.

A year after the Reading raids, two Federal Judges in Manhattan and St. Louis simultaneously ruled that the FBI's evidence against two men 'caught' in the celebrated Candyman case was false, and deliberately so. Contrary to FBI warrant affidavits and subsequent publicity (e.g. Unit Chief Heimbach, CJHR, 2002: 9) those signing up to one of the many sites on *eGroup* did not automatically receive child pornography. How many blameless others there were amongst the 1800 alleged 'paedophiles' investigated remains to be seen; but, the fact that only 60 convictions had followed suggests that any number of Candymen far from being evil monsters were possibly oblivious to the child pornography being distributed on site. The reaction of the parties involved in these two cases is informative. While the defendants' lawyers saw the rulings as a victory against endemic illegal searches and seizures in the US (see Redden,

2000) and hoped that police officers would stop bearing false witness while judges examined warrant applications more thoroughly in future, it was business as usual at the Justice Department. While vowing to continue vigorously prosecuting purveyors of child pornography, nothing was said about blatant perjury and media exaggerations (Weiser, 2003). This failure to face up to one cause of child protection scandals is, unfortunately, all too common, and masking such practices behind the appeal to protect children is a form of exploitation in itself. Why so many people are 'in denial', and believe that admitting mistakes or dealing with malpractice undermines child protection when the numbers of falsely accused or convicted continues to grow along with the chronic waste of resources should worry everyone who really wishes to protect children, and not only because of the subsequent number of children unnecessarily separated from parents, care damaged, and caught up in confabulations with its lasting harm. Just ask the children 'saved' from a 'satanic ring' in Ayrshire. But, no: the authorities prefer to punish those who continue to deny their guilt by then refusing parole (*Guardian*, 16.10.00) on the basis that if convicted one has to assume the 'offenders' guilt; even though those found 'not guilty' are still considered guilty, but 'got away with it' (*Daily Mail*, 29.05.01).

If this seems too far fetched, one need merely remember that we were faced with the same extensive scepticism and scorn when questioning the validity of 'Satanic' allegations over a decade ago, but hundreds of children suffered, before the truth was finally admitted (La Fontaine, 1994). In one case that UK law prevents us from naming, a baby literally seized from the maternity ward still does not know that her 'parents' are actually adopters, because a High Court ruled that it would be too traumatic to reunite the then four-year-old with their parents whose innocence was finally accepted. What will they say when they finally find out who they are? The failure to address past mistakes like the Playtime Nursery case in Brecon (*Guardian*, 20.05.00) ensures they are constantly repeated, and the fact that

numerous miscarriage of Justice Inquiries have failed to address the core problems is demonstrated by the fact that the Shieldfield disaster featured several of the 'professionals' involved in the previous Cleveland, Nottingham, and Bishop Auckland debacles! That was no coincidence. At least the Shieldfield accused were finally 'compensated', which is more than can be said for many care home social workers and teachers who have lost jobs and had careers destroyed even when compensation fuelled motivations were exposed in court (Home Affairs Committee, 2002: Ev31) or during Appeals (*Telegraph On Line*, 19.02.03). Such cases reveal how much damage can be caused by taking all complaints at face value, and being entranced by 'the seriousness of the allegation', rather than really investigate the claims, a necessity still not appreciated by some child protection workers (*Community Care*, 08.11.01).

Last year, a secondary school teacher faced complete ruin when his credit card number was found on the Operation Ore list. Taken into custody, he was not believed when he claimed he had not used his card for such a purpose, and he faced losing his two children as well as his reputation. It mattered not that he had no images on his computer; he had obviously accessed Landslide Inc. His card number said so. Fortunately, he was meticulous enough to keep his credit card statements, enabling him to demonstrate that he had challenged the Landslide Inc. payments at the time. It was only then that an alternative explanation was sought, and it transpired that the school's technician had copied the teacher's credit card number to purchase over 140,000 images (*This is West Country*, 12.02.03). Nor was he the only Ore suspect to have suffered before a stolen or lost card was found to be the cause. One offender had used his mother's number (*NewsandStar*, 20.01.03). Another had copied the credit card numbers of customers at the garden centre where he worked (*This is Brighton and Hove*, 01.02.03). No fewer than 14 per cent of those raided in Sussex were guiltless for similar reasons too (*This is Brighton and Hove*, 17.01.03).

Over-reaction?

Given the proliferation of Internet paedophilia and the involvement of the previously unknown and unsuspected, many believe it is impossible to overreact; but wasn't that the same justification for what became disasters in the past? Do we really have to wait another ten years before we admit the real cause for such problems, and eliminate them?

There is still widespread ignorance of what the Web consists of. One Bristol Judge believes that 80 per cent of the Web is devoted to pornography sites! (*This is Bristol*, 20.05.02). Many people also exhibit a tendency to always expect worst case scenarios. The Deputy Education Minister for Wales wishes to prohibit mobile photo phones near children's changing rooms to defeat paedophiles (*icWales*, 11.02.03) yet, when a similar fear of 'stalking by text' occurred the year before, it transpired that most of those engaging in such behaviour were one half of a broken teen relationship or parents 'getting back' at estranged partners by harassing the children (*Guardian*, 17.10.02: 7). Then there is the continuing distrust of the Internet per se; one mother lost custody of her children because the Family Court judges thought it is disreputable for separated mothers to meet one's sexual partners on-line (*Guardian*, 23.05.02). When children go missing, Internet contacts are immediately suspected too (*News of the World*, 11.08.02). Prosecutors and others are also prone to hyperbole: each case is the worse the commentator has ever seen. Such a claim was even made in a Coventry court though the case concerned was to be immediately followed by another with far worse material (*icCovertry*, 10.02.03).

Another more understandable reason is the as yet unproven fear that there is a high correlation between possessing or downloading images and being a 'hands on' offender (Jenkins, 2003). Dr Andres E. Hernandez's, 'Self Reported Contact Sexual Offences by Participants in the Federal Bureau of Prisons' is frequently cited as evidence of this (e.g. CJHR, 01.05.02: 2; 6) yet, like similar claims touted 20 years ago 'proving' a link

between soft-core pornography consumption and rape, such 'studies' start with contact offenders and then considers how many had used the material concerned, rather than the other way round: the scientific approach (see Best, 2001; Thompson, 1994). To demonstrate the danger of such calculations one need simply compare convictions with the total number of Candyman investigations which produces a ratio of guilty to 'innocents' of 1:30; but, we would not be so sensationally unscientific to suggest such an exercise 'proves' that for every true case there are 30 false cases. While Hernandez certainly did provide viable data on undetected offending, which was extensive; and while collecting child pornography suggests a proclivity in that direction: what Candyman reveals is that the numbers and extrapolated estimates bandied about can be exaggerated. Whether or not those do so to secure funding (*Sunday Times*, 1.12.02: 7) these numbers are being used to justify acting before investigating, which can never be a wise move. To date, Operation Ore, which involves some 7,300 UK residents has led to 40 children being taken into protective care (*Guardian*, 18.12.02: 7) but until the final tally is in, it is unwise to make assumptions.

Then there is the other, smaller, side of the equation, no one has been brave enough to deal with. While the Patrick Greens of this world deliberately exploit teens entering groups like 'Younger Girls for Older Men' (*Guardian*, 25.10.00: 7) to suggest that we need to be more proactive about the under-aged using such sites is *not* blaming the victim or ignoring exploitation; it is recognising that despite extensive publicity, teens *are* still placing themselves in danger in some chat rooms, and often foolishly *pretending to be older*. One Reading PhD student discovered this alarming situation by checking participant's chat room claims with their original MSN identity; and a Basingstoke 14-year-old met men who booked hotel rooms at her behest, not once, but three times (*Times*, 09.06.01). The Hong Kong trial of Toby Acton apparently raised similar questions (*Daily Mail*, 16.04.99: 26) and Cincinnati police were bemused to discover that the young teen targeted by Ian Waddup from the UK had repeatedly defied her parents and even skipped school to meet him at the airport. Indeed, his plans were exposed because his parents found the 'love letters' she had been sending as part of a year long Internet liaison (*Guardian*, 08.04.99: 13) which also revealed her determination to fly back to the UK with him on her 16th birthday (*Times*, 12.02.99: 3). While there is no excuse for taking advantage of naivety, we need to consider, address, and discover why some teens place themselves at risk too. Though media reports imply UK predators are being caught by police posing as children in chat rooms (*Guardian*, 6.01.03: 1) anecdotal evidence from the US suggests that the number of 'travellers' – people attempting to arranging meetings – may be extensive (CJHR, 2002: 28-30 and 37). As a result, the number of adults who may arrange to meet teens believing that they are meeting someone older can also increase. Until such possibilities are recognised, those doing so are unlikely to report the problem, enabling child protection measures to be activated, for fear that they will be blamed. Likewise, lumping everyone who deliberately targets children and teens through the Web under the same label (*Daily Mail*, 27.04.00: 7) will not aid our understanding or help encourage the search for potential solutions to this problem. As late as three years ago we addressed 200 police and probation officers who had never heard of hebephilia, although such basic differentiations can be vital in addressing offending behaviour.

We also need to recognise that the chances of teenagers coming across illegal material, has increased in line with its proliferation. A March 2003 Report by the US General Accounting Office concluded that child pornography is easily found and downloaded on file sharing networks and that juveniles were at 'significant risk of inadvertent exposure'. Using 12 words that could be associated with child pornography they were confronted with 1286 files, 42 percent of which were dubious. A similar 3-word search by US Customs led to 341 images of which 44 were child

pornography. Using innocuous words, such as cartoon characters or singers names can produce similar results (NEWS.com.us, 25.03.03). Yet, despite this risk, naive 13 and 16-year-old males who download what they see as *age appropriate* material rather than look at topless 'Page Three' models are being declared 'sex offenders' (*Daily Mail*, 28.03.01; *Daily Telegraph*, 15.05.01 and 03.07.02). If the New Zealand experience, where 20 percent of all police investigations concern teens collecting such material, *is* replicated around the world, we will criminalise a large number of male teens for failing to understand the illegal origins of such material. Even though the police's simplistic approach to such practices is not shared by the major children's charities (*Guardian*, 18.07.02: 21) prosecutions continue.

Perhaps the biggest problem, however, is that the Law frequently does not lay down the exact means as to how it is to be carried out in practice; and nowhere is this more apparent than the law relating to child pornography and the Internet.

Virtual paedophiles

Despite extensive cooperation between law enforcement agencies across the Atlantic exemplified by Operation Ore, the US and UK developed completely different approaches to Internet paedophilia because of the way their courts have dealt with legislation.

US enforcement efforts, which already suffered from a lack of funds (CNN, 08.04.97) and the unconstitutional provisions of the Communications Decency Act (CNN, 02.12.97) almost came to a halt following the Supreme Court decision in *Ashcroft -v- Free Speech Coalition* 535 US, which declared that the prohibition of images of youthful looking adults or created by computer graphic software were 'overbroad' and thereby unconstitutional. It was not to be an offence to have non-obscene images or even other undesirable depictions of children, including sexual situations, when no child was involved in the making of the material. As a result of this decision, drawing a distinction between 'speech' protected by the First Amendment and measures designed to stop sexploitation of children, defendants began to claim that as their collections *could be* virtual pictures and prosecutors were faced with the absurd task of having to prove that the child depicted existed in real life. This was an almost impossible task. In six years of trying, the FBI had identified only 80–90 of the thousands of victims they uncovered (Unit Chief Heimbach, CJHR, 2002: 10 and 25) and Mr Allen of the National Centre for Missing and Exploited Children has demonstrated the impossibility of distinguishing between real and high quality virtual pictures of children (Figure 1). This threatened to make the law unenforceable, even though there was no evidence to suggest that the material involved depicted anything other than real children (Unit Chief Heimbach, CJHR, 2000: 6).

A Child Obscenity and Pornography Prevention Bill 2002 was quickly drafted by the Justice Department, but came under fire for both its strict liability offences which would inhibit any scholarly research, and for other measures which transgressed previous Supreme Court rulings (see ACLU, 8.05.02). However, the Bill did offer an 'affirmative' defence for those charged with possession, as opposed to production, if they could prove that the material did not consist of real children; i.e. reversing the burden of proof imposed by the Supreme Court. What annoyed law enforcement was that:

> *Child pornography is not merely an aberrant form of free expression it is a criminal tool, used to seduce and manipulate child victims, break down a child's inhibitions, and make sex between adults and children appear 'normal'.*
> (CJHR, 2002: 17).

…and that even high quality virtual pornography could still be used by contact offenders to entrap children (Allen, CJHR 2002: 18). At a House of Representative Sub Committee on Crime (01.05.02) impressive testimony was offered by Lt William Walsh of the Dallas PD Youth and Family Support Division, one of the thirty Internet Crimes

against Children Taskforces funded by Congress. It was this taskforce that ran Operation Avalanche with the Postal Inspection Service against Landslide Inc. which uncovered 36,000 American subscribers. Walsh revealed that the follow-up operations uncovered numerous 'hands on' offenders including one man who had assaulted his own daughter over several years, and another man prepared to pay for sex with a 12-year-old. Walsh was convinced that the case had exposed the tremendous consumer demand for the material, and that the profits would attract organised crime (Walsh, CJHR, 2002: 212).

Further lobbying and committee hearings then led to the PROTECT Act 2003 which continued with the affirmative defence, but now required defendants to show that the depictions involved were produced by using virtual creations or youthful looking adults, as registration of performers common to pornography products in the US was extended to logging virtual productions. It also became a crime to use pornography to persuade a minor to perform an illegal act (PROTECT Act Report, 7).

Making pornography

Like the US, UK courts also exercised increasing control over legislation, but in the opposite direction, increasing rather than reducing the images subject to law. During 1999, a series of legal cases covering downloading from the Internet threatened innocent Web surfers and researchers alike, as the Director of Public Prosecutions sought to equate both viewing material on the Web with possession of it (through one's cache), and downloading material with 'making' it, thereby undermined the legislators' original intent behind the Child Protection Act 1978. This had been designed to protect children from the experience and ramifications of appearing in child pornography, through four, sequential, crimes: the taking, or the permitting to be taken, of an indecent photograph of a child; the distribution or showing of indecent photographs of children; the possession of such indecent photographs in order to distribute or show them; and the prohibition of any advertising matter offering such photographs for distribution or exhibition.

Several rationales were offered by the original Bill's sponsors. The first, 'legal', rational was to prosecute those taking obscene photographs but not assaulting the child (HC, 10.2.78: Col. 1834. para. 5; HC, 5.5.78: 543, 4) and the second, 'social', rationale was to reduce any sex offending related to the pornography (HC,10.2.78: 1839, 3). Mr Townsend was not concerned with simple nudity, and, although today's readers will find it hard to believe, he was not concerned with the consumer either (HC, 10.2.78: 1837, 9–10; 1854, 2]. The child's welfare was paramount because, as Mr Bottomley explained, such sexploitation created a 'distorted personality and a twisted view of life' (HC, 10.2.78: 1855, 5; 1857, 6). This sentiment was widespread, and used as the core rationale in Baroness Faithful's summation in the House of Lords (HL, 5.5.78: 579, 3). The Home Office supported the Bill for this reason too; arguing that they sought to stop the corruption of children for 'perverted sexual pleasure' and the 'cynical desire to profit from the perversions of others' (HC, 10.2.78: 1843, 3; HL, 5.5.78: 574, 2; 576, 1; 578, 2). This desire to 'strike' at both 'those who took photographs and made films for profit, and paedophiles who may use the material to lure children into sexual activities helped distinguish the nature of legitimate possession from a dubious one (HC, 10.2.78: 1843, 3).

Legitimate possession, written into the 1977 Bill, was originally defined as 'scientific and learned study'; a deliberately wide definition to safeguard academics and others researching paedophilia and child sexual assault. During the debate, however, more defences against possession charges were *added*, beginning with parents who took pictures of their own children, whether or not someone thought them indecent, unless the pictures were for financial gain. Other defences included those campaigning against paedophilia and child pornography, those handling the material for

medical purposes, and those engaged in educational activities. As these groups were referenced as *examples* of the *kind* of people who could claim a legitimate defence, they were not an exclusive definitive list. Ironically, the only proposed defence to face an objection was the original one, 'learned study'. One MP suggested some pornography could be passed off as 'learned' though he offered no examples (see HC, 10.2.78: 1880, 5) another feared the phrase would cover 'a multitude of sins', though he could not suggest what (HC, 10.2.78: 1892, 7) and Lord Ingleby was 'not entirely happy with the defence' either, though he did not say why (HL, 5.5.78: 570, 4). Consequently, during a full debate in Committee, the Government and movers both agreed to create an even more inclusive defence rather than offer an inflexible predetermined list of legitimate researchers (HL, 18.5.78: 539, 3; HC, 14.7.78: 1943, 1–2). These exemptions even covered distributing and showing, though not 'taking', as there 'could never be a legitimate reason for the taking of an indecent photograph of a child' (HL, 18.5.78: 539, 3). Consequently, to act as if such defences were restricted to the enforcement agencies – the current practice – ignores the inclusive meaning given to 'legitimate interest', and the movers specific rejection of an amendment seeking to restrict defences to those working 'solely in the course of justice' or 'connected directly with duties or purposes concerned with the furtherance of the objects of this Act' (HL, 18.5.78: 540–555; HC, 14.7.78: 1937–1943). However, by adopting Lord Scarman's suggestion that the Courts could always be relied upon to decide if the legitimate reason was viable if there was a dispute (HL, 18.5.78: 545–6; HC, 14.7.78: 1956, 5) further changes in the law and the current social climate now means that most statutory defences can only be invoked in court rather than during the early stages of an inquiry.

Simple possession became an offence in the Criminal Justice Act 1988 (S.160), after police complaints that their investigations into sexual assaults were hampered by an inability to prosecute possession given that paedophiles used the photographs to seduce children. However, further defences, such as not knowing the nature of the photograph, or to have received it without prior request, or to have disposed of it within a reasonable time, were automatically added, being a typical feature of all obscenity legislation (see Robertson, 1979). This new emphasis upon the obscenity involved was made explicit by John Patten, whose stated aim was to 'act against the market' in child pornography and to end 'the encouragement of paedophilia' it caused (HC SC H, 15.3.88: 592; 596) though he also re-emphasised that possession was not a crime 'in all circumstances' (HC SC H, 15.3.88: 593) referencing the need to protect organisations campaigning against child pornographers, and readily accepting others offered by Mrs Taylor (HC SC H, 15.3.88: 593). Taylor, whose primary concern was child protection, did not want all pictures of children being outlawed, or see the law used against 'those who offend against an intangible standard of propriety which is difficult to define' (HC SC H, 15.3.88: 599). She also raised numerous classes of people who should not be prosecuted, and was given Ministerial reassurance that they would not be. These included: those engaged in educational purposes (HC SC H, 15.3.88: 598–599) 'medical people and social workers' involved in cases, and others who must see such material, 'without problems or accusations arising there from' (HC SC H, 15.3.88: 598–9). She also insisted that 'the law should not be so poorly and widely defined' that there was any repetition of the infamous incident in which parents had been arrested when trying to collect nude pictures of their own toddlers from a photo shop. Such cases demonstrated that Lord Houghton's fears, expressed in the original debate back in 1978, that 'the damage is done' long before the DPP could review such charges (HL, 5.5.78: 557) were justified.

In short, the legislation was supposed to offer protection for many people beyond the law enforcement agent, whose own handling of the material has since expanded in practice to forms of entrapment (*Cassidy -v- HM Advocate*) including posing as procurers (*Guardian*,

23.05.00: 12). Every one of the protected groups, along with those engaged in research and teaching, is supposed to have a defence to possession charges; and that defence would also have applied to those viewing material on the Web, as the COPINE researchers have, if it were not for the CPS and judges who took it upon themselves to rewrite the Criminal Justice and Public Order Act 1994, and decided that even accidentally coming across a sexploitation site amounts to an illegal act.

In such cases, there may be less need to query the person's 'possession' than the motive behind the prosecutions; but there are other grey areas too. Apart from the teens accessing material discussed above, anyone surfing the 'Net' who stumbles across child pornography by accident and moves on is left with an image in the cache. Even if the viewer – disgusted by the image – made no attempt to deliberately download and keep the image, they could still be held accountable. This risk has increased now that one merely has to come across the growing number of ill defined 'teen' sites, chat rooms, or suffer one of those 'ad attacks' – whereby the attempt to escape an unsolicited porn site leads to the sudden proliferation of dozens and dozens of advertisements for other sites, flooding the computer screen ten times faster than one can close the 'windows'. The only way out is to crash your computer. Absurd scare-mongering? Hardly, the Thames Valley Police have already tried to prosecute one of the hundreds of thousands of victims of 'spammers' who scan on-line PCs for the 'open proxies' left by download software companies to place 'trojans' on the users machine. Early in June 2003, one such virus was sent to over 1 million PCs in order to send out adverts for incest pornography sites (*Guardian*, 13.06.03). Under the existing law, each one of these victims could be subject to a prosecution if any advert contained an under-age image despite it being unsolicited, as Mr S. discovered to his cost.

Mr S

The first attempt to use a 'making' charge to secure what would previously have been possession was *Reg. -v- S.* in which a school teacher fell foul of an unpleasant trick, if not deliberate entrapment of the kind used in the US (*Guardian*, 24.01.03). As a result of 'chatting' with someone presenting their self as a grown woman, Mr S was sent unsolicited child pornography during 1997. A shocked Mr S deleted the material; or at least he thought he had: he did not realise that the image was still effectively contained on his hard drive. He had also told his house-mates about his experience, and even more foolishly showed them the offending article, which they then used against him during a dispute over their unpaid share of the telephone bill. Ignoring the origin of the complaint, the police recovered the images and Mr S was prosecuted *not* for possession, but that 'he took *or made* an indecent photograph or pseudo photograph of a child contrary to Section 1(1) (a) of the 1978 CPA', an amendment introduced by the Criminal Justice and Public Order Act 1994 [Part VII (2) (a) (i)]. Yet this was not the intent behind the Amendment.

As the *Statutory Instruments* 1994 [Part IV] made perfectly clear, the phrase 'or to make' was inserted into the 1978 Act to cover the threat of *pseudo photographs*, which unlike those in the US, were to be prosecuted. The new Act defined a photograph as 'the negative and positive version' of an image on photographic film or paper; photographic images which could be seen on computer screen were referenced as 'data stored on a computer disc or by any other electronic means which is capable of *conversion* into a photograph'; a *pseudo photograph* was an 'an image, whether made by computer graphics or otherwise howsoever, *which appears to be a photograph*'; i.e. what in the US is called a 'virtual photograph'. 'Making' only applied to the product – i.e. something that was *made* – by using a computer graphics programme. Without such a package, it is impossible for the user to make a pseudo photograph. To claim that Mr S had 'made' the images he had been sent, was a misnomer; the concept of 'making' a photograph by downloading, copying or converting a data file into an image did not

exist in law. No one in the world of computers ever used the term 'making' to describe opening, downloading, or copying files; and nor did anyone in Parliament. During Standing Committee B, which discussed the Bill in detail, the only time 'making' was used was when the speaker referenced pseudo photographs (e.g. David MacLean; HC SC B, 15.2.94: 733, 4; Mr Evans, 751, 1) which were being targeted to prevent people 'making' composite or manipulated images, claiming they were not 'real' photographs to circumvent the law (HC SC B, 15.2.94: 733, 4–6) but using them 'to lure children or convince them that what is happening is all right' (HC SC B, 15.2.94: 745, 3). This innate link between the term 'making' and pseudo photographs was even made explicit by McLean, worried that paedophiles could use graphic packages to get round the law (HC SC B, 15.2.94: 735, 7) it had nothing to do with real photographs at all, nor even photographic images on computers, downloaded or otherwise, which were referred to as 'read' or 'looked at' material (as in HC SC B, 15.2.94: 733, 8). People sending illegal material were to be dealt with by an extended definition of 'publishing' to include the transmission of electronic data that could be converted back into photographic or pseudo photographic images between computers (15.2.94: 732, 5; 736, 6 and 9) but this did not apply to copying images one already had, which was never mentioned during the Committee stage or the debates in the House. A perfect description of how one 'makes' an indecent pseudo photograph was also laid out, just as it had been in the Home Affairs Committee, which referenced the Shakespeare case – where a man *had* made a pseudo photograph (16.12.93: 29–40). The phrase 'otherwise howsoever' didn't cover downloading or copying either. As the Minister of State explained, this phrase was included to try and catch *future* trends and changes involving methods of storage that was not by a disc or laser tape.

Represented by Elwyn Jones and Co., Mr S prepared to argue that the charge of 'making' was contrary to the legislators' intent; but he had other defences too. He was unaware of the contents of the attachments to the e-mail when it was sent; once he knew, he deleted it; he didn't know that the image was still on his hard drive; and he did not have the software to retrieve it. These defences also challenged the CPS's concept of 'possession'. As Mr S *had* deleted images he didn't like, want, or ask for, and as he was unable to retrieve it utilising his own software, did he really posses it? This was not analogous to throwing illegal material into one's dustbin, which before collection means that the item is still in one's possession by being retrievable, it is merely an incidental feature of computer technology that an erased image can be retrieved (see Hill and Fletcher Rodgers, 1997: 364–5). After all, in order to see the deleted images, the police had to use sophisticated software beyond the means of ordinary users like Mr S.

Not sure of their own argument, the CPS also attempted to cover their case with several bizarre claims exploiting ignorance of computer use amongst the judiciary, asserting that it was impossible for someone to: receive material in an e-mail without knowing its content; or download material from the WWW without knowing the contents; or view material on the Web without knowing that the image would also appear in the cache. Such claims were common in the early days of computer prosecutions. In one Reading case, during 1998, they even claimed that users could not copy material *en masse* from a hard drive to a jazz drive or even work on a computer without knowing the contents of *all* the files! The moment such claims were questioned by a knowledgeable defence, they would be dropped.

These dubious tactics were not confined to argument; but were also applied to evidence. No attempt was made to record or produce Mr S's 'image' file record which could have been used to chart all his computer's activities as it records file names, dates, size and time of access. Such evidence, which could help determine the truth of a case one way or the other and is far easier to obtain than a deleted image, was used selectively: produced when it

could prove guilt, ignored and not produced if it would prove innocence. Even more incredible, the police made no attempt to trace the person who sent the material, one 'samanthajames@hotmail.com'; and one is left perplexed as to why they were so anxious to have Mr S declared an evil paedophile for receiving unsolicited material, but completely ignored 'Samantha' who had clearly wilfully and knowingly committed a crime. Could it be that 'Samantha' was a police officer?

Whatever the reason – misuse of legislative definitions, erroneous claims about users' knowledge, or masking entrapment activities – one week before the trial, the CPS decided to discontinue proceedings in January, 1999. Not that this meant Mr S's problems were over; they were only beginning. To face a charge of sexual assault or sexploitation carries serious ramifications; and although Mr S was effectively exonerated, his teaching career was over. For the 'crime' of being sent a picture he never asked for, Mr S is now deemed 'a risk to children'. He will not be able to teach again.

Bowden

Like Gary Glitter, Jonathan Bowden came to the police's attention after a computer shop checked the contents of his computer taken in for repairs. He had downloaded pictures of young boys, printing some and storing others. He was subsequently found guilty of 'making' child pornography; but this decision applied to all his downloads, printed copies, as well as the one pseudo photograph he had actually constructed. At Appeal, his counsel argued that he had merely downloaded the pictures, and apart from one, had not 'made' them. The judges reduced his sentence; but they agreed that downloaded images as well as printing them constituted 'making'. They did so by first ruling that the word 'making' should be given their 'natural and ordinary meaning'; and second, that as *Pepper -v- Hart* [1993] had ruled that references to Parliament could be ignored when legislation was ambiguous, there was no need to consider Parliament's intent in this case. They could take this course because the defendants submission had argued the word 'making' should be read as creating and not encompass downloading or printing out, and that the word was ambiguous, which it was not. The Crown's counter submission was that as many of the pictures originated outside UK jurisdiction to download was to create (i.e. make) new material which may not have existed within the jurisdiction. As neither submission specifically likened the 'making' clause to the pseudo photographs it was designed to encompass, the symbiotic link in the Parliamentary mind disappeared from UK law for ever.

This was bad news for Dr Atkins, a Bristol University expert on D.H. Lawrence and J.M. Barry who had been prosecuted for 'making' teen pictures he had downloaded while conducting research into hebephilia. He had been found guilty of possession rather than 'making' because none of the material was pseudo photographs, and even that was somewhat controversial as he had written several articles covering the issue of sexual maturation. If Atkins' Appeal submission had been heard before Bowden, history may have been different; but now to maintain precedent, the Appeal court reversed the lower courts decision: Atkins was now guilty of 'making', because of Bowden; although the court reaffirmed that academic study was a defence for possession.

The problem now was that if anyone wished to study trends in Internet paedophilia they would no longer be able to mount a statutory defence to a possession because they would now be charged with 'making', which has no defence. As a result, the courts have inhibited any independent authorities on the subject, and make UK studies like those conducted by COPINE impossible.

Theory and practice

The new, wider, definition of 'making' not only undermines the possibility of academic study, in doing so it prevents those charged with

breaking the law with any defence expertise; and whatever we think of those who take, make, buy, or trade in child pornography, that situation is not good for justice. Worse, producing a win-win situation helps ensures the kind of heavy handed policing which encourages false allegations (see Redden, 2000).

For example, having failed to discover any crime, rather than turn their attention to those who made the false allegations, the police submitted the contents of a legally privileged Appeal case file Dr Thompson was working on to the CPS for prosecution! Needless to say, this was dismissed by the CPS, as was the request to prosecute old NAMBLA leaflets, which he had used during his PhD, and for quotes in classes covering the history of paedophilia and hebephilia in his Human Sexuality, and Child Protection courses. Failing that, the police then sought a Destruction Order on his collection of pornographic wholesaler catalogues which Dr Thompson had used to identify the illegal material amongst a collection in *Reg -v- Web*. None of these materials had anything to do with the original 'investigation', and these actions suggest that law enforcement not only refuses to admit errors, allowing those who deliberately make false allegations to escape the consequences, but that they also oppose *any* study of such subjects or educational provision; the very situation Parliamentarians strove to avoid happening. It seems bizarre to say the least that despite the importance Thames Valley Police put on eliminating child pornography, they do not want psychology or sociology students, who will provide the next generation of psychologists and social workers, to know about the origins and nature of paedophilia and hebephilia.

Pushing the law to its limits is not restricted to child sexploitation; but it is amazing what people consider justifiable. Until the High Court ruled otherwise (*R -v- T*) the CPS even sought prosecutions for 'showing' child pornography when the offender had shown it to no one but themselves (Law Report, *Times*, 12.02.99: 43). Creating a 'wallpaper' file has been deemed 'making' a pseudo photograph (*R -v- Mould*). As feared, it was not long before those surfing the web were prosecuted for having come across child pornography. Although he was technically guilty, and had to sign the Sex Offenders' Register, the judge appealed to the Local Authority not to consider Andrew Maddock 'a risk to children' and re-employ him. Maddock, who was given an absolute discharge, had been surfing adult sites, and occasionally came across images of children. He had made no attempt to deliberately download or save the pictures; but, the offending page images were still, unknown to him, on the shared computer he used, and Maddock was reported to the police. St. Helens Council promptly began disciplinary proceedings against Maddock and his wife, who will not now be able to proceed with plans for an adoption (*Daily Mail*, 24.07.01). Under the US PROTECT Act, such an event would not be considered a crime.

Indeed the law as it stands is becoming more ambiguous and contradictory. While the motives of defendants who took photographs are deemed irrelevant when determining if a picture is indecent (*R -v- Graham Kerr*). Tom O'Carroll's collection of street children images was deemed 'indecent' because of who he was (*The Times*, 10.08.02). In *R -v- Smith*, the defendant was found guilty because he had agreed to receive e-mail pictures, even though he didn't know they would be indecent. On Appeal, it was determined that while opening an e-mail attachment was not in itself a crime; as he asked for the e-mail he was guilty. In *R -v- Jayson*, while there were other grounds to believe his actions were deliberate, the Prosecution actually argued that because any image one saw on one's screen was automatically stored in the cache, the surfer would be guilty of 'making' that image. On Appeal, the Judge ruled that browsing child pornography pictures amounted to 'making' the moment an image was displayed on the computer screen. He did so because there was evidence in that case that the browsing was deliberate; but, how would others who were not deliberately browsing for them prove such

an image was accidental, such as the result of an 'ad attack' which occurs precisely when one tries to leave a site. The Jayson ruling could, of course, also make any deletion of an unsolicited e-mail irrelevant, as the offending article could still be recovered.

One legal authority has suggested that the problem with penalising someone because their computer 'makes' a copy in the cache at the same time as an e-mail is opened is that one could not possibly have committed the act knowingly. In many cases:

> The offences are now so broad and overlap to such an extent, but with such inconsistencies, that it is desirable for Parliament to rationalise the scheme with a properly structured hierarchy of offences reflecting wrong doing.
> (Vencatachellun, 2002: 661).

The core problem now is that 'making' charges prevents anyone mounting a 'did not know' defence, whether they did or not. Gillespie has suggested that a new defence – to have attempted to delete an image one did not solicit – should be created to avoid such problems (Vencatachellun, 2002: 662). Another possibility, as with all pornography, is that as the designation 'indecent' or 'obscene' does not exist until a court rules upon the article, and because there is a considerable amount of material, such as that lifted from continental nudist publications, that depends solely upon the eye of the beholder, any number of people could be committing crimes unknowingly. In the case of *Reg -v- Smith*, the offending pictures were those of the daughter of an internationally renowned artist, who has exhibited all over the world. The offending attachment was send by someone calling themselves Yvonne Nystrom at smallthings@hotmail.com, who had seen that Smith was posting material at a fans newsgroup. No effort appears to have been made to prosecute Nystrom.

Why the law cannot distinguish between such cases when bogus defences are relatively easy to spot defeats us. Accidental downloading is unlikely when dealing with files that take minutes to download (*This is*

Nottingham, 15.02.03). 'Erotic writers' hardly need to visit child pornography sites to write (*icNewcastle*, 11.05.02). When someone claims to be 'writing a book on the relationship between art and child pornography' to explain 368 illegal images (*This is Somerset*, 04.03.03) one could ask where is the draft of the book? The same could apply to those claiming to be selecting subjects to paint (*This is Grimsby*, 10.01.03) where are the paintings? If self styled net detectives were going to inform the authorities of their finds (*icBirmingham*, 30.01.03; PA, 10.02.03) why had they failed to do so before the authorities found them? Do teachers really need to access material to see how easy it would be for their charges to find them? (*This is Hull*, 04.01.03). And yes, when University lecturers in Sexual Health claim that they were downloading pictures for a lecture on sexual development (*The Times*, 23.06.00: 14) one could ask what is wrong with existing text books and the alternative sources available?

Compared to these excuses, a real academic defence should be easy to mount and assess by learning from the two cases in which it was dismissed. In *R -v- Wrigley*, the Court denied his Appeal that he was conducting research because: he had not discussed conducting the 'pilot study' of contact and non-contact paedophiles responses to different material with any tutor, he knew it would be difficult to secure permission to use pornographic pictures, he had no dated research notes, and he had offered a different account when first interviewed. The Prosecution could also offer evidence that he had a sexual interest in young boys.

In *R -v- Atkins* the prosecution claimed that he had neither the permission of the police, the Home Office, nor his University's Ethics Committee. This hardly made sense given that when questioned, during our research into the case, the Home Office and three police forces told us that they could not give such permission. Ethics Committees do not, of course, always cover such research either. At Reading University, for example, Web research merely requires the agreement of the Head of Department as the Ethics Committee deals

with face-to-face contact between people. In any event, few Ethics Committees would exercise the power the CPS infers that they have; which is precisely why the only major study undertaken to date had to be based in Cork rather than a British University.

In contrast to these cases, Dr Thompson: had *not* downloaded any material, or even visited a site with such a facility; he was not studying child pornography, he taught courses which contained classes and essays on paedophilia, child pornography laws, and child sexual assault; he was supervising PhD students at Reading and was to be the external examiner for two PhDs at Glasgow and Cambridge; and he was a recognised expert with over 100 cases to his credit, many of which were high profile. However, the determined effort to find anything to justify the raids despite the allegations behind them being false and the failure to seek out those making the false allegation could have an adverse effect on any study in the UK outside those related to offending behaviour. We know of only two contemporary PhDs covering paedophiles and hebephiles accredited at UK Universities which involved face-to-face interviews and reading literature, as well as the two at Reading, which approached the subject at a tangent: one a study of anti-paedophile demonstrations, the other a study of 'Chat Room Etiquette' (in which the potential to uncover illegal activity was covered by a Protocol). None of these four PhD students have downloaded material either; yet two have been harassed by law enforcement (e.g. *Guardian*, 10.09.01) and another has abandoned his study. There has to be another way. There is a pitiful number of independent studies on what is probably the most talked about social issue in the UK during the last decade; and the attempt to undermine such research does not bode well for the future. Likewise, why should Stephen Whitelaw, head of a company which produced tracking software, have to go to court to exercise his statutory defence. Given that he was quickly cleared of unlawful possession of a CD-Rom containing illegal material which was seized at Glasgow airport, as he returned from a conference covering illegal material on the Web, why were the facts not obvious to Her Majesty's Advocate? (*Daily Record*, 24.01.03).

The need to find other solutions also applies to the constant efforts to outlaw any pictures of children existing in the public domain. Apart from the reported investigations of art galleries – Saatchi which exhibited Tierney Gearon's pictures of children (*Guardian*, 10.03.01: 1) and Rhodes and Mann, which exhibited Annelies Strba's daughter in the bath (*Evening Standard*, 17.12.02) – the number of prohibited areas for cameras and videos continues to grow; as we finalise this article, local authority sports centres are now off limits (*The Sunday Times*, 30.03.03). Far from winning, we are losing the battle against child sexploitation because we are in danger of designating any picture of a child outside the home, an illegal article; and even then parents still find themselves being investigated having been reported by high street photo developers whose sensibilities have been offended. Give or take David Hamilton's work which is still available in high street stores, we are allowing ourselves to be dictated to by what one imagines paedophiles may find stimulating and situations in which assaults or false allegations could occur, as when Department stores abandon Santa grottos. When this paranoia also affects the legal system – the reluctance to post Internet case judgements on the Internet least 'the facts described improperly excite the attention of those who commit this kind of offence' [1 Cr. App. R(S), 161] – it is time to review the single minded 'prosecute at all costs' approach, especially as this has reversed the whole purpose of the 1978 Act.

Moreover, it is precisely because the public regard child sexploitation as a hideous crime that we need to be even more careful that those accused are afforded a rational and reasonable investigation, and a viable defence. Steps must also be taken to prevent law enforcement behaviour that fuels tabloid mob hysteria (Hall, 2003) which now ensures that the ostracism which used to follow convictions,

then followed arrest or charges (Lawson, 2003) now occurs the moment one is accused. When innocent and guilty alike are hounded across the country or 'outed' locally, to be driven from their houses, or worse, it is time to reconsider the law. Not only are the simply accused now fatally attacked; passers-by when told the victim is a paedophile, believe 'that's fair enough then' and walk away from the murder scene (*The Sun*, 20.11.99;18.11.99; *Bristol Evening Post*, 17.11.99; *icWales*, 18.01.03). This hue and cry, and threat to life and iimb means that we need not only to be more careful when leaping to prosecutions, we also need to consider the potential long-term effects. Society has enough problems securing teachers, scout masters, or sports coaches for children already (Thomas, 1999) and the police would not have suffered from so many resourcing problems if a little more care was taken first in sifting dubious complaints and unnecessary actions from those needed to advance child protection (Bennetto, 11.03.03 b). As the *Guardian* newspaper has observed:

> *There is no more venerable suspect than someone accused of paedophilia. It is regarded as the most heinous of crimes, by both the public and prisoners alike. Many arrests never lead to trial, yet once named, the suspects life is ruined, even if he is eventually found not guilty.*
> (Editorial, *Guardian*, 18.01.03).

However, they failed to record that for those falsely accused, and even blatantly so, there is little redress. Newspapers, for example, can effectively say anything they want about the accused with no responsibility. When Southport businessman Alan Campbell sued for false claims, his initial award of £350,000 was reduced to less than a tenth of that on Appeal, which meant, due to their costs, he ended up paying the *News of the World* for being libelled by them (*icLiverpool*, 2.08.02).

We disagree with Mathew Parris (2003) who argued that mere possession should not be a crime, and we understand that given the large number of hitherto unknown devotees, separating the guilty from the innocent would not always be easy; but that is precisely why

the legal safeguards established by
Parliamentary debate should have been
maintained and not made meaningless by
those ignorant of Parliamentary intent, the
vagaries of computer operation systems, and
the practices of pornographers.

When people such as ourselves can be
subject to such extensive damage when we
have never visited any site let alone
downloaded a single picture, solely on the
basis of a malicious phone call, and then find
that we have no redress against media
falsehoods, we need to consider why it is that
the system cannot tackle one evil without
creating another. False allegations, false
convictions and vexatious 'investigations' do
not help end child sexploitation; they get in the
way, and demonstrate a level of incompetence
and obsession that helps explain how and why
the problem became so huge in the first place.
We pointed out years ago that child
sexploitation was increasing because police
forces were wasting resources trying to outlaw
adult pin ups, and that law enforcement had
the wrong priorities! (see Thompson, 1994). We
take no pleasure in saying 'we told you so'; nor
in now having to issue a warning about going
too far the other way and criminalising
innocent people. As with deliberately leaking
names of the accused to the press, what does
the need to issue such a warning 'say about the
professional ethos, the institutional morality,
and the managerial competence of our police
service' (Parris, 2003).

References

Books and articles

Aaronovitch, D. (2003) Don't Look Now. *The Observer*, 19.01.03: 29.

Akdeniz, Y. (1999) *Sex on the Net: The Dilemma of Policing Cyberspace*. Reading: Garnet Publishing.

Akdeniz, Y., Walker, C. and Wall, D. (Eds.) (2000) *The Internet, Law and Society*. Harlow: Pearson Education Ltd.

Bell, S. (1988) *When Salem Came to the Boro*. London: Pan.

Bennetto, J. (2003) Media Helping Paedophiles Escape Charges, Say Police. *Independent on Line*, 11.03.03.

Best, J. (2001) *Damned Lies and Statistics*. Berkeley: University of California Press.

Ceci, S. and Bruck, M. (1995) *Jeopardy in the Court Room*. Washington: American Psychological Association.

Guardian Online (2003) Cut Child Porn Link to Abusers. *Guardian Online*, 23.01.03: 2.

Hall, M. (2003). Are Paedophiles Victims too? *Independent On Line*, 18.02.03.

Home Affairs Committee (2002) *The Conduct of Investigations into Past cases of Abuse in Children's Homes. Fourth Report of Session 2001–02. 1.* London: HC 836-I.

Independent On Line (2003b) Awfulness That Drives the Huge Inquiry into Internet Child Pornography. *Independent On Line*.

Jenkins, P. (2003) *Beyond Tolerance: Child Pornography on the Internet*. New York: NY University Press.

Lawson, M. (2003) Victims of a Nudge-nudge Culture. *Guardian*, 18.01.03: 20.

Parris, M. (2003) Child Abuse, or a Crime in the Eye of the Beholder? *The Times*, Opinion, 18.01.03.

Quayle, E. and Taylor, M. (2002) Child Pornography and the Internet: Perpetuating a Cycle of Abuse. *Deviant Behaviour*, 23: 4.

Redden, J. (2000) *Snitch Culture*. Venice, CA: Feral House.

Robertson, G. (1979) *Obscenity: An Account of Censorship Laws and Their Enforcement in England and Wales*. London: Weidenfeld & Nicolson.

Rodgers, Hill and Fletcher (1997) *Sexually Related Offences*. London: Sweet and Maxwell.

Thomas, D. (1999) Damn This Demonising of We Men. *Daily Mail*, 27.07.99: 10.

Thompson, B. (1994) *Soft Core: Moral Crusades Against Pornography in Britain and America*. London: Cassell.

Thompson, B. (1998) *Case of R. -v- Atkins: A Commentary on Charges of 'Making Photographs'*. Reading University.

Vencatachellun, G. (2002) Indecent Pseudo Photographs of Children. *Criminal Law Review*, August.

Weisler, B. (2003) Judge Discards FBI Evidence in Internet Case of Child Smut. *NY Times*, March 7.

United States Sources

ACLU (2002) Letter to Representatives Smith and Scott on H.R. 4623, The Child Obscenity and Pornography Prevention Act 2002. *www.aclu.org* 08.05.02.

CNN (1997) Internet Measures to Protect Children. *www.cnn.com* 02.12.97.

Frieden, T. (1997) FBI: Internet Paedophiles A Growing Threat. *www.cnn.com* 08.04.97.

Judicial Committee, House of Representatives (2003) *The Protect Act Of 2003 Report*. Judicial Committee, House of Representatives 108th Congress, 1st Session, Calendar No. 7, 11.05.03.

NY Times (2003) Judge Discards FBI Evidence in Internet Case of Child Smut. *www.nytimes.com* 07.03.03

Subcommittee on Crime, Terrorism, and Homeland Security (2002) *Enhancing Child Protection Laws After the April 16, 2002 Supreme Court Decision, Ashcroft v Free Speech Coalition*. Subcommittee on Crime, Terrorism, and Homeland Security. 107th Congress, 2nd Session. 01.05.02.

Newspaper Articles

06.11.02 Porn Shock at BT Call Centre.

13.03.03 Kazaa Used by Child Porn Fiends: Paedophiles Swap More Than Music.

14.02.03 Teacher's Nightmare.

15.02.03 Top Birds Expert Has Child Porn off the Net.

17.02.03 Man Pleads Guilty to Making Child Porn Pictures.

21.02.03 Child Porn Swoop: 121 Computers Seized.

21.05.02 Child Porn Swoop: Man Released

23.01.03 Billericay: Child Porn Man Jailed.

24.01.03 Father Stabbed in Barbecue Row.

31.01.03 Torment of an Innocent Man.

BBC (2001) How I Lured Paedophiles Online. www.news.bbc.co.uk 07.08.01.

BBC (2001) Paedophile Jailed Over Internet Pictures. www.bbc.co.uk 06.07.01.

BBC (2002) Two Britons Charged Over 'Paedophile Ring'. www.bbc.co.uk 20.03.02.

Cambridge News (2003) Computer Expert Downloaded Child Porn. www.cambridge-news.co.uk 31.01.03.

Community Care (2001) False Allegations Cost us Dearly. *Community Care*, 18/14.11.01.

Community Care (2001) J'Accuse. *Community Care*, 18/14.11.01.

Community Care (2001) Scales of Justice. *Community Care*, 18/14.11.01.

Daily Mail (2001) Headteacher Ruined by Lies and a Witch-Hunt. *Daily Mail*, 29.05.01.

Daily Mirror (2003) Express Executive in Child Porn Quiz. *Daily Mirror*, 14.03.03.

Daily Record (2002) Hi-Tech Whiz-Kid Denies Porn Rap. *Daily Record*, 4.01.03.

Daily Record (2003) We Found Rope Noose Under Our Son's Bed. He Was Ten: Every Family's Nightmare. *Daily Record*, 11.03.03.

Daily Telegraph (2001) Boy 13, Placed on Sex Offenders Register Over Internet Child Porn. *Daily Telegraph*, 15.05.01.

Daily Telegraph (2002) My 16-Year-Old Wanted Computer Pictures of Girls His Age: Now He's Branded A Paedophile. *Daily Telegraph*, 03.07.02.

Daily Telegraph (2003) Man Made False Claim of Abuse in Care to Get Compensation. *Daily Telegraph*, 19.02.03.

Dewsbury Reporter (2003) Child Porn Man Fined. *Dewsbury Reporter*, 07.02.03.

Evening Standard (2002) Detectives Question Gallery Chief Over Portrait of Girl, 12, in the Bath. *Evening Standard*, 17.12.02.

Evening Standard (2003) Police Trainer Spent £9,000 on His 'Unquenchable Thirst' for Child Porn. *Evening Standard*, 27.02.03.

Express and Star (2003) Porn Terms. www.expressandstar.com 03.03.03.

G2 (2002) Is This a Pornographic Photograph? *G2*, 18.12.02.

Gloucester Citizen (2003) Porn Photos Priest is Jailed. *Gloucester Citizen*, 28.02.03.

Grimsby Evening Telegraph (2003) Net Porn Artist is Free. *Grimsby Evening Telegraph*, 15.02.03.

Guardian (1999) Net Paedophile Jailed in US for Corrupting Minor. *Guardian*, 08.04.99.

Guardian (2000) Nursery Owner Cleared of Abuse. *Guardian*, 20.05.00.

Guardian (2001) Police Obscenity Squad Raid Saatchi Gallery. *Guardian*, 10.03.01.

Guardian (2002) Internet Chat Site Clue to Missing Girl, 13. *Guardian*, 02.04.02.

Guardian (2002) Is it Art or Child Porn? Why Gallery Faces Prosecution Over Picture of a Girl in the Bath. *Guardian*, 18.12.02.

Guardian (2003) Pornographers Hijack Home Computers. *Guardian*, 13.06.03.

Lancashire Evening Post (2003) Child Porn Man Put Behind Bars. *Lancashire Evening Post*, 22.02.03.

Manchesteronline (2002) Crack Detectives Cage Net Pervert. www.manchesteronline.co.uk 06.04.02.

Manchesteronline (2002) Five Years for Pervert who Collected Child Porn www.manchesteronline.co.uk 27.05.02.

Manchesteronline (2002) Shameful Secret of the Sick Collector. www.manchesteronline.co.uk 27.05.02

News & Star (2002) Child Porn on Mum's Computer. *News & Star*, 20.01.03.

News (2003) Child Porn on Peer-to-Peer. Simon Hayes, www.news.com.au 25.03.03.

Observer (2001) Paedophile Fear Exaggerated. *Observer*, 09.09.01.

Plymouth Western Morning News (2003) Officers' Tenacity Traps Internet Pornographer. Plymouth *Western Morning News*, 21.02.03.

Press Association (2003) Teacher Who Downloaded Child Porn Images Walks Free. *Press Association*, 10.02.03.

Scotsman (2001) Suicide Man is Cleared. *Scotsman*, 04.05.01.

Scotsman (2002) Sheriff Wrong to Free Man, Court Told. www.scotsman.com 31.05.02.

Sunday Times (2003) Sports Centres Ban Taking of Child Photos. *Sunday Times*, 30.03.03.

The Sentinel (Stoke) (2003) FBI Helped Snare Child Porn Man. *The Sentinel* (Stoke), 26.02.03.

Times (1999) No Offence to Show Indecent Film of Child Only to Oneself. *Times*, 12.02.99.

Times (2001) Girl, 14, Met Men for Sex Via the Internet. *Times*, 09.06.01.

Times (2001) Man Freed After Girl's Fantasies Exposed. *Times*, 22.03.01.

Times (2002) Doctor Faces GMC Over False Sex Claim. *Times*, 01.08.02.

Times (2002) Paedophile Campaigner Jailed Over Child Snaps. *Times*, 10.08.02.

Times Opinion (2002) Child Abuse or Crime in the Eye of the Beholder. *Times Opinion*, 18.01.02.

Yorkshire Evening Post (2003) No Hiding Place for Perverts. *Yorkshire Evening Post*, 08.02.03.

On-line Newspaper Articles

icBerkshire (2002) Child Porn Addict Gets Six-Year Prison Term. *icBerkshire*, 24.12.02.

icBerkshire (2002) Paedophile Exposed on TV Jailed. *icBerkshire*, 01.03.02.

icBerkshire (2002) West Berks' police in Internet Porn Swoop. *icBerkshire*, 02.05.02.

icBirmingham (2003) Cabbie Porn Shame. *icBirmingham*, 13.01.03.

icBirmingham (2003) Man Copied Child Porn. *icBirmingham*, 30.01.03.

icBirmingham (2003) No Worse Than Stamp Collecting. *icBirmingham*, 27.02.03.

icBirmingham (2003) One Goes to Prison, the Other Walks Free. *icBirmingham*, 27.02.03.

icBirmingham (2003) PC Sex Trial: Girl Denies Lying. *icBirmingham*, 07.03.03.

icBirmingham (2003) Police Computer Unit Upgraded. *icBirmingham*, 12.03.03.

icBirmingham (2003) Porn Man's Web Search. *icBirmingham*, 04.01.03.

icBirmingham (2003) Saved From Child Abuse Hell. *icBirmingham*, 26.02.03.

icBirmingham (2003) Shame of Child Porn Son, 33. *icBirmingham*, 07.03.03.

icCheshireOnline (2003) Google Refuses to Remove Filth From Site. *icCheshireOnline*, 14.02.03.

icCheshireOnline (2003) Net Porn Police Officer Jailed. *icCheshireOnline*, 07.01.03.

icCoventry (2002) Paedophile Jailed for 9 Months. *icCoventry*, 10.08.02.

icCoventry (2002) Pervert to be Sentenced. *icCoventry*, 09.08.02.

icCoventry (2003) Child Porn Case, Man Avoids Jail. *icCoventry*, 03.03.03.

icCoventry (2003) Janitor Faces Porn Charges. *icCoventry*, 14.05.03.

icCoventry (2003) Two Admit Child Porn Offences. *icCoventry*, 10.02.03.

icHuddersfield (2003) Ex-Social Worker is Fined Over Net Porn. *icHuddersfield*, 07.02.03.

icLiverpool (2002) Cheshire Software Vital to Police Raid on Web Child Porn. *icLiverpool*, 25.04.02.

icLiverpool (2002) Libel Damages Cut by £320k. *icLiverpool*, 02.08.02.

icLiverpool (2002) Scandal of Child Abuse Witch Hunt. *icLiverpool*, 15.05.02.

icLiverpool (2002) Training School to Beat Cyber Crime. *icLiverpool*, 20.02.02.

icNewcastle (2002) £3,500 Fine for Techno Porn Pervert. *icNewcastle*, 20.05.02.

icNewcastle (2002) Abuse Claim Experts Drop Bid for Appeal. *icNewcastle*, 19.07.02.

icNewcastle (2002) Abuse Victim's Mother Speaks. *icNewcastle*, 25.04.02.

icNewcastle (2002) Accused Worker Calls for a Change. *icNewcastle*, 04.08.02.

icNewcastle (2002) Child Porn: Two Arrested. *icNewcastle*, 21.05.02.

icNewcastle (2002) Computer Clerk Facing Jail Over Website. *icNewcastle*, 14.07.02.

icNewcastle (2002) Girl's Rape Seen Round the Globe. *icNewcastle*, 25.07.02.

icNewcastle (2002) Nursery Families Win Huge Payout. *icNewcastle*, 09.08.02.

icNewcastle (2002) Nursery Workers Showed Honesty. *icNewcastle*, 20.06.02.

icNewcastle (2002) Writer Faces New Claims. *icNewcastle*, 11.05.02.

icNewcastle (2003) Child Porn Teacher Sentenced. *icNewcastle*, 05.01.03.

icNewcastle (2003) Police Arrest 22 in Child Porn Sweep. *icNewcastle*, 18.01.03.

icTeeside (2003) Scouting Master on Child Net Porn Charges. *icTeeside*, 04.02.03.

icWales (2003) Morgan to Meet Police Over Paedophile Crackdown. *icWales*, 11.02.03.

icWales (2003) Pair Deny Murdering 'Paedophile'. *icWales*, 18.01.03.

thisisBrighton&Hove (2002) Adviser Jailed for Porn E-mail. *thisisBrighton&Hove*, 05.01.02.

thisisBrighton&Hove (2002) Jail for Web Sex Offender. *thisisBrighton&Hove*, 19.01.02.

thisisBrighton&Hove (2003) 112 Suspects on Child Porn List. *thisisBrighton&Hove*, 17.01.03.

thisisBrighton&Hove (2003) Child Porn Man Jailed. *thisisBrighton&Hove*, 01.02.03.

thisisBristol (2002) Cyber Cops go On-line. *thisisBristol*, 29.03.02.

thisisBristol (2002) Dad's Child Porn Shame. *thisisBristol*, 20.05.02.

thisisBristol (2002) Hospital Man Jailed for Net Child Porn. *thisisBristol*, 18.03.02.

thisisBristol (2002) Man Jailed Over Internet Porn. *thisisBristol*, 23.03.02.

thisisDevon (2002) Man Guilty of Porn Charges Took His Life. *thisisDevon*, 25.02.02.

thisisDevon (2002) Man in Court Charged With Indecent Assault. *thisisDevon*. 20.04.02.

thisisExeter (2003) Kiddie Porn Policeman is Sent to Jail. *thisisExeter*, 25.01.03.

thisisExeter (2003) Policeman Caught in Child Porn Raid to Keep Pension. *thisisExeter*, 10.01.03.

thisisGosport (2001) Man Loses Sex Slur Slip-up Court Fight. *thisisGosport*, 09.07.01.

thisisGrimsby (2003) 60,000 Sick Child Images. *thisisGrimsby*, 10.01.03.

thisisGrimsby (2003) Angry Parents Warned Against Vigilante Action. *thisisGrimsby*, 13.01.03.

thisisHull (2003) Ex-Deputy Jailed in Child Porn Swoop. *thisisHull*, 04.01.03.

thisisLancashire (2002) Wheelchair Paedophile Jailed. *thisisLancashire*, 07.02.02.

thisisLancashire (2003) FBI Help Track Child Porn Man. *thisisLancashire*, 08.01.03.

thisisLancashire (2003) Indecent Photo Case is Dropped. *thisisLancashire*, 08.01.03.

thisisLancashire (2003) Jail for Man Who Downloaded Child Porn Pictures From Internet. *thisisLancashire*, 25.01.03.

thisislocalLondon (2003) Mysterious Death of a Suspected Sex Beast. *thisislocalLondon*, 29.01.03.

thisisNottingham (2002) How Net Closed in on an Evil Child Abuser. *thisisNottingham*, 06.04.02.

thisisNottingham (2002) Paedophile Jailed for 120,000 Images. *thisisNottingham*, 27.04.02.

thisisNottingham (2003) Judge Slams Sex Orders. *thisisNottingham*, 18.01.03.

thisisNottingham (2003) Spared Jail for Net Porn. *thisisNottingham*, 15.02.03.

thisisSomerset (2003) Doctor Jailed for Child Porn Offences. *thisisSomerset*, 04.03.03.

thisisSouthampton (2001) Child Porn Man Fined £2,500. *thisisSouthampton*, 09.07.01.

thisisStaffordshire (2003) Paedophile Targets Girl Using Library Computer. *thisisStaffordshire*, 11.03.03.

thisisthenortheast (2002) Indecent Images Verdict Awaited. *thisisthenortheast*, 26.03.02.

thisisthenortheast (2002) News in Brief: Pornography Charge Denied. *thisisthenortheast*, 12.04.02.

thisisthenortheast (2002) Probe into Suspected Child Porn Continues. *thisisthenortheast*,. 22.05.02.

thisisthewestcountry (2003) IT Chief Jailed for Child Porn. *thisisthewestcountry*, 12.02.03.

thisisWiltshire (2003) Films Were Stored on Computer. *thisisWiltshire*, 10.01.03.

thisisWiltshire (2003) Man Filmed Tots Playing. *thisisWiltshire*, 10.01.03.

Scottish Legal Cases

AJE -v- HM Advocate, Appeal Court, High Court of Judiciary 42/98.

Kirk -v- The Procurator Fiscal, Kirkcudbright, ScotHC 104 [2000]

Ogilvie -v- HM Advocate, ScotHC 69 [2001]

Millbank -v- HM Advocate [2002]

Lillie & Reed -v- NCC, High Court of Justice, Queens Bench Division, Case HQ9903605, HQ9903606 [2002]

Cassidy -v- HM Advocate [2000]

Reported English Legal Cases

R. -v- Bollingbroke, Court Of Appeal, Case 2000/00505/W1 [2000]

R. -v- Clark, 2002 unreported.

R. -v- Cuddeford, Court Of Appeal, Case 00/4821/X5 [2000]

R. -v- Graham-Kerr, Court of Appeal R 302 [1990]

R. -v- Jayson, Court Of Appeal [2002]

R. -v- Leighton, Court Of Appeal, Case 1999/07167/Y2 [2000]

R. -v- Monkford, [2003] unreported

R. -v- Smethurst, 165 JP 377 [2001]

R. -v- Smith, EWCA Crim 683 [2002]

R. -v- Toomer, Powell & Mould, Court Of Appeal, Case 200004398/Y3 – 200005577/Y3 – 200005812/W3 [2000]

R. -v- Wild [no.1] EWCA Crim 1272 [2001]

R. -v- Wild [no.2] EWCA Crim 1433 [2001]

R. -v- Wrigley EWCA Crim 44: Case 99/01497/Z5 [2000]